Heart Of A Victim In Harm's Way

*Surviving nightmarish deeds of darkness
as a spouse reveals secret sins*

Rosy Latur

PublishAmerica
Baltimore

First printing

ISBN: 1-59129-675-7
PUBLISHED BY PUBLISHAMERICA BOOK PUBLISHERS
www.publishamerica.com
Baltimore

Printed in the United States of America

Dedication

This book is dedicated to the memory of a fireman that lost his life in the line of duty, my hero, Frank (Jack) Butler. Also to my children, Joe, Greg, Angela and Frankie and grandchildren, Megan, Shane, Joshua, Justin, Drenda, Chance and Jonah.

Acknowledgement

I wish to acknowledge and give Glory and Honor and thanksgiving to the Awesome God Almighty, Jesus Christ the King of Kings and Lord Of Lords, the Savior of the world who gave his life for all mankind. Praise and worship God for who is, for all he did and all he does for his children and for his forgiving mercy and loving-kindness.

God Bless my family, friends and Publish America for giving my book the chance they said it deserved. I couldn't have completed "Heart Of A Victim In Harm's Way" without the support of my children and their spouse's Richard, Shelly and Renee. Each child and every person I'm close to contributed to help me through trials and tribulations. Joe and Shelly thanks for your love, supporting and helping me survive financially and all the extra moola, Greg and Renee thanks for supporting me with your love, encouraging words and understanding.

Angela and Ritchie thanks for your love, watching over me and helping me with problems that arose whenever I called on them. Thanks Frankie for loving me, all the tender loving care you shower me with, your thoughtfulness and caring concern for my health.

Thanks to my very dear friend and confidante Denise whom encouraged me to write and stood by me 23 years accepting me just as I am, never getting on me even when I deserved it. Thanks to dear 25 year close friend and relative Soni encouraged me to lock myself in my room and write and for making me laugh and giggle when were both depressed. Thanks dear close friend Sharon for the many times I leaned on you and your wisdom in the Lord. Thanks to Mark and Heidi for their kindness and standing by me as part of my life too. Thanks Sandy and Gail you're both sweet and loving. Thanks brother Frank and Dwayne.

I appreciated and thank Dr. Richard and my councilor Diane who became a dear friend too as she comforted, wept and laughed. Thanks Attorney Mariclare for all your kindness and sympathetic words of wisdom "Let Go and Let God." Thanks to Accurate Answers owner, Detective Heige Thanheiser who became my friend. No matter how busy he was, he went above and beyond the call of duty to help me uncover truth and reality.

Table of Contents

Chapter One

Life In Loony Land

I had no way of knowing I was marrying an underhanded, unscrupulous self-seeking individual heavily involved in pornography. A sex addict leading a secret double life that took over every semblance of sanity. My husband shoved his addiction down my throat on a daily basis. Not openly in front of me. He kept his secret hidden in deception that transgressed, betrayed and degraded everything I believed in.

My view of enslavement to an addiction is on the same level equivalent to a hostage held captive within your own soul. I came to the conclusion addictions have a hold on the addict's heart as well as what they crave with a particular addiction. My husband's heart grew colder and distant with each passing day. I felt nothing or no one could penetrate the wall of steel immorality builds between "reality and darkness" between "love and hate."

I hid behind a smile and lived in denial trying to cope in a marriage based on nothing more than deception and illusions. It became a way of life where only the grace of God kept me safe in an unsafe environment. I tried to hold my life, marriage and family together with obstacles I had to overcome to survive in his loony land of chaos and confusion.

I equated my husband to the little dude in the LiL Abner cartoon strip. Dressed in black, a black cloud followed him everywhere he went. As he walks down the road there were storms, lightning hail, fire, accidents and pandemonium on all sides of him. He not only walks away unharmed he didn't notice anything that was happening all around him.

I can't prove all my spouse's behavior and problems were caused by pornography. I can prove it didn't help. It magnified them so it wasn't any one thing but a deadly combination of different personalities that brought death to our relationship.

One evening as I watched the news showing the after math of a tornado I compared my marriage and living with my husband to a tornado whirling, kicking up dust and debris, destroying everything in its path. The reaction of people after the tornado passes and they are surrounded by destruction of everything they strived and worked for as it lay in ruin everywhere is the way I felt inside from day to day struggling to hold everything together as Tornado Konn blows and explodes and destroys himself, his wife, our marriage and everything in his path and it lay in ruin.

I was trying to make sense out of senseless. Trying to understand something I couldn't understand. I wasn't aware of the controlling manipulative mind games my husband started to play as we dated or the hold he began to have on me. He had a plan that viewed me as an easy target, an easy victim.

I need to write with complete honesty after living in the midst of dark deception, lunacy, violent discord and perverted sexual fantasies where there is no truth and reality in the outlandish lewd, twilight zone my husband Konn Rodent lives in. Grabbing my hand he pulled me in to dwell with him.

I couldn't conceive my husband would be an individual heavily involved in pornography. He didn't say anything out of the way, never made sexual innuendos, never used bad language and never told a dirty joke. He depicted his character to be that of a perfect gentleman, opening car doors and implemented all the romantic mannerly things women like. Amazingly he never held my hand or kissed me goodnight or made a move on me. He never touched me, not even accidentally. Not showing some form of affection should have sent a signal. Instead I thought he was being careful for he knew when we started dating I was apprehensive.

He was an expert on women. Compared to Konn's knowledge I was naïve and gullible, like a country bumpkin visiting the city for the first time. He knew exactly the right moves to make to pull me into uncontrollable madness of swirling patterns he exists in.

I thought playboy was the height of nasty magazines. I didn't know anything about sexual addictions or what the entire pornography scene was promoting and I didn't want to. I definitely didn't want it brought into my life or in my home where I was raising a teen-age daughter and grandchildren running in and out of our home all the time. Along with their friends, my friends and the neighbors. Plus my three other children and in laws dropped in any old time and sometimes spent the weekend. My family and I were astounded as we witnessed my spouse's mania. My husband didn't worry about what he did in front of anyone. He never showed embarrassment or at least want to hide his head in a hole.

I wanted so badly to see something, anything that showed remorse for the conduct he displayed in front my family and me. I was humiliated for him and for myself. He went about his business like nothing took place and all is well in la la land.

A fraction of my hubby's secret habit made its debut one Sunday morning. He was sitting in the front room reading the Sunday paper or so I thought. I didn't know he had a porno magazine between the pages. I rushed him into getting ready for church and apparently he forgot the magazine and left it between the pages of the paper.

He didn't know my older daughter; Angel came over and took the paper home every Sunday while I was in church. We lived next door to one another in a duplex we purchased together so both our immediate families would each have a reasonable place to raise our children in a decent area. We had a key to each others house in case one of us got locked out.

After we left for church she came over, got the Sunday paper, took it to her home to read and snarf my coupons. She poured herself a cup of coffee and got comfy in her favorite chair to enjoy a leisurely Sunday morning. She opened the paper lo and behold there was a filthy magazine Konn was looking at while pretending to read the sports page. On first sight she thought it was a movie magazine called celebrity sleuth. She turned a few pages and almost fell out of her chair. It was filled with lewd sex acts. Women with women, men with men, group sex and other perverse acts. Angel was so upset at the contents and infuriated her twelve-year-old daughter Marty viewed nudity on the back cover of the magazine as she picked it up out of the paper and opened the pages.

She knew more than I did as to what the magazine represented. My granddaughter was never allowed to come over to our home unless her parents were with her. Marty was told she could never be alone with Konn under any circumstances.

In due course after several hysterical events Konn performed in front of my family my other grandchildren were not allowed to come to grandma's house unless their parents were with them. At family functions the grandchildren had to stay near their parents and weren't allowed to wander around the house.

Several neighbor girls told my granddaughter they felt Konn stared at them in a strange way. Their mom thought he was kind of spooky and they couldn't walk in front of our home again. Due to Konn's screaming, running in and out of the house, tearing down the driveway and kicking down the front door several times, a few of the neighbors children weren't allowed to play outside if Konn were home. No matter how much I loved my family and respected my children's wishes. It didn't matter what anyone said about my mate I stood firmly committed toward protecting and trying to please Konn first. He was my husband and I was going to stand by him through thick and thin.

The controversies between my marriage and family lay heavy on my heart all the time. I was put in a position of middleman between my family and my husband. It made me sad not to be able to have a closer relationship with my grandchildren for the choices I made to be with my new partner for life Konn Rodent. Before the issue occurred Angel permitted Konn and I to escort Marty and her friends to the zoo, out to eat and various places. For some reason Konn liked to take people places and explain the history relating to the sites. It hurt when my grandchildren were restricted and couldn't run in and out of my house any time or visit without their parents. They were never allowed to go places with Konn and I again.

Angel didn't just drop the episode. She confronted and chewed Konn out. She told him she turned a few pages and it was more than a nude magazine, which in itself would have been bad enough for anyone to have access to. Let alone a newly wed hiding it in a Sunday paper looking at the degrading acts before he sets foot in the house of God while his wife is getting ready to worship with him. She adamantly told me the sexually explicit magazine represented perversion and wasn't fit for anyone's eyes let alone a man professing to be a Christian.

I thought she was making too much of the incident. I treated it lightly and told Angel he's been a bachelor 5 years he probably looked at nude magazines because he was alone. He has a wife now. I told her not to worry it's nothing to be concerned about. I'll ask him to throw it away and never bring anything of that nature into our home again. That was the start of protecting Konn but I must have been protecting myself too I didn't want to think of him owning a porno magazine of that magnitude.

Angel was trying to safeguard me. She knew I led a pretty sheltered life with her dad whom loved her mom and never looked at another women sexually whether it was in a pornographic magazine or on the street. Even after I learned of Konn's depravity and survived through the nightmare I didn't comprehend everything Angel was trying to tell me until the moment I wrote the words and relieved the incident. I finally realized the revelation of the incident my daughter tried to warn me of was the type of magazine and circumstances that signified where his mind and heart was right from the beginning.

The seriousness of everything the disturbing material represented flashed before me. I couldn't help but remember the way it pierced my heart the first time he said Rosie, I never loved you, your not the women meant for me. Recall of those words hit me like a ton of bricks because those words held true as the abusively toxic relationship progressed to a point of no return.

The flashback relating to the hidden magazine was saying so many things I didn't grasp during the moment in time it happened. A most important point Konn's deception in the hidden pornography episode introduced was the appearance of Konn's dishonest addiction and immoral cheating. I discovered the lies, dark deceitfulness and craving lust to partake of depraved, distorted sexually explicit nudity of people engaged in perverted poses along with his habit of cavorting and chasing strippers began long before he met me.

The promises Konn made as he professed to accept Jesus were as twisted and illusory as the addiction he tried to hide. He put me though hell as I slowly learned he's more deeply disturbed than I could ever imagine in my wildest dream. It was traumatically overwhelming to stumble across women's underwear and immoral paraphernalia hidden throughout the house in the coming months. Covering his tracks to hide the addiction minutes before church then sit piously with his wife as though he's the pillar of the community. His conduct revealed it didn't matter that he is about to go to church, worship God and teach children's Sunday school directly after the deception. It should've been obvious he wasn't going to give up pleasure seeking habits for God either. At the time nothing was obvious to me.

Equally disturbing after he satisfies his passion visioning sex with nude women posing in various sex positions with various partners is the fact that he would tell me he loved me seconds later. I'm living proof and can attest to the cliché "Love is Blind." The treachery related to the hidden pornography and sex addiction laid the foundation for the rest of his behavior throughout our relationship. All the stories I relate regarding the most intimate experiences of my life stem from the same occurrence. At the time I had no idea so many things were intertwined in the twisted depraved activity. Dishonesty appearing days after we said our wedding vows confirms he never gave our marriage a chance to get off the ground. It was over before it began. Divorce just made it legal.

I trusted him when he said he didn't know it was in the car. He was looking for something, came across the magazine and stuck it in the Sunday newspaper to throw away when he came in the house but forgot it was in the paper. He told me he is a married man now and he'd never have anything to do with pornography items again. It's okay to pin a tale on my behind for believing his story. Ultimately his behavior showed he was not trustworthy. My partner taught me not to trust him Living in the midst of my husband's obscene addiction I watched it take over his judgment and eventually take over the already strange everyday patterns he survives in.

Sometimes I was so shocked by his twisted behavior in the midst of frenzied confusion I couldn't react for days. I couldn't believe what I was hearing or seeing and what was happening. Violent psychotic reactions one minute and the next minute he acted like nothing occurred as though whatever he did was the norm and maybe to him it was.

The abuse changes from day to day from physical to verbal to sexual to emotional to mental to mind games to control and manipulation from one to the other, over and over, back and forth like a snake sitting very still in a coiled position. Suddenly the snake strikes then goes back into the coiled position, sits very still, very quietly and stays in that position. Then boom it strikes again and again. The snake never gives you a chance to heal from the first strike before it strikes again.

I always thought it was best to deal with problems as they happened. Put them out in the open, talk them over, be done with it and go on. I used to think every issue had to have a solution and everything could be solved and resolved. After Konn moved in I changed my mind. There were some things pertaining to his mannerisms that couldn't be resolved for he wouldn't acknowledge the problem. There by he doesn't have to resolve anything. I didn't know how to handle the type of problems he gave me to deal with. Just when I thought I had a handle on the problem at hand the situation went in another direction so fast I couldn't keep up with it all. Some of it was so deranged unlike anything I had been exposed to or even heard of. He always managed to skirt around the truth. It was like being on a merry go round that never stopped; the music went on and on and played the same old song.

My teen-age daughter Francis and I were awestruck at the things we seen happening in our home. She became frightened when he yelled and acted psychotic at two in the morning. She wept in fear she was so worried he was harming her mom. We didn't live with the standards his behavior displayed to the beat of a different drummer. There wasn't any confusing chaotic turmoil in our home before Konn moved in. The biggest decision I had to make was what to have for supper.

I asked Konn if he'd take a chemical imbalance test but he wouldn't. I didn't know if this was the problem. I just thought it might help. It certainly couldn't hurt. I may not have known what his behavior would have been clinically diagnosed as by a professional but one thing I know for certain. I have been around for 60 years I know behavior that's disturbed, ludicrous, and immoral and showed no natural feelings or affection. His solution to having his own way and avoid answering questions was to lie, cry and shout, hyperventilate, throw himself on the floor and hold his breath. Run in and out of the house; deny everything with anger, and violence. Kick the dog, kick the door down, wildly throw and break things, twist his glasses to smithereens, pound his head with his fists or whatever objects were handy, self inflict bruises and cuts on him self and sometimes on me.

One day I asked him where he went when he vanished eleven hours during the time he was supposed to be on his job. He grabbed a beer bottle sitting on the dresser and whacked his forehead gashing his head open blood was spewing all over the place. Another time my husband hit himself in the eye with his fist and gave himself a swelling black eye. Then told everyone I hit him. My hubby jumped up and down on the floor so hard he shook the house. He'd make a loud commotion, run outdoors yelling and screaming then drive away like a wild maniac. He attempted suicide twice. I called 911 and he took off like a bat out of hell then called to see if the policemen left and asked if he can come home.

No matter how insane his reactions looked he had a motive for all of it. His behavior was enacted to control and manipulate every situation to avoid the issue he needed to give some answers to. By the same token his behavior took away what I had to say and he wasn't allowing me have an opinion on any issue?

Any question can set him off. If I ask what the weather was like when he opened the door to pick up the paper his reply was a loud snotty commentary. After living with his arrogance a year sometimes I'd purposely ask questions I knew would bug him. After displaying each and every academy award-winning performances portraying "Mr. Nutso" clamoring he didn't have any problems and never did anything wrong I was his only problem. Every thing he did and said was my fault for accusing him of cheating. I had to see a councilor or he was getting a divorce.

Witnessing the way he hurt himself in the bizarre behavior literally broke my heart. I cried for days whenever I looked at him. I couldn't take seeing him inflict pain on his body any more than I could take it when he hurt and inflicted pain on me. It was a sad state of affairs to learn Konn wanted to keep me distressed, perplexed and fearful. He counted on it. No one knows better than me how hard this must be to conceive. I stood speechless and in shock after each encounter.

At first I tried to impede Konn from physically hurting himself. I wasn't strong enough to hold him. I was trembling and my insides shook. After each encounter I'd get physically ill and almost pass out. It was very traumatic knowing I couldn't do anything to stop him so I began to simply walk away while he was in the act of hitting himself.

Most of his routine was geared at forcing me into letting him do whatever he wants to do with out question. And everything he wanted was spelled W-O-M-E-N and S-E-X and I-M-M-O-R-A-L-I-T-Y. His ultimate goal was to be married to a slaving robot with out a brain while he continues to live as a single person. The tantrums worked to his advantage. I wasn't a robot and it hurt immensely to see him harm him self. After each distressful ordeal I started to space off trying to talk things over. I tried everything I was ever taught and everything I wasn't ever taught but it was to no avail. Nothing was ever resolved. One problem piled on top of another until they grew into volatile explosive situations. Dominating every second. He would do whatever it took to have power over everything. If one way doesn't work he finds another way until he gets what he wants.

Konn has been a computer programmer for 30 years. I used to contemplate him as having a computerized brain that seemed to be ticking away minutes of the time bomb he carries within him self and it would eventually self-destruct. Between the habits with porn and sudden changes with different personalities he maneuvers I began to think he programmed his brain the same way he programs the computer. If it doesn't work one way he will adjust the program to work another way. But it is still the same program and only he knows how it works. He wasn't concerned if anyone got hurt or who got in the way he was going to accomplish what he set out to do.

I'm sure there are others that have been subjected to some of the same situations I had to cope with. I was not out there alone. But as time marched on I began to believe some of the things my husband did had to be a first. Before meeting Konn Rodent I was a widow four years after the untimely death of my husband, a volunteer fireman who died in the line of duty after he answered a fire call to help fight a blazing prairie fire. I watched him as he drove down the street one minute and the next minute I was told he was dead. The world as I knew it was dead too.

I did only what I had to do to survive and take care of my thirteen-year-old daughter. The death of my husband provided income for us so I didn't have to work and was able to stay home to take care of Francis. We weren't rich by any means we were just surviving.

I isolated myself so much of the time. I didn't know how to step out and have a life again. Joking with my friends one day I told them if I were ever going to meet someone God would have to plant them in my front yard. After living in the midst of Konn's strange mannerisms a few months I wondered if some strange planet really did beam the abominable alien I married onto my front yard.

Chapter 2

The Dating Game

It isn't easy to reveal the most intimate details of sexual abuse perpetrated by the alien stranger that slept next to me. Nothing could have prepared me for the unbalanced behavior I witnessed. My face still turns beat red simply writing the words.

I graduated from the old school of tales where we didn't talk about sex. I never even talked about sexual things to my children. I made my deceased husband Franklin tell the children about the "Birds And The Bees." Occasionally I joked a little and repeated slang remarks I heard when I was growing up like, if you want to know about sex, go out on the street and learn about it the way I did.

In the quote-good old days we were told, "babies came via the stork." As children we were kept in the dark. I remember my mom told me if you kiss a boy you would go blind. I was so scared waiting to see how long it would take before I lost my sight!!!!

There were consequences to growing up in that particular era when we were told fairytales concerning what went on in mom and dad's bedroom that we were not supposed to talk about. As a result I wasn't prepared for relationships. I made many mistakes trying to learn about sex in the streets as the slang of the times said to do. We have come a long way baby. Fifty years ago the worst most talked about smutty obscenity in this country was when Clark Gable said "Frankly Scarlet I Don't Give A Damn" in the movie "Gone With The Wind." A lot of people were shocked by the movie industry letting loose with the word "dam." Censorship was running rampart and it was not the answer either.

It doesn't take a genius to see the so-called sex revolution went from one extreme to the other. Today every other word depicted in most movies is the F- -K word plus every other naughty word related to the f word is used more than a story dialogue. Nudity, depicting explicit sexual acts are in most of the Hollywood movies.

On our first date Konn and I went to a movie I suggested. I was enjoying the film and being on a date with him. As the movie progressed two of the movie stars were engaged in a graphic naked sex scene. It seemed like it went on forever. I was actually embarrassed sitting next to Konn while the scene was on the movie screen. I didn't glance his way once throughout the rest of the movie.

One other evening when we went to the theater every other word in the show was the f- - - word. I asked Konn if we could leave and he was very accommodating to exit the theater. I couldn't take hearing the filthy language it hurt my spirit. I thought if Hollywood's intelligence in making movies was no greater than the language it used then it insults my intelligence to sit through an entire movie where the dialogue is nothing but filthy swear words.

I didn't just fall off the banana boat I was aware of what was happening with changes subtly taking place allowing the billion dollar industries selling nudity and pornography and all it promotes depicting sexual freedom. The freedom of speech analogy was used to eventually invade everyone's life and homes with x rated scripts, nudity and naked people engaged in sex acts. This liberation included people that didn't want adult entertainment to invade their lives and homes. It took away their rights not to have to deal with all the immoral independence was promoting through freedom of speech. Even sit coms began to write scripts based on sexual innuendos and clean wholesome comedies and family sit coms have become a thing of the past. The magazine that doesn't have at least one sex article written in it is far and few between. The movie channels that once showed decent movies are became nothing more than x-rated channels. Soliciting prostitution is right at your fingertips in phone books and on the Internet. The Internet provides every kind of perversion in a matter of seconds whether you adhere to wanting it or not. Email addresses including children's are saturated with ads ranging from incest to bestiality to teen girls, college girls, children, fat women, skinny women and the list goes on and on.

There is no way to block out sexual innuendo from children's view or hearing. It is everywhere they look and in most everything they hear. Block the TV and computer with gadgets the children will still have access to all of it in some other way or in some other form. The adult pornography and entertainment sites can be opened by a five year old whether there is a block on the computer or not.

The computer can't distinguish someone's age as porn ads flood the children's e-mail addresses along with adults that don't want perverse sex ads polluting their email either. I've heard some of the clichés like; there's nothing wrong with nude sex scenes in the movies or in pornography paraphernalia. A little of it is okay it makes you horny. There's nothing wrong if a person wants to sleep around with everybody and their brother and jump in the sack with some one they knew ten minutes and other excuses made to justify distorted morals and values. I didn't have to accept the 90's lifestyle of anything goes in the morals of the times. I decided to do my own thing too. I could reject what was offensive to me; I didn't have to partake of it if I didn't want to and I didn't.

I didn't consider my preference to live a moral lifestyle made me a square. I'm a happy go lucky person that loves having a good time, laughter and playing. I was spontaneous, ready to rock and roll anytime. I'd drop all I was doing to run wherever. I rode on the roller coaster 100 stories high on top of the stratosphere building in Vegas. My motto was I'd try anything once, " if I can't do it, it can't be done."

Konn was very much aware of how I felt about pornography from our first date on. He knew he was involved in a different lifestyle than I was. He seen and heard me take a stand against immorality. There could have been no doubt what so ever he knew I wouldn't condone being with someone morally depraved. He didn't have to continue to see me. One of the first things I told Konn on our first date is that I was a Christian that wants to live by the principles Jesus teaches in the Bible. I actually told him I don't fool around or jump in and out of bed with anyone because it's the trend of the 90's.

I didn't want to hide my love of God and the personal relationship I committed myself to have with Jesus as number one in my life over my daily living and in my decisions.

Confessing to be a Christian didn't mean I wasn't as fallible as the next. I stumbled and fumbled, made mistakes, sinned and fell short many times. But it was my goal to strive to be a truly dedicated Christian witness. In order to sincerely walk the talk it is essential for people to see the love of Jesus in my behavior without saying a word. I didn't adhere to the theory I could do whatever I wanted to do and it was okay because God loved me. It is my belief Christianity is a process that requires progress. It is a responsibility. I alone was accountable for my actions as well as my words. It was my choice to choose Jesus as my Savior. I wanted God in my life and in my marriage. I prayed and I desired God's guidance. As the months rolled by I found I was not as strong in my faith as I thought I was. I got caught up in mind games and brainwashing sabotage masterminded with the wrath of Konn. I grew weak in spirit and in my faith. I admit some of my behavior and words weren't very Christian like, heck it wasn't even very lady like. I lived around the garbage of filthy smut Konn moved into my life and into home. At times garbage is what came out of my mouth. What goes into someone is what comes out of him or her. Like the old saying "birds of a feather flock together."

Konns behavior was based on personal habits that went into his heart for they were the things that came out of his heart. He stood for nothing and gave nothing. After months of listening to Konn blame me for all his behavior I began to blame myself. I don't excuse all I did to protect my sanity but I quit being so hard on who I am personally. Meeting Konn was my own doing and demise. After being alone four years the loneliness and the void I felt started to overwhelm me. I thought all I wanted was a companion to go to a movie with once in a while, have a cup of coffee with or just go for a ride.

I told my friend Veronica I was ready to meet someone but I didn't know how to go about meeting a man. I didn't want to meet a jerk so I thought it would be safe if I met someone a friend already knew was a Christian. Veronica called one day and said I have someone I want you to meet that is a Christian too. Her husband suggested a bachelor they both knew. He did computer work for both their businesses almost two years.

I said okay and she introduced me to Konn Rodent shortly before Easter March 1995. After the formality of introducing us Veronica and her husband Don drove their two children, Konn and I to a restaurant for coffee and cokes. On the way home Don was going to drop me off first so Konn could see where I lived. I asked Don to take Konn home first. I'll give him my phone number and if he calls I'll give him directions to my home then. I was afraid to let anyone know my address. I didn't want strangers to know I lived alone with my teen-age daughter. When sales people or repairmen came over I pretended to have a husband. Moving from a small town to a big city was like a culture shock and was scary at first.

I called Veronica the next day and told her I didn't want to go out with Konn. He was funny looking. She told me he had an auto accident when he was twenty. His car caught on fire and he was badly burned on parts of his body. One ear was smaller than the other and he had skin grafts on his neck that were kind of yellow looking. Half of Konn's head was permanently bald. Hair couldn't grow back in the area he suffered extensive burns. He wore a funny looking hairpiece that only covered a small area of his head and he combed the hair he still had on one side of his head over the hairpiece. He carried himself well. He knew exactly how to hold his head so his scars wouldn't be as noticeable. He wore a baseball cap all the time. Konn's sister told me before he was in the accident the night he graduated from high school he was the most handsome man she had ever seen.

He always made sure he sat with his good side next to you. He had other burn scars on his arms and chest. I wouldn't have called him unattractive despite his burns but it was the first thing I noticed. It did kind of bother me. Aside from the burn scars he looked a little shifty.

Veronica was upset I didn't want to see him again. She lectured what is the matter with people that won't give a person with a handicap a chance. He's intelligent almost like a genius. He taught at a college at one time. He is such a nice Christian man. I felt bad I was looking for excuses and being superficial and I decided to give him a chance.

A week later Konn called and asked if I want to go with him and Veronica's children to a football rally. I was glad the children were going so I wouldn't have to be alone with him. I said okay.

We went to the rally and the children sat between us. I barely spoke to Konn but I kept glancing at him. He was good with the children. I could see they were genuinely fond of him. A few days went by and Konn asked if I'd like to go with him, Don and Veronica to play keno. I said okay. I never played keno before and I hadn't dated or been alone with another man in over thirty years. I was very nervous the day we were to go on our date and I had an anxiety attack. I wasn't sure how to reach him so I called Veronica and asked her to tell Konn I was sick. Later in the day he called and said he was sorry I didn't feel well and we could make it another time. I felt bad breaking the date and a few days later I asked Veronica for his phone number. I called and said I was feeling better if he'd like to see a movie with me sometime. We set a date to meet on Saturday. I was still nervous but I didn't panic. I was determined to make it out the door this time. We went to a movie and stopped for a cup of coffee afterwards. It wasn't easy for me to go on that first date.

After I got home I cried all night. It felt like I was cheating on my dead husband. After we broke the ice we began to see one another very slowly at first. After six months we started to see each other quite a bit.

Konn recognizes exactly what it takes to please a woman. He does the one thing he knows women love. He took the time to make himself available anytime day or night and was always very accommodating. He had his own business and didn't seem to care if he made any money or not. He took off work whenever he wanted to.

He was always on time and gave his undivided attention. Konn led me to believe it gave him pleasure to do anything I asked of him. It didn't matter what I wanted he'd do it for me and with me. He knew I was leery of him but discerned exactly what to do and what to say to gain my confidence. I began to feel safe with him.

When I was with Konn I didn't notice him ogling women. There was a few times I thought he was looking fixedly at someone I'd glance at him and he looked away immediately. He didn't have the transfixed look on his face I came to know oh so well after I married him. Sometimes I felt like he was on guard and went out of his way to avoid looking at women. Except for Veronica, he did stare at her with an impishly sick grin on his face.

She was the only other person I knew of that he made himself available to and spent time with. It was nothing to me. I didn't care if he and Veronica had a close friendly relationship. Konn and I were just dating and having fun together. We weren't romantically involved at this time. Besides Veronica and I had a close friendship too. I thought our personalities had some similarities. When we were together we joked and laughed all the time. We confided things to each other and were in contact with one another all the time. I don't know how Konn would have time to be a womanizer when we dated. All I seen him do was juggle his time between Veronica and me like a bouncing ball. I did notice Veronica egged him on and flirted with him sometimes. Occasionally I did feel like I was in a triangle with the three of us involved in the same friendly relationship. Her husband accepted Konn and Veronica's close friendship and the time they spent with each other so I figured it must not have been a big deal.

I blew off the ambiance I felt between Veronica and Konn when we were all together. We were all friends. We all hung out together. Some times Konn would pick me up and we'd visit with them in their home. The four of us went to some of the children's church and school programs and we celebrated a few holidays and meals together. Konn and I liked their children. We both spent time with them and babysat. He gave the children lessons on the computer and gave them much more time than I did.

We we're becoming good friends. At first friendship was all I wanted from him. When showing me the sights of the city he seemed to get a kick out of the childlike reactions I had with all I was seeing for the first time. He made it seem as if the city was nothing more than his very own playground.

He was born and raised here and knew the town like the back of his hand. He'd explain the historical sights in detail and made it all sound very interesting. His personality would change from intellect to little boy as he escorted me places that were of interest to him. I thought we were attracted to one another because the child in both of us that didn't have a chance to emerge when we were growing up came out in the excitement of being with someone that had similar qualities.

We were always doing something and it all seemed carefree and fun. I was coming out of my shell. I began to love teasing and kidding with Konn. He acted thrilled with what ever I said and he teased me too. We went for long walks in the park and had kiddy water gun fights. Sometimes we went to the lake in town at five am in below zero weather to feed the geese. They were all huddled up in one spot and so hungry flocking around us honking for more food. Afterwards we went to a diner to have breakfast. Veronica said Konn told her he was having a good time with me. But then she said don't fall for Konn because I'd just get hurt he only wants someone to do things with. He didn't want us to become serious. For some reason I took offense to the comment but shrugged it off. I just wanted to do things again too and Konn was more than willing to do them with me.

He liked surprising me. One day he picked me up and wouldn't tell me where we were going. He seemed especially energized as he drove me to a place way out in the country to a spot with a huge lake, camping grounds and picnic areas. The scenery was gorgeous and I fell in love with the surroundings.

We went for boat rides on the lake. As we came ashore I'd kick off my shoes and walk in the water at the edge of the beach watching the sunset and taking in the beautiful scenery around the lake. There were blue herons, ducks, geese, pelicans and sea gulls in the water and flying all around us. One beautiful star lit evening I was walking on the beach dreaming away in my own little world I spontaneously jumped in the lake with all my clothes on. Konn jumped in right behind me. The water was warm and the lights around the lake sparkled in the water. Splashing and laughing in the water I knew then I loved being with Konn. I didn't want the evening to end.

It didn't matter where we went he would go out of his way to show me good times acting as if he lived to entertain me. I learned he acted fond of whatever anyone loves and if he didn't like something he let you think he did. Learning as much as he could about a person gave him the key to having a power hold over whoever he's impressing at the time with out them being aware. Controlling everything with knowledge he acquires through his efforts to know all he can about whoever he's luring into his trap. His efforts were merely to please himself not the other person. He had me Bamboozled. I thought he was Mr. Nice guy.

He acted as though he liked having me to do things with too. He also liked the idea of having someone that had a cool car, a home, finances and someone willing and ready to run with him at the drop of a pin.

Continuing the façade. He knew I loved animals. One day he drove for miles to show me funny looking sand hill cranes that looked like turkeys. They flew to Siberia and stopped in certain spots around the state every year to mate before making their long voyage. They mated with one bird for life and did a funny little jig like dance when they spotted the crane they wanted to mate with. We did so many things I didn't even know I liked doing. Many of which were a first for me. I was busy raising my family for so many years I didn't have time to wile away the day. I was happy to have some one to share things with me again.

It felt good to have Konn take an interest in me. I liked the attention and the feeling that he thought I was cool. After spending so much time together I became impressed and infatuated with him. I started flirting in a non-sexual way. I looked forward to roaming here and there. We were both spontaneous. We played all the time. I began to call him my playmate. I'd call and ask him if he wanted to come out and play with me. He laughed and went along with anything I said.

I don't think calling him my playmate is funny or laughable now. If I had known he was setting me up to zero in on me with dishonorable intentions the word I would have used was womanizing playboy. But I didn't know. I continued to be fond of him. I wanted be as close to him as I could possibly be.

One day as were driving down the highway I told him I thought he had a flat tire. He leaned halfway out the car window. His hat flew off his head and went flying down the road and landed in the middle of the highway. I never saw anyone check a low tire in that manner before. It struck me funny he didn't pull over to the side of the road to check the tire and I giggled my head off. I was never around someone like Konn. Eventually I became fascinated with everything about him. His agenda was packed full of surprises. I did think he was mysterious at times and some things he did were unusual. But I thought he was fun to be with so I ignored his idiosyncrasies. I began to look at him in a different way and suddenly he was very handsome in my eyes. I stopped noticing his scars.

My family and a few friends were concerned I wasn't behaving like mom. I was gone most of the time and acting like a teenager and they were acting like my parents. They kept track of what time I got in and where I went. They were having bad vibes concerning Konn. They kept asking me what do you see in him? I replied it's like having a playmate he makes me laugh. I feel alive again. I ended up falling hook, line and sinker for Konn. I can't explain why or how. It just happened. There were warning signs but I ignored them. I was drawn to him like a silly teen in love for the first time. I continued to tell my family I see something in him no one else sees. I have plenty of flaws too so I defended my relationship with Konn like the old adage says, " we don't love someone because they are perfect."

I didn't realize some of the things he did that I thought were funny were really nutso. Nor did I recognize he has a motive for everything he says and does. I was like an open book. He knew more about the things I liked than my children did. He learned exactly how to react to my personality and what it would take to reel me in all the way. I trusted and believed him. Konn told me I was so darn friendly to everyone. I could talk to someone one time and they'd remember me the next time they seen me. It didn't matter where I went or what kind of store I was shopping in there were always people around that were attracted to talking and laughing with me. He seemed impressed with the way people were drawn to me.

Konn and I talked about showing affection one night after we dated eight months. I began to think it was a little weird he didn't even try to hold my hand so I told him I didn't think there was anything wrong with holding hands or sharing a good night kiss after all the time we spent together. Konn said he didn't hold my hand or kiss me goodnight because he thought if he did I would think he wanted to marry me. I thought his reply was one for the Guinness book of records.

I never told him how I felt about him. Up to this point we never talked about love or marriage. This was the first inking I had of where he was coming from in our friendship. I expressed he shouldn't flatter him self I didn't want to marry someone like him. I was merely having a good time being friends and going places with him.

That wasn't exactly the whole truth. He was acting egotistical and I wasn't going to give him the benefit of the doubt. I had thoughts of marriage. Thoughts of wondering if I want to remarry and sometimes I did wonder what it would be like to be Konn's wife. We were together all the time. At times I wondered why he wants to be around me every day if he didn't think of me in a serious way. After I reassured Konn I didn't want to marry him he must have felt relieved I let him off the hook. For out of the blue he told me for never having touched my hand he fanaticized about me more than he ever fantasized any women he ever knew. I took it as a compliment. I thought it was such a cool thing to say. I honestly believed the remark meant he thought I was good looking and I was hot. After our conversation he did begin to hold my hand and kiss me goodnight. I told a close friend the remark Konn conveyed about fantasizing me. She said do you know what that means. I said yes it means he thinks I'm pretty. She said no, it means he fantasized sex with you. I said what's wrong with that. Doesn't that mean he's attracted to me and thinks I'm hot like sexy looking. She tried to explain what it meant I didn't heed her words. I couldn't believe he meant his words in a sexually harmful way. He had been so nice and as yet he hadn't done anything to make me think otherwise.

As the months rolled by Konn and I were inseparable. He started to really lean on me. He had a change of heart and began to tell me he loved me, wants to marry me and spend the rest of his life with me.

We had our ups and downs especially when we became serious about one another. There were moments I had doubts. We both broke it off a few times but never for more than an hour or a day. But there was one really serious down that came between us. I almost wiggled off his hook he caught me on and swam downstream as far away from him as I possibly could.

It was a very grave indiscretion. I changed my mind real fast. I didn't want to marry him anymore. I sternly told him to get lost I never want to see him again. Veronica and Don were having marital problems. He filed for divorce and was out of the house two days and Konn made a move on Veronica. He took her a dozen roses and a poem he wrote telling her of his undying love. He told her if she would have him he would dump me. It didn't dawn on Konn some people having marital difficulties do work out their differences and reconcile. Don was a good man and he loved Veronica and his children despite the fact they had some problems. They patched things up shortly after Konn made his move on her. They're still together loving one another and raising their children.

Veronica called the moment Konn left her place and told me things he said to her. It took him five minutes to reach my home from her place. He came in, kissed me, said I love you honey are you ready to go to church. It's time to help the photographers take pictures for the church directory.

I couldn't believe he could walk in my home act so nonchalant within minutes after confessing his love to Veronica. Looking him in the eyes I quietly sobbed Konn how can you kiss me and say you love me seconds after taking roses and a poem declaring your love to a mutual friend. To say he was surprised I knew what he had been up to is putting it mildly.

She told me everything now you can tell the truth too. What does Veronica mean to you? He said I love her I want to have a chance with her. I wanted someone like her 29 years. Now I'm the one that is surprised for he practically lived with me and made a commitment to marry. We had been seeing one another over 14 months.

I did what any fiancée in my position would do. I threw him out but not before I called Don in front of him and said Konn was no friend of his or mine. He just told me he's in love with your wife. He's been pursuing her right under your nose in your home the entire time. Konn stood there looking a little green as I talked to the other friend he betrayed this morning. I got off the phone. I looked at Konn standing sheepishly with his hands in his pockets and his head lowered. I asked him to look in my eyes as I spoke. Konn the poem and roses you gave her was precisely what I asked you to give me after you asked me to be your wife.

I said it would be sweet and romantic if you wrote me a poem with the day you decide our wedding should be and put the poem in a card with a dozen roses. As I open the door and see you standing with roses in your hand I'll know you picked our wedding day. I'm sure you know how much you've hurt me with a cold-hearted willingness to dump me and give a married woman my romantic idea that was meant to be a precious bond between us. She got the roses and the poem and five minutes later I got the shaft, dishonesty and deceit as you gave me a kiss looked me in the eye's and said I love you Rosie directly after telling another man's wife you love her. I consider your kiss to be the Judas Kiss of death. I can't fathom how it was easier to dump me for your friend's wife with no feelings or regards to how the adversity would affect me. Nothing about me seems to matter in your quest to have what you declared you wanted for 29 years over our engagement. Which takes in the 16 years you were married to your ex wife.

I loved you and shared all I had so you wouldn't have to live in the city mission. I would have helped you without the proposal of marriage and without the misleading confusion.

I'm flabbergasted you can fake love and fake wanting me for your wife so convincingly. The whole time you're with me your chasing another man's wife you claim is merely a friend. Your physical body was next to mine but your heart was yearning to be with Veronica. Get out of my house and out of my life.

He went directly to see Veronica after I threw him out. She finally told him she just wanted to be friends and nothing more. One hour after she rejected him Konn came back over to my home and knocked on my door. I didn't answer it.

A few minutes later he called and said I'm at the church are you coming. You committed to working here too, it's your responsibility to come up and help. I told him to call Veronica and ask her to help and hung up the phone.

I called a close friend and asked her to come over. I was so distraught I needed someone with me. His remarks about my commitment to help at church almost threw me over the edge.

Later that evening he called and said please don't hang up I just want to ask one question, will you marry me. No click. He called fifty times a day for several weeks. I didn't give him a chance to say a word. When I heard his voice I hung up the phone so hard it's a wonder it didn't break his eardrum. He put notes in the mailbox proposing marriage and asking me to meet him. One time when he called I listened very quietly, he said please give me another chance. I love you Rosie. I'll do whatever it takes to make this up to you. Please marry me. I didn't say a word I hung up the phone. I didn't want to speak to him let alone marry him. He called unrelentingly and I kept hanging up until one night he called and was crying so hard, panting and hyperventilating. His speech was unintelligible. I thought he might have been in an accident and was hurt. I should have hung up or at least bought a one-way ticket to another country. But I made the fatal mistake of listening.

Sobbing hysterically Konn said he realized how much he missed me the moment he knew he lost me. He didn't really love her he was only infatuated. Rosie, your the woman I really love. If you give me a chance I'll spend the rest of my life making it up to you. I promise I will never look at another woman. I will never ever leave you. Please marry me I can't live without you. He sounded weak and helpless I talked a few minutes. Stop calling and stop asking me to marry you. I don't want to be with someone that can look me in the eye and lie as deviously as you did for over a year. Your dishonesty is appalling. You broke trust that should have been a bond between us as two people that loved one another.

Your behavior is not that of a Christian. I don't want to marry someone that doesn't know or accept Jesus as his Savior. You don't know how to love a woman the way God intended a man to love her. Leave me alone and don't call ever again.

Still sobbing uncontrollably He called back and asked me if I'd pray with him he wants to renew his commitment to Jesus. I had misgivings but the sound of his voice sounded sincerely desperate. I gave in. Regardless of the unkind betrayal I couldn't help myself I had never refused to pray with anyone and I was still very much in love with him.

He wept so hard when we finished praying he couldn't speak. I melted and my heart went out to him. I was like an evangelist. It was in my heart to witness the saving grace and love of God every opportunity I had. It was a delight to be a small part of helping anyone pray as they accepted Jesus for their Savior allowing God in their heart and life and spend Eternity in Heaven.

I believed the second he accepted Jesus his sins were washed away and he is a brand new person, a born again Christian. I got caught up in the moment and agreed to see him in a few days. Konn looked relieved and genuinely glad to see me. He appeared to be lonely and looked like a lost small humble child. I caved in and said I'd marry him but he couldn't see Veronica again. Nor could he continue to do any more work for her. Even though he accepted Jesus I had mixed feelings.

I didn't blindly trust him any more. He had to build trust between us all over again. He promised he'd spend his life building trust and will never put anyone between us again. I said I forgave him but the entire experience left scars. I wasn't upset with just Konn. I was perturbed with Veronica too. It doesn't excuse Konn. He's responsible for his crafty behavior. But I did think she was partly to blame for his amorous overtures toward her. She knew he had a romantic crush and was infatuated with her. I felt she enticed him to believe he had a chance. It was partially the reason I thought without her in the picture and Konn accepting Jesus we could be happy together.

There was no doubt in my mind after I told Veronica Konn asked me to marry him she and I were constantly competing. We both tugged and pulled him in two different directions vying for his time and attention. Several times I asked her to be honest with Konn right up front and tell him she wasn't interested in him romantically. I felt she liked the attention, the gifts and all he did on the computer that saved her a great deal of money. They confided in each other and he was cognizant of what was going on with her in every respect and aware of her marital problems. Some remarks she made were misleading. They called each other all day long and they knew where one another was at all times. He was at her beck and call. I thought she had him do some things her husband would have been glad to do.

Don believed Konn was harmless and just lonely. He accepted the close friendship between his wife and Konn and accepted him running in and out of his home all the time any hour of the day. There was only one time I seen Don peeved at Konn and Veronica. We went to their house one evening to celebrate Veronica's birthday when we arrived Konn made a beeline into the house. I stayed outside to say hi to Don. In a few moments they both came running out of the house laughing and bouncing in step kind of giddy like. Konn said Rosie is it okay if I use your car to take Veronica to the store? Don glanced at me and could see I was taking in the way Konn and his wife acted around each other. I didn't say anything but I wasn't happy he brought me to a party and wants to leave with Veronica for a while. Don looked at them and sternly said no. You both stay here if you need something from the store I'll go get it.

I don't know if Don knew Konn bought his wife 12 birthday gifts? Some of the presents were very expensive. It was obvious he thought a great deal of her. I said something to Konn about buying another man's wife 12 gifts. He said it was because she helped him when he was down and out. It was perplexing to see them together, hear some of the comments they made to each other and at times go places together without any one tagging along. I did believe Veronica when she told me she would never sleep with him nor did she want to be involved romantically. But there was no mistaking she wanted him around for some reason.

I wasn't exactly sure what the reason was aside from using his computer talents. I thought she might just like having guys think she is attractive and wait on her hand and foot. What women didn't? I know I did. I told her I was in love with Konn. I asked her to ease up and give him and I a chance to be together. I wasn't aware of the stories Konn told her while he was telling me a different story for I trusted him then. Several times I talked with him about things I felt were happening between them. She has a wonderful husband that might like to spend time alone with his wife. It shook Konn up. He flew via express to her house and told her every word I said in his own version.

My daughter Angel cleaned house for Veronica. One morning she went to clean and Konn and Veronica were sitting at the kitchen table teasing and carrying on. They decided I was jealous of Veronica and were joking about a book on jealousy she intended to give me for a Christmas present. They didn't seem to care my daughter was there and heard their conversation. Konn went downstairs to work on the computer and Angel went down stairs and told him it was going to hurt her mom if Veronica gave me a book on jealousy. He should ask her not to give it to me. Konn said there wasn't anything he could do about it.

Angel told me about their conversation but asked me not to say anything to them. I didn't say a thing to either one. I gave a Christmas Party for Veronica and her family. I bought her a nice gift. After we had our meal Veronica handed me her gift. She and Konn smilingly exchanged glances as they watched for my reaction as I opened the gift containing the book on jealousy.

I said thank you. I got my bible and quoted the scripture in Matthew 7 verses 3—6 that pertain to "take the log out of your own eye before you try to take the splinter out of your brother's eye." I ruined the amusing time they were looking forward too at my expense. Don sat very quiet directly across the table from me and didn't say a word. There came a day Konn and Veronica had a disagreement He didn't speak to her for several months. At this point he was using my home and phone number for his business. She continued to call him all the time and left messages but he wouldn't return her calls.

It was nice having her out of the picture. It finally gave us a chance to be alone without any interference from a third party. It was during this time I became serious about Konn and he led me to believe he was serious about me. I looked at us as being romantically involved now.

After not speaking three months Konn and Veronica made up. The first time he went to her home after their long estrangement she called while he was visiting with her and told me she and Konn were going out of town to see an evangelist. She asked if I wanted to go with them. Needless to say it ticked me off. I told her Konn and I are going steady and she couldn't fill his weekly planer anymore. He's already committed to go with me on that same evening to see my daughter perform in the school band. I asked to talk to Konn. He wiggled out of the corner he painted himself in committing to both of us for the same evening. He got on the phone and said don't worry we're going to the concert its top priority with me. He made a few adjustments here and there and much more careful about cutting down on some of the errands he did for Veronica and cut down on the time he spent with her.

But the tug of war between Konn, Veronica and I started up again. Konn was trying to please her at the same time he tried to please me. He played Veronica and I for all it was worth. He was thrilled to have two women wanting his attention. Much later I learned he really does like two or three women in his life at the same time. If one doesn't work out he has another one lined up so he's never without a woman. Replacing the one that got away and the one he throws away immediately he has a fresh supply at all times.

Veronica tried to warn me without telling me actual things he was saying to her behind my back at the same time he's telling me he loves me to my face. She didn't tell me Konn said he'd dump me if she would have him until he made a move on her. It probably spooked her when he called her on some comments she made that might have led him to believe she was interested in having him as more than a friend and he tried to corner her into going out with him and possibly become romantically involved. She inscribed a few books she gave him that said she thought a great deal of him and their friendship and telling him how intelligent he is. Knowing Konn had a crush on her there's no way she didn't know the inscriptions were misleading and could easily be misconstrued by someone as infatuated as Konn was with her.

Veronica and I discussed our viewpoints regarding some things he did between us. Regardless of what the issue was we confided to one another she still wanted him in her life and so I did too. Sometimes we were just being silly and chuckled about things he did that seemed funny in a weird sort of way. Konn had a strange habit of driving up and down the street in front of both our homes at different hours during the day. Don was gone two days when Konn drove by her house so often one morning the paperboy was going to call the police. He told Veronica there's a strange car driving up and down the street past her house at five am. She warned Konn not to drive by.

It was a hard decision and a sad situation we had to sever our ties with Veronica and her family if we were going to have a life together. I loved Veronica, Don and the children. I didn't want the children hurt. But they were. The boys loved both Konn and I. They always said if we get married they'd have both of us together anytime they wanted.

Konn wrote Veronica a letter and put it in her mailbox. He told her he could never do any work for her or see her. I love Rosie I don't ever want to take a chance on losing her again. I thought it was a good start to making amends and we are on our way to a lasting relationship. After I filed for divorce I contacted Veronica. We talked over some things that happened between us. We became friends again. She told me she did tell Konn if anything ever happened between her and Don she would go out with him. Knowing Konn the way I do now he probably took that to mean she would marry him if he threw me away.

Being gullible, naive and in love at the same time is no picnic. The entire episode is in the past. I believed from now on it was going to be smooth sailing. We're going to live happily ever after. Konn is truly a Christian now and he's going to do right by me. Everything is going to be wonderful from now on. I was pumped and raring to get on with it. Now that we both know for certain we want to spend the rest of our lives together it's time to plan for our wedding. Konn clung to me for dear life. He wouldn't let me out of his sight. He wasn't going to take a chance of losing me for any reason now. He had big plans for me. The only explanation I can come up with as he performed the drama of barraging phone calls laced with tears, promises and prayers to God was to catch me in the trap he set, then come in for the kill. He must have felt it was his duty to destroy who I was and what I stood for along with my dreams, future plans and finances.

Chapter Three

The Wedding

No matter how much I loved him it was set in my stone I would not marry someone if they didn't recognize a need to have Jesus as number one and strive to live for God. I couldn't imagine any one going to the extremes Konn went to in order to woo me back. How could I know he wasn't sincere when we prayed together? I trusted when someone made a commitment of that magnitude it was for real.

I forgave Konn but he never gave me a chance to forget for there was no end to the deceptive bedlam. At first I wasn't aware of the controlling manipulating mind games he added to the enhanced turmoil. They were his games and he made the rules. He could act so fine one minute and be an evil enemy in the next. I didn't know he was like a predator viewing me as an easy target, an easy victim.

Separating the person I fell in love with and believed him to be and the twisted wicked person that turned on me with the wrath of Konn was much more than confusion. Sometimes I used to ask him would the real "Konn Rodent" please stand! The baggage he moved in with him included his suitcase full of surprises. He always kept one handy to give me at the most inopportune times.

Konn knew he was the only man I was involved with in the last five years since my husband died. He told me I was the first woman he had been involved with since his divorce five years ago. I was ready to reach over in the night and feel the warmth of my husband sleeping next to me. I desired everything that goes with two people loving each other. I figured since we were both single five years we'd both be hot to trot, chasing one another around the kitchen table night and day. Konn gave me one of the surprises he kept handy for such an occasion.

Sometimes I wonder about myself I woe de oh doe through life as a dreamer and a romantic. I don't always think with my head, I think with my heart. I loved Konn and regardless of all his behavior he held my heart. I felt complete when I was with Konn. In my dreams we were two hearts beating as one. The things I look at from my end is that I married him in good faith. I was loyal, devoted and loving toward him. I can only account for my own emotions and feelings. What he felt for me good or bad was his feelings

Our wedding day finally arrived. I could hardly contain myself. I was like a cat on a hot tin roof when I went to the flower shop and picked up the flowers and a hair clip I had decorated with lily of the valley flowers. I made all the arrangements two months before our wedding. I was trying to save money so I did most of the decorating. My son in law and Konn's son in law took a few pictures. It was a small wedding with a reception in the church afterwards. Blue is my favorite color so I had the flowers, decorations and our wedding cake adorned in blue and peach colors. I would have liked a beautiful wedding gown and a lace veil but I settled for a white lace dress I bought on sale for $30.00. I bought Konn a dark blue suit from the good will store. I economized as much as I could because all we had to live on was my income until Konn found a job. I desired to have the music and all the preparations for the wedding blend in harmony.

We exchanged our wedding vows Friday evening at 7:00 pm May 24, 1996. Our pastor performed the ceremony at North Glory Church. Accompanying myself on guitar I sang "The Wedding Song" to Konn then we lit a unity candle together.

My daughter in law sang a beautiful Christian song. My son and daughter were best man and woman. The director of music from our church played the piano. She played "The Wedding Song" as we walked up the isle to the front of the church. At the end of our ceremony she played "We've Only Just Begun" as we walked down the isle. I was walking on a cloud. I was happy and proud to be Mrs. Konn Rodent. We were newly weds and I couldn't wait for the honeymoon to begin.

My pastor was such a kind quiet spoken man. He made me feel very special when he told me I was a beautiful bride and the decorations and wedding was done in a sweet manner. I appreciated his comments because although I didn't have much to spend on the wedding the simplicity of the decorations stood out and was more than adequate. The morning of our wedding day I wrote a note in my journal that said, thank you Jesus for letting me have Konn Rodent as my husband, to share my life as my companion, provider, best friend and lover. Share intimacy, the day, the storms and the sunshine. Someone to hold my hand, dry my tears and be there to lean on. Instead of giving each other a gift on our wedding night Konn and I decided to write one another a love letter. After I wrote in the journal I wrote Konn a love letter to give him later that evening but he welched on our agreement and didn't write me one.

After a small reception the women from church prepared, we left and went to eat at a fancy restaurant. We rented a room for one night in a motel close to where my home was located and where Konn would be living with me and with my teen-age daughter Francis. We we're waiting a few weeks before going on a short honeymoon to Las Vegas.

I didn't want to be far from home the first few weeks of our marriage. I felt I needed to be with Francis and try to help her adjust to the changes taking place in both our lives.

She was preparing for her upcoming graduation that was to be held May 19. It was her special day. I wanted her to be the center of attention and enjoy the thrill of finishing high school. I definitely didn't want to spoil her graduation by telling her I was going to marry Konn. She despised him. But regardless of my intentions I ended up making her very unhappy.

After the graduation ceremony we celebrated with our family in an exclusive restaurant. She didn't want to invite Konn to share her special day. But I invited him anyway. I didn't want to hurt him either. I loved both of them. They were both pulling me in opposite directions. I felt torn me in half. His attitude wasn't any better toward Francis than hers was toward him. As I sat across the table from Francis I glanced into her eyes and felt guilty and miserable. I knew my plans and happiness to marry Konn was going to affect her.

I kept thinking this is my life. I choose to be with Konn too. Somehow I had to find a happy medium between the two of them tugging on me. I had to stop feeling awful over every decision I made that involved either Konn or Francis feeling hurt in the choices I make.

I waited until two days after graduation before I told her I was going to marry Konn and it was only two days before our wedding. I seen the hurt well up in her eyes and I could feel her pain. It made me feel bad for her and for me. I tried to explain I loved her as my daughter and I loved Konn as my husband to be. She wouldn't attend our wedding. Francis was thirteen when her dad died and we clung to each other. I felt remorseful over the time I took from her and gave to Konn when she needed me the most. I didn't comprehend the full extent of how lonely she was.

I thought because I was home most of the time if she needed me I was there for her. But I wasn't there for her. I was only there for Konn. I tried to go to most of her school functions. All the time I was there my thoughts were on him and she knew they were.

Francis and I argued about Konn. She hated the thought of him living in her home. I thought she was used to him being around all the time he practically lived here anyway and I could handle being a mother and a wife again. I didn't realize how different and difficult it is when it consists of two ready-made families living together.

She never acknowledged or spoke to Konn the entire time he lived with us and Konn never spoke to her. They ignored one another over four years. I didn't see what I was doing to my daughter when he started to dominate most of my time and thoughts. I only seen what I wanted and I wanted Konn Rodent. I was lonely for more than companionship with someone around my age. I wanted to reach out and touch someone in the comradely that goes along with having a partner. I thought it was going to be awesome to have Konn by my side in every way. There was a twelve-year difference between Francis and the other three children. They were married and had their separate life apart from me with their mates and raising their children.

I didn't like having to depend on them to take me places and do stuff for me on their time schedule. I yearned to have someone to do things with when I got the itch to do them. I didn't want to wait for some one to schedule me into their busy agenda. Sometimes I felt I was kind of a burden. Besides hanging out with my children all the time was not the same as having a husband to share my life with. It was tiring to hear people tell me if they had a great husband like I had and he died they wouldn't ever want to be with anyone else again. Like I was supposed to be content to kiss the emptiness and not want the things most women want. I still yearned for them. They meant well but they were getting on my nerves. I was not dead and buried, I was alive, and I felt like I still had a lot to offer. I liked to think I could still attract someone.

There were a lot of things I wanted to do besides go to the grocery store. I teased with a few people working in the store telling them I had no life. Shopping in the store was the highlight of all I did in the last four years. All my children were against my marrying Konn. They didn't like him and they definitely didn't trust him. They were upset he was going to be part of our family. I stood by Konn. I told my children he accepted Jesus and he is a Christian. Now that he has God in his life he will treat me the way God intended a husband to love and treat his wife.

Angel was a no nonsense person she questioned Konn's motives for wanting to marry me after his adventures with Veronica. He basically told her the same things he said to me. She didn't believe anything he had to say. She was fearful he was out to take me financially.

I had a little money in the bank from an inheritance their father left us. I was trying to save it for the children if anything happened to me. I was already giving up $100,000 I received in monthly payments from a death benefit. I would lose the money if I remarried. The benefit came from workmen's compensation which is a State insurance and the laws governing stipulations in the policy while collecting the insurance are written by the State and there is no way to recoup it back. The minute I said I do I forfeited the rest of the payments. I looked at giving up the money as an investment in my husband's ability to earn an income for the both of us. Konn had a talent with computers and he could earn a great deal of money as a computer programmer. Angel also worried about a mutual contract between us on our homes. She believed Konn was going to try to have his name put on the deed. I tried to ease their minds by having a pre nuptial contract drawn up. Konn had to sign it before I would marry him.

He agreed to sign it. I hired an attorney to draw up the contract and two days before our wedding he tried to get out of signing it. I was adamant. I told him I can't and I won't marry him if he doesn't sign the pre nuptial agreement.

I wasn't just protecting my children I was protecting myself too. I loved him dearly but I wasn't going to entrust him with my children's home and inheritance they had before he came into my life. Angel said I never thought I'd say this to my mom but can't the two of you just live together without being married. She cried through out the wedding ceremony. She couldn't stand Konn and she was heartbroken that I followed through with marrying him. One of my son's wouldn't attend the wedding. He called me the day of our wedding and said mom don't marry him you don't know him well enough he's already hurt you. I told him I love him. I want to be his wife. Then he called the pastor and asked him not to marry us.

Family and friends alike tried to warn me about Konn. They all said the same things. They all seen a side to him I didn't see. I continued telling everyone I see something good and kind in him they didn't see. I felt he had been hurt in life and carried a lot of pain inside. At times he seemed like a lost unloved child I wanted to hold and comfort. I had some of the same feelings as a child I still carry within too. I felt a kinship kind of like karma

41

towards Konn. I wanted to show him he was lovable and valuable as a person and he could count on me. The more they did to convince me it was a mistake the more I clung to Konn and the more determined I was to marry him. I thought wow I defied the odds I was confronted with. First by Konn, by my family and friends and the obstacle of the money I chose to give up to stand by his side. I believed it all worked out in the name of love. I didn't just love Konn I was in love with him. I had to be with him. I used to tell him I had with drawls when he wasn't with me. Contemplating my thoughts I'd often wish I knew why he was the person I met married and divorced. But I don't. It is my mystery. I once thought it was a spiritual love and a spiritual battle and believe I'm not to far off. Maybe God will reveal it to me one day.

Meanwhile Konn is my husband now and I want to be the best wife any man could hope to have. I was going to treat him like a king. I wanted the best of everything for my partner. However my husband chose to terrorize and put me in harm's way. I don't ask why did he treat me sadistically cruel and traumatically abuse me every humanly way possible. My question is how could he choose and make decision's he knew would destroy me? (I was his wife that should have meant something to him.)

There was no doubt Konn had to know I loved him a great deal to marry him with the disadvantages and negative aspects he had going into marriage. He had absolutely no possessions and didn't have a dime to his name.

I couldn't help notice when we dated most of the time his clothes were wrinkled. Sometimes there were coffee stains and Ink stains spattered all over the pockets of his shirt from not closing his pens. Some of his clothes had holes in them and some were too tight or too long and nothing was ever coordinated. I could tell he attempted to keep them clean but most of the time he looked disheveled. Cleanliness was a priority with me. Why I didn't run the other way when I seen him coming to pick me up was beyond my conception.

I didn't know Konn was sleeping in his car. He started looking really unclean and now he was unshaven. He had the same clothes on for days. After a few days his clothes were filthy and they smelled bad.

I could put up with the mismatched clothes he attempted to keep clean. But I couldn't stand it when he began to wear the same dirty clothes for days at a time. Nor could I take the smell that followed him around and permeated the air when he walked in. When he walked out I grabbed a can of room freshener and sprayed wherever he sat. I didn't want to hurt his feelings but I couldn't see him if he was going to look and smell like a garbage can.

The next time he came over I asked him to peel off his clothes so I could wash them. He told me he didn't have any other clothes to change into they were the only clothes he had. He gave no explanation as to why he didn't have any other clothes and I didn't ask. I gave him my bathrobe to put on and washed and dried his clothes. He put them on and I had him drive me to a clothing store. I bought him some underwear and new clothes. I decided to keep them in my closet and take care of keeping his clothes clean and neat. I told him he could come over early every morning to bathe and shave. Several days later I learned why he didn't have a change of clothes. One of the patterns of habits he transpired was not to tell me anything when I stood looking puzzled as to why he behaved mysteriously unlike anyone or anything I ever encountered. It seemed I found out things he didn't want to tell me days later after the fact.

His nephew called. Evidently Konn's mother was upset and changed the locks on her doors so he couldn't get back into her apartment. He said he put Konn's clothes and all his belongings in a storage locker and called to tell me he stuck an envelope between my screen and front door containing a key and the address of the storage locker. He told me he was tired of Konn abusing his grandmother and wants him out of her apartment. I told his nephew I didn't know anything about the situation between Konn and his mother. I was a Christian woman and we were just good friends. I was helping Konn because he needed someone to help him. When he said Konn abused his Grandmother I chose to think maybe his mom was a little demanding and he didn't do something she asked of him.

One of his friends gave his mother my phone number and she called my home all the time especially after she put her son out in the cold. I saw Konn do many things for his mom. He was always running errands for her and shopped for most of her groceries. I was with him when he took a TV to the nursing home when she broke her hip. He was always taking her to the hospital emergency room. I thought his mother might have been a little upset he spent less and less time at home and was with me most of the time now. He knew I felt sorry for him when I heard of the predicament concerning his mom. He played on my sympathy for all it was worth.

One night he called at midnight from a store that stayed open all night located close to where I live. It was ten below wind chill out doors and he couldn't start his car. I drove to the store and he's standing in the bitter cold night air waiting for me to jump-start his car. He had very little money if any at all. A few times I loaned him a few bucks for gas. He was freezing and looked pathetic. I invited him to come over and warm up over a cup of hot cocoa. After he drank several cups of the hot liquid I told him he could stay and warm up and get some rest sleeping in my bed tonight. I slept on the sofa. I didn't want my daughter to be frightened if she came upstairs and seen he was here in the middle of the night. From that night on he just kind of moved in on me. He stayed in my home as much as he possibly could. I didn't care if he stayed. I was afraid he'd freeze to death if he slept in his car again. I was acting with my heart again. Sometimes when my head seems to be in China and I'm thinking with my heart it gets me into trouble.

I couldn't fathom being the only one that cared if he lived or died on the streets in zero weather. I would have done whatever it took to ease his hardships. I didn't pay attention to the word abuse his nephew used in describing the situation between Konn and his mother. I couldn't believe he harmed her for all the things I seen between them were positive things. I thought it was sweet and nice of him to do so many things for his aged mother.

Another key to my forgiving Konn came through meeting his mother for the first time. Shortly after locking him out she called and wept everyday asking to speak to Konn. He wouldn't speak to her. My heart went out to her when I heard the forlorn sound of her aged lonely voice weeping into the receiver. She was really sorry she locked him out of her apartment. We haven't met personally yet we just talked on the phone. She asked if I'd have lunch with her sometime and I agreed. We met several weeks later in a nearby restaurant. While we were having lunch I told her I broke it off with her son. We are not getting married after all. She said it made her sad for she was so happy he met someone with my qualities. She pleaded with me to marry him. I confided some of the events pertaining to Konn and Veronica and why I wouldn't see him again. She kept asking me to see him and give him another chance. That evening she called and said she was sorry she asked me to marry him after what he did to hurt me.

As the story goes Konn and I made up weeks later. I told him how sorry his mother was and the only mommy he'd ever have. I kept asking Konn to please speak to her. But he still wouldn't talk to mom for five more months. I finally got them together on a mother's day and the two of them went back to their old routine as though nothing ever occurred.

In the mean time it wasn't long after she locked him out that I heard he slept in his car. My daughter told me several times on her way to work she saw Konn sleeping in his car down the street from our home. I couldn't tell

Angel I was aware of it and I was helping him. He hung around so late I didn't have the heart to send him out in below zero weather knowing he had no place to go. I'd try to sleep on the sofa but it made me nervous to let him stay in my home all night long and I never slept soundly. I made him leave at 5 am. I didn't want my family to get the wrong idea and think I was a hussy.

I wasn't aware he merely went down the road close to my address and slept till around 9 am then came back to my home. I didn't tell my family everything about my relationship. I began to feel as if they were my parents and I was the child they needed to discipline. We were a close family and they're for one another. The children loved me so much they worried and watched over me after their dad died. But sometimes I felt smothered like I couldn't deal with all the things that happen as your immediate family grows into four separate entities with their own families.

The children leaned on me and I leaned on their dad for everything including some problems that arose with the children from time to time so when I had to do it alone I'd get overwhelmed. If the children would say mom you used to be able to do this or that. I had to remind them I didn't do it, dad did. Sometimes I thought they didn't grasp the enormity of how abandoned, alone and frightened I felt at being thrown into a world I didn't know without their dad. He was like an eagle that covered me with his wings so nothing could harm me. He was my best friend. When he died I think we all kind of fell apart. Our little corner of the world was never the same. There was a void in each of our lives. He was a pillar and the rock in our family. He treated me like a queen He never raised his voice to me. I ruffled his feathers and irritated him sometimes and he never got on me, not once in all our years together.

Sometimes when I did or said something I shouldn't have said it would upset him and he never said a word. His silence would get to me. I'd feel guilty I could even think of saying what I did to begin with. I'd apologize immediately. We disagreed but we didn't argue heatedly or fight with one another. We were total opposites. He said potato and I said patato. He was quiet and I talked a lot. I was flighty and at times I didn't think things out. I tended to jump in with both feet in my mouth. He took his time to think things out before he made decisions. When he died in the line of duty the town gave him a hero's burial.

The newspaper honored him with several articles. One title said "Franklin Latur Had A Gentle Spirit." He didn't have to tell anyone he was a Christian his behavior showed the love of Jesus. I can accurately say he was one of the few people I have ever known that truly showed the light of Christ in all he said and did. He never wavered or got weary of helping others. It was nothing for me to help people either they always came to our home knowing Franklin would do all he could to help them. I picked up the slack and did what I could so he didn't have to carry the full load of all their needs. Our doors were always open to those less fortunate. They came over to eat when they had no finances to buy food and we loaned them money. We gave a home to some of our children's friends that had no one that cared about them.

So when I met Konn I didn't look at what he had monetarily. I didn't care that he didn't have anything. I only cared about helping him have something. As we dated I thought I saw a few of my late husbands qualities in Konn and I was attracted to those qualities. Later I realized I told him some things I liked in a man. With his acting ability he performed those qualities.

A few people stopped in when Konn was here and they told him they thought a great deal of me and I helped them in various ways when they had no one else to turn to. I'm guessing the idea to use me for his personal financial gain manifested after hearing their stories. I came across articles in the paper where a few men shared their views on what they looked for before they zero in on certain women and take them for all their worth. They said they like to pursue Christian women they are trusting and easy to fool. They got that right!

Konn didn't know how to get his life back together so he used me to do it for him. He was intelligent enough to know he could use my love for Jesus, my Christian principles and my love towards him to get back on his feet. At this time I'm still in the dark as to what his motives are toward me and Konn is still my shining knight. The two weeks we waited to go on our honeymoon passed. It's time to fly to Las Vegas for three days and nights. I'm excited, happy and ready to rock and roll.

Chapter Four

The Honeymoon

Hooray! It's honeymoon time. We're on our way to Las Vegas. I had never been to Las Vegas. I never gambled before. I was looking out the plane window as the lights of Vegas came into view I could hardly sit still. The night sky lit up in the beauty of all the lights sparkling everywhere. The plane landed. I flew out the door and up the runway. I was in awe of the sights that greeted us in the first few minutes. I was like a kid in a candy store. It was like visiting a foreign country. I stood enthralled when we walked into the hotel. I took in the gambling scene, the sights and sounds. I kept bugging Konn to let me play something. He said I could play after we are situated in our room and get something to eat.

I was giddy by the time I put my first quarter in a slot machine and pulled the handle. I went from one machine to the other. After ten minutes my husband said he was tired and wanted to go to our room. The hotel was huge with so many things going on all over the place I was afraid if I didn't go with him I'd get lost.

I loved our room; the view was fabulous. When I came out of the bathroom Konn had already nodded off to sleep. He looked beat by the time we got to the room so I thought what the heck we had two more evenings. I joined him and fell fast asleep. Early the next morning we had breakfast and read the information on a few things we wanted to do. As we got off the elevator I scoped out directions so I'd know the route from our room to where the action was and back to the room without getting lost. We went to Hoover dam and took in as many of the sights as we could the first day. It was still fairly early in the evening when we got back to the hotel. My hubby said he was pooped and wanted to rest for a little while. He dozed off immediately. I couldn't sleep so I went back downstairs and learned how to gamble.

I was having a good time entertaining myself. He hustled me in and out of the gambling rooms so fast I didn't have to time to wander around. I thought Konn would play a few games of cards, maybe gamble a little but he didn't play the slots or gamble at all. After a couple of hours I went back to our room. He was still sleeping. I woke him up and told him I went downstairs and won a few dollars. I asked if he wanted to get something to eat but he said he was too tired and just wanted to watch TV awhile. My husband acted strangely indifferent showing no emotional excitement relating to being a newly wed. He didn't act like the man that told me he hadn't been with a woman in five years. Even if he had been with some one he didn't act like a groom on his honeymoon with a new bride by his side.

Konn seemed content to just hang out with me as if we were nothing more to each other than good friends. The next day we went to see a pirate show. I perceived how eagerly Konn came to attention when the pirates ripped a girl's dress off in one of the scenes. His face looked glazed and transfixed watching her every move. No matter what was happening during the show he never took his eyes off the partially nude body. I poked him once and called his attention to the action in a fight scene the actors were performing on the pirate ship. He glanced over to the area for a second and his eyes roamed directly back to gawking at the half nude showgirl through out the rest of the action packed thriller. I wasn't sure he knew if I was still sitting next to him. When the show was over I asked what was your favorite part. Grinning from ear to ear he said when the pirates captured the girl and ripped off her dress. At first I laughed and ignored it.

I started to worry and wonder if he knew the reasoning connected to going on a honeymoon and why he wasn't showing any interest in me. I looked forward to having a few days alone with my new husband for we wouldn't have a lot of privacy raising a teen with friends running in and out along with my other children and grandchildren. Plus I had to take time to become acquainted with his family and it would take time for Konn to find a job. Between the two of us we'd have a total of nineteen people that became both our families now. Konn's family consisted of a daughter, son in law and his mother living in the same town as we did. He had one sister that lived in another state I had not met as yet. I liked his family. I didn't mind knowing I'd have to help Konn take care of his frail aged mother. We were going to have a lot of hustle and bustles facing us when our trip was over.

I wanted us to savor every minute getting to know one another intimately in the limited time we had. I didn't like him paying attention to a girl in a slinky bikini. I want him to look at me that way and notice his new bride was ready to be desired as the woman he loved as his wife. He acted as if I were invisible. Being ignored during the special time we should be having on our honeymoon was stirring me up. Yes, I had little green horns popping up.

All the attention he gave me when we dated seemed to disappear. I wanted it back. I need my husband to show in actions he loved and accepted me all the way. I looked for excuses for his behavior. Maybe he really was just tired from the activities of the past two weeks and a little nervous about his new life with me. Maybe I was making too much of the way he stared at the showgirl.

I thought he would be as excited being with me as I was to be with him. I was very nervous too but I was lighthearted and ready for him to show he was anxious to know me intimately too. I felt he acted like making love was a chore or it's a dirty job but someone has to do it. He wasn't the least bit romantic or affectionate. I desired to be all that I could be getting to know him better.

It's our second night in Vegas and his behavior still seemed oddly detached. Rejection started creeping in. He seemed to be having a good time in all we did outside of our bedroom. I was becoming perturbed and hoping his behavior toward me was not a preview of what the rest of the show would be like that's about to start. Starring two people whose lives became entwined as man and wife till death do we part? We had one day and night left in Vegas. My husband occupied the entire day and night with activities. He made sure we ran our butts off all day long. We went to the Stratosphere hotel and rode the roller coaster on top of the 100 story high building. Then we went to the hotel's amusement park. We gave the rides a workout and took in several shows. We ate everything in sight and walked a long way. That evening we rode the bus to see the City of Lights lazar show and we ate some more.

When we got back to the hotel we prepared for the trip home. We left early in the morning and as we're riding on the transit to the airport I teasingly asked if he remembered to bring the camera and film with all the pictures he took of his favorite part of the pirate show. I thought he'd just tease back. Instead my words upset him immensely. His face looked contorted and livid.

His entire personality changed in a second. He was mean and hateful so I decided to say how I really felt concerning the way he stared at the bathing beauty unaware his new bride was sitting next to him feeling neglected. He got so angry it's a wonder smoke didn't come out of his ears and nostrils.

When we reached the airport he got off the transit, grabbed his bag and hurriedly walked away from me. I didn't know much about traveling and a feeling of panic came over me as he left me standing there to fend for myself.

I called out to him in a nice manner to wait for me. He started walking faster. Seeing he was not going to stop and wait I belted out his name real loud so people in the vicinity noticed and turn their attention on Konn. He had no choice but to stop and wait for me to catch up. He said I looked ridiculous. I began to sob quietly as we kept walking at a steady pace. When we reached the terminal area he sat directly across the isle from me scowling.

Still sobbing I looked at him and apologized even though I felt I didn't do anything wrong. All I did was make a remark he didn't like. My hubby smiled and said okay, that's better. He gave me some coins to play the slot machine. I figured giving me a few dollars to play the slots was my reward for apologizing to him for something he did toward me. I loved Konn very much. I always shoved everything I didn't like under the rug. He didn't see the stars in my eyes whenever I looked at him. I didn't see the contempt and control building a nest in his heart surfacing in his eyes when he looked at me. Seemed like forever before we were finally seated on the plane. He gave me the silent treatment.

The honeymoon I looked forward to, as one of the happiest times we would share was a bomb waiting to explode. The fun times I envisioned both of us having on our trip are lost forever. I couldn't capture the moments back. Sitting in silence next to my hubby as we flew closer to our destination I was thinking about the events that took place in the last three days. I looked at him and it was as if I seen a sign clicked on over his head saying "beware." For he showed no emotion toward the angry unloving, uncaring, ungentlemanly conduct he displayed through out the entire time we were in Vegas.

Konn's reaction over an insignificant comment I made was more than I could understand. I thought he could have laughed it off or said something like; come on stop kidding or just plain old knock it off. Simply anything normal would have been okay.

I had no idea my remark was hitting upon something he chose to be number one in his life long before he chose me. I was in for the long haul before I learned he was leading a secret life.

I didn't know when he's faced with truth and reality he freaks out and his behavior becomes irrational and violent in vehement denials to everything he knows he is actually doing. Reasoning things from my perspective I thought if he wasn't aware his eyes were lustfully focusing on everyone but his wife he should have known after I asked him to pay attention to me. As my new partner he could have respected my request and given a little consideration toward behaving like a tender loving husband to the newness of being alone together as man and wife.

At first when I made the comment about the camera and the pictures I wasn't trying to be maliciously sarcastic. I was trying to make light of a tense situation arising between us. If he had blown it off or talked it out with me I probably would have thought the issue was nothing more than a figment of my imagination.

Konn said he became angry in the airport because he didn't like to tease or kid around and that he was a serious quiet person that didn't like to talk much. This was another shockaroo after all the teasing; kidding and horsing around and talking we did in the last year and a half. He was aware of my personality trait to clown around long before we tied the knot. He led me to believe he was attracted to the way I loved to tease and joke around. Laughing, having fun and making light of things was the way I over came some of my fears. Especially riding the roller coaster on top the stratosphere. I was terrified of heights all my life.

Unmistakably on our wedding night Konn lost his sense of humor plus other traits and qualities he portrayed that I was attracted to before he said I do. He definitely made it very plain he couldn't take being teased. Later on after many of his perverted habits and trickery to hide his addiction began to unfold I used the trait of teasing to annoy him.

The end to our drama in Vegas wasn't over yet. It started up again when I had the film developed. His niece sent us a beautiful picture album with our name and the date of our wedding engraved on the front cover. It had a glass frame above our names to place a wedding picture. It was a small album and didn't have room for too many pictures. I thought it would be romantic to designate the small album merely for pictures of our wedding and a few photos of us on our honeymoon. We asked people in various locations if they would snap our picture. When he opens the album I want him to see special memories of us posing together and notice me standing by his side. I was going to put the rest of the pictures from Vegas in a bigger album. Although

I put the unpleasant irritations of Vegas on a back burner I still had a funny feeling about the after math of cruelty Konn displayed in the airport. It annoyed me when the pictures were developed and seen just how many pictures he actually took of the partially nude showgirl.

After I finished arranging pictures I showed the album to my husband. He wasn't paying any attention to the pictures of us nor did he notice the way I arranged them in sequence of things we did. He zoomed through the pages searching for something in particular. He became irritated when he couldn't find what he was looking for.

It was apparent he was looking for the photos he took of the showgirl. Sure enough he asked where they were. I gave him one of the envelopes that contained some of her pictures. He proceeded to take some of our pictures out of the folders and gave her front page billing in the first few pages of the small wedding album. It hurt my feeling immensely.

I proceeded to take the revealing pictures back out and put ours back in. This is our wedding album of special memories. I'm going to buy a bigger album to put all the other snapshots in so they are all together in one album. Konn started yelling uncontrollably. He grabbed the pictures of the showgirl that I took back out of the album, reached for the scissors, cut them up and threw the pieces all over the floor and left. I stood thunderstruck.

I couldn't conceive why he was throwing a fit of insurmountable rage. I wondered if he thought I had a brain fart and didn't pick up on the way he was frantically looking for the pictures showing exposed nudity of a stranger that seemed more important than his wife's wishes and welfare. His actions showed he didn't accept or respect the romantic way I felt about our special time as a married couple starting their life together. More than that I was beginning to feel he just plain didn't accept anything about me.

I was puzzled at his unusual behavior. However I learned it wasn't unusual to him. He knew what he wanted and needed in his own little perverted sexual world that had no place for his new wife to sleep in. Once again a sign popped up over his head that said. "Beware" Only this time there were flashing red lights.

There were still quite a few pictures of the showgirl mixed in with other snapshots in another envelope. I found all of them and threw them away. The twinge of guilt I felt thinking I might have bum rapped his motives disappeared. I had no more doubts about the vibes I felt watching him slip into another world engrossed in lusting after her body parts. I'm very sensitive and cry easily. My feelings were extremely hurt. The violent uncontrollable reaction still didn't give me a clue as to how far he would go and what he was capable of doing to hide the habitual hang up I still didn't know about yet.

Every time he lost his temper it was more volatile than the time before. Minutes later he acted like nothing occurred. He would come in the house and say I love you honey. I didn't get it and I fell in headfirst. I forgave him and acted like nothing occurred too. It was always in my nature to forgive people. I couldn't stand strife. I didn't like to be around people that fought.

I filed the showgirl incident under the category of history and laid it aside. But I didn't lay aside the knowledge that it was not my imagination it was a real encounter. I did see something happening when he tried to convince and control my thoughts into believing I falsely accused him of something he didn't do. He said there was nothing wrong with the way he reacted toward me at the airport or in his out burst during the picture drama. If this were true he went to a lot of trouble over nothing.

The violence was a warning I didn't heed. I didn't understand where it was coming from. At first I never said much of anything during his flare-ups that took me by surprise. Even if I wanted to say something after the initial shock wore off he never gave me much of a chance to say anything. He always took off and I stood speechless. Which was kind of a first for me because I always had a come back and something to say.

I liked having my input and putting my two cents worth into circumstances that included me. Especially when the situations were harmful and humiliating. I didn't know how to deal with the transformations taking place in Konn's mannerisms. There were so many changes coming at me so fast I couldn't keep up with them. I started to pick up on some of Konn's body language. For instance, if he was on the phone I could tell whether or not he was talking to a male or a female. When he talked to women whether it was on the phone or in person his entire personality changed. The tone and inflection in his voice took on a syrupy sweet flirty tone.

The changes that came over him when women were near him and as he spoke to them reminded me of a spider artistically weaving a web. Then the spider patiently waits in the cleverly woven web till the unsuspecting bug falls into the woven ambush and is caught in the trap the insect set for his prey before it kills and eats them.

When he spoke to men His voice was mediocre and the look on his face was indifferent. It took a little while before I caught on to various approaches he used when he communicates with men and women and the other one he used to communicate with me. There is a type of look that say's there's a pretty woman or there's a handsome man. I like to glance at nice looking people and pretty things that catch my eye. Most people do. Konn had a habit of turning his entire body and stare mesmerized at women not caring or unaware if I am standing or sitting next to him.

After I became acquainted with some of his body language I started to pay attention to men's reactions to a pretty woman. I never really gave it much thought before I met Konn, now I was curious. One day as I was getting out of my car to go into the grocery store I noticed an exceptionally nice looking girl walking in the store. I singled out several men walking in the vicinity as the pretty woman approached the store. One man almost fell over as he turned to stare without ceasing, he reached his car opened the car door then looked back to see if he could take another peek at her but she was already in the store. The other man I observed walking out the door briefly glanced at her and looked away. I figured the first man had motives for staring in the obvious manner he scoped every step she took. My observation of the second man is that he looked at the pretty woman, admired her beauty with no motives and went about his business.

Most people know there are different kinds of body language. Some times even in an innocent conversation between a man and woman you just know when some thinks you're hot. What really matters is what a person does with the knowledge of knowing they are attractive. With the exception of one woman as we dated Konn didn't stare at females when he was with me. I would have picked up on the habit for I was sensitive to the way I seen him looking at women at the start of our honeymoon.

After a few months it started to irate me when we were in a fine restaurant, in church, at the movies, in his office, standing on the street or wherever we went I'd see him turn his whole body and stare spell bound at every pretty women in his path. It would have been acceptable if he looked at a pretty woman and turned away after she passed in front of him. Like looking but don't touch or as I learned later on don't fantasize sex with them either. I didn't like seeing his face and body turn as she passed by and watch her until she was out of sight.

What began to really bother me was when I noticed his entire countenance changed. There was a transfixed lustful look on his face, his eyes glazed over and he's unaware of anything going on around him. He wasn't conscious of someone watching him back as he looks ludicrous and goofy as he watches them. I said something to Konn about the irritating habit of acting as if I was invisible whenever any woman was in his sight. Of course he said it was my imagination and there was no such thing as body language.

Our eyes are usually a dead give away to every emotion we feel. I couldn't hide my feelings my eyes always gave me away. They are green but at times seem to look the same color as some of the clothes I wear. When Konn and I split up my son Paul said mom, your eyes look like the eyes of someone that has been totally betrayed.

The first things I notice about someone are their eyes. My favorite song to my husband was 'I only have eyes for you.' He never once noticed the way my eyes lit up when he walked into a room. Before Konn I believed everyone's eyes showed what he or she feels. Most people's eyes do give him or her away. I'd ask him to look into my eyes when we were speaking seriously. I needed to see if I could see any truth in his eyes as we spoke and I wanted him to see truth in mine. I loved blue eyes they're my favorite. I noticed the color of his eyes right off. It was one of the things I was attracted to. As we dated I didn't notice anything out of the way for when I looked at him I had stars in my eyes and they clouded seeing anything more than the color blue. A few times I thought his eye contact was saying he was in love with me. As an accomplished artist in deception even his eyes were deceiving.

My husband could look me in the eyes and say I love you seconds after betraying me, seconds after telling another woman he loves them. As time went by, as I looked into his eyes I seen vagueness, contempt, violence, hatred, and anger flare outward. Sometimes they looked crafty, shifty and suspicious and they darted to and fro. After marriage I didn't see any light or softness in them when he looked at me. Nor did I see the look of love or desire I desperately wanted to see.

Seeing his steely blue cold eyes transfixed on woman I recognized he was really raping them with his eyes. I don't believe there is any other way to describe the act of fantasying women sexually without their consent except to call it like it is and it is called rape. I think it is a power play to control them because they were not aware he was using their bodies for his entertainment. I think he assumed a bigger thrill if he can gain their confidence to have them think he's a nice kind man as he uses their bodies without their knowledge.

I started to hear comments from females that were aware of the way he stared and made them feel he is engrossed in undressing them with his eyes. Sometimes I had a tough time keeping their confidence sometimes I wanted to let him know they felt he was pond scum.

Both my daughter in laws and my daughter Angel said they caught him gawking as if he were undressing them with his eyes. My best friend and several co-workers told me the way they felt when he gazes at them looking dumbfounded. One female told me he spooked her when he leaned on her desk not saying a word for ten minutes just staring at her with a weird look on his face. Three other friends we took to dinner said they seen Konn staring at the waitresses, women sitting next to us, the ones that got up from their table and left the room and women walking in the room. They said his eyes darted to and fro all the time we were in the restaurant. I was almost relieved to hear them say that for I didn't want to feel I was reading things into the truth of what I was becoming aware of dealing with someone that acted like every woman wanted his body.

Everyone noticed as I made lighthearted conversation he rolled his eyes at every thing I said. There were way too many women in the course of time telling me the same things. If Konn knew the stories they told me he would have gone berserk. He believed he was God's gift to women. Believe me a womanizer is not a gift from God.

Chapter Five

Secret Sex Addiction Emerges

Everything pertaining to my husband seemed one way when it was really another. I couldn't distinguish between the exasperating sequence in Konn's reign of terror and the man that said the words I love you all the time. He escorted me wherever I wanted to go and let me do what ever I desired. He was very generous with money. I could buy anything without question. He was kind one minute and the next a raving maniac. I couldn't make heads or tails out of anything. It was getting harder to discern what was real and what wasn't. I functioned in the maddening abuse and lunacy trying to focus on things that appeared to be positive and good.

At this point I didn't comprehend the good and positive was twisted within the same madness. Wickedness and evil saturated his behavior until there was nothing good or kind to hold onto. I never thought anyone could ever have power over me. I was a free spirit with a mind of my own. I pretty much did what ever I pleased most of my life. I was completely mesmerized by the man I loved and became totally brainwashed. Instead of concentrating on what my husband did when we stepped outside of church I tried to hold onto the person that went into church with me. I looked at the way we studied the bible and books about God. I thought it was relaxing and I enjoyed reading books together. We'd each read a page then discuss all we read in depth. I fell in love with the idea of sharing God together as couple.

We taught children's Sunday school together several years. He took an interest in children learning and worked on bible lessons several evenings a week. My husband taught the children, I handled skits and music and explained the salvation message inspiring children to ask Jesus into their heart. I was careful to see he taught truth in the lessons he prepared. Some of his interpretations seemed vaguely off the wall. At times we ushered together. I led the church in worship before service once a month and Konn always acted proud of the different programs and special music I was involved in. At Christmas time we played Joseph and Mary in a Live Nativity scene.

We worked well together in church. We came across as a loving couple. People there thought of us as loving happy go lucky newly weds. I wasn't pretending when I showed affection and held onto Konn wherever we were. I liked treating him lovingly in public or in private. I wanted it to be that way all the time.

Konn was always ready and willing to do whatever came up at church functions. We became members and attended services in this particular church every Sunday a year before we were married in it. I fell head over heels in love with the stranger I shared my heart and my God with. The nice guy showed an additional true color when I asked if he'd go with me to our first family function to hear my two daughters music recital. I want him to feel a part of the family. He was okay as I approached him but quite suddenly didn't feel good. I said the program is only 45 minutes. We don't have to stay for refreshments we can leave right after it's over. He went begrudgingly.

When it was over I said if you want to get the car I'd be right there. I want to take a moment to tell everyone good job. I was in the kitchen a few minutes everyone was milling around telling the girls they gave a great performance. My husband thundered in grabbed my arm tightly; in a loud voice that got everyone's attention he said let's get a move on. We are leaving immediately right this minute. Trying to ease the situation I joked around and said I've got to go now the warden wants me to leave see you all later. The rude awakening was totally uncalled for in the midst of the children's joy at their accomplishment and happiness I felt for their talent and performance.

The second my friend and daughters made it home after the program I said let's go somewhere and grab something to eat. I didn't tell him I was leaving. I wasn't totally under his spell yet. I called from the restaurant and told him to get out of my life. I don't want you in my home when I'm done eating. You're not going to treat me like a barbarian. This was my daughter's special time. They worked hard on singing lessons all year so loved ones can see them perform. I hung up the phone.

In a few minutes he came running into the restaurant. Looking worried he said what's the matter. What did I do? Konn I'm sure you know I'm not used to anyone manhandling and humiliating me in front of my family, friends and everyone at the recital. The fits of temper your displaying over nothing is repulsive. You're not going to treat me as if I don't have a brain and need you to tell me what to do. Let's nip this in the bud. I can't stand mean people. I'm not going to be around someone that feels they can mistreat me any time they dam well please. I was merely being kind and saying good job to everyone with the good manners I had before I met you. I was only in there a few minutes. I was coming out to the car when you stormed in like a storm trooper.

He said I love you I won't ever do that again, don't be upset with me you're my wife.

Okay it's over but stop acting like a brute. I decided I wasn't going to take down the same sign that kept appearing over his head with flashing red lights that said 'Beware.'

Subsequently in due time I learned the reason he didn't want to go the recital. He would become distraught and cried real tears if I didn't want him to drive me to my appointments. Konn wanted to drive me everywhere and drop me off and I'm stranded until he picks me up. That way he doesn't have to worry about me walking in on him when the sexual addiction whacks his brain. He can't wait to be alone to take part in sexual fantasies with his parade of imaginary women. He had an ample supply of the sexually explicit wicked videos and magazines. At length I did walk in on him and each time I did I was shocked to find he had more than magazines hidden.

I believed the tears were sincere and every time he cried it touched my heart. At first I thought it made him feel good to drive me places like he is doing something loving for me. It was incredibly hurtful to be taken in all the while his motives were to get me out of the house so he can be alone and take part in the cycle of self-seeking preference. Full filling his sexual needs as he continues to neglect mine with corrupting dishonesty to hide a secret that destroyed all I believed I would have in a loving husband and in our marriage.

He didn't seem happy to have a family he could do things with. I was a family oriented person and loved doing things with my children. Konn had a daughter and son in law he never paid any attention to either of them before I came into his life. I couldn't believe he ignored them they were both so sweet. I pulled his family into the fold. They were my family now too. I treated them as if they were my children and his mom was my mom. I invited his family to do things with us and included them in all the holiday celebrations. I bought them things trying to make up for the years he neglected his child. I helped him take care of his mother. We took her to ice shows, the circus, plays in the park and concerts. We did whatever she wanted to do and took her wherever she needed to go.

Most of the time Konn made me go everywhere with him. When we were both home he wouldn't let me out of his sight and always held onto me. Not in a sexual way but it was more like a suave persuasive hold that was controlling my movements. The only time he didn't want me with him was during his vanishing acts and when he wanted to indulge in sex without including me. Shoving everything disturbing to the back of the closet it was time to settle down and get on with the next order of business on our agenda. I was going to lose my income soon so the next project was to help Konn find a job. My partner wouldn't make the effort to look through the ads so I went through newspaper ads by myself everyday. I had to call his attention to certain advertisements because I didn't know computer lingo yet so I wasn't sure which jobs he was qualified to do that would be of interest to him. There were a lot of jobs listed for the kind of work he was capable of doing. It was right before the Y2K scare and companies and state governments needed to be computer ready for the year 2000.

Konn was not a bit motivated. Sometimes I wanted to set a firecracker under his butt to get him going. I repeatedly asked him to write a resume and make extra copies. I needed them to put in the envelopes I had ready to send off to ten different places. When he finished writing the information I put it in envelopes and prayed over the sealed resumes before mailing them. I asked God to bless us with a good income. It took several months before we began to get some responses. Meanwhile I encouraged Konn and helped support us financially. I bought him new work clothes and all he needed to get started in a new job.

After his first divorce He lived with his mother and didn't have an income or a job in almost ten years. Before we tied the knot I shared all I had with him and allowed him to run his business from my home and use my phone number to receive calls from customers. I thought all Konn needed was to know someone loved and cared for him since no one seemed to be concerned about Konn's welfare before I started to help him. I wondered how he could ignore and not see the love I put into everything I did for him and with him. I wanted the best of everything for Konn. To reach out and touch his heart in a way no had ever done before. I can't put my finger on why I thought at times he seemed so darn helpless and pathetic. That is, when he wasn't acting arrogant and superior.

We finally received several replies on the resumes. He had a few interviews but nothing came of them. Then bingo. One of the job's came through. Konn asked for $30,000 a year they offered him $45,000. We were pumped. Now we'd both have health insurance neither one of us had. Plus life insurance and the rest of the goodies that came with the job.

I believed the employment was an answer to prayer and a blessing from God. I thanked God for watching over Konn and blessing us with this wonderful job. I always included prayer in everything I did. I don't know how or when it happened but somewhere along the way I threw my hands up in the air and gave up trying anymore. It seemed like everything I tried backfired. I grew weak in my faith and slacked off going to God for guidance. I started to take matters into my own hand. Not only did I mess up big time, I ended up hurting myself even more. I didn't walk away from God. It was just that I became weary when everything I held dear and all that was wholesome, clean and good seemed to disappear as the darkness Konn created overshadowed all I tried to do. It over powered everything I sought after striving to live a moral righteous life.

At the time God blessed us with an income I still thought of Konn as being a born again Christian even after witnessing quick-tempered unkind flare-ups. Thinking he was as fallible as the next and made mistakes along the way as we all tend to do at times. The only thing about my philosophy is there was always much more involved than the simple analogy I gave to everything.

After not having a job almost ten years I looked at securing the job and income for both of us as an affirmation God blessed our marriage. Konn was a blessing to me and I was a blessing to my husband but we still have the free will to conduct our marriage in the blessings of God or blow it and do our own thing. I honestly believed from the point of his conversion before marriage my husband was truly going to fear God and be a great husband. I believed if a man knows and loves God he will know how to love and treat a woman the way God intended a man to treat her. Likewise A woman who knows and loves God will know how to love and treat a man the way God intended her to treat him. Equating my beliefs I thought my husband and I would be equipped to weather the storms of life together the moment he accepted Jesus. I had the misfortune to believe the deceptive confession.

There were numerous people my husband was in contact with that accepted him as being the nicest sweetest person. He was charismatic and very good at all he accomplished both in computer programming and craftiness. At one point I thought the same nice things of him. I was smitten and delighted just to be near him.

As time marched on and Konn exposed me to vicious revolting brutality it was exasperating to hear people give me their rave revues of how kind and good my husband is. The main thrust to the business he owned was a church software program he wrote. When he took me to churches to service his program I met many pastors, priests and people working in the church offices that knew Konn for several years. They all told me he was a wonderful man and how lucky I was to have him. Their opinion on my husband's reputation was a big influence and played an important role in my decision to forgive Konn when he broke trust during our engagement. I thought that many people associated with Christianity couldn't be wrong about someone's character. If they all think that highly of him then he has to be okay. It was one of the reasons I stood by him and remained firm in my decision to marry Konn after he accepted the Lord regardless of my family and friends negative advice.

Without further ado I'm ready for the good times to begin. It felt great to know we were going to have a steady income with plenty of money to start our life together. Konn was smart and knew his business. Besides the church software program he wrote, sold, and maintained throughout the area he was in on writing some of the first ATM programs. He was a troubleshooter in other countries if they had problems with the program. I was confident he could get a job if I helped him. Sometimes it takes money to make money and it took quite a bit to get him going. We were a family now and I was glad to be able to help him. The firm he would be working for was from out of town. They rented the entire 4th floor in one of the finer hotels downtown. Konn was one of the first hometown men they hired. They were still remodeling the day he took me to see where he'd be working. He showed me the entire fourth floor where the offices would be located and introduced me to his boss and the man that hired him. I wasn't part of the business world. It was all new to me. I was exuberantly childish about things that were a first in my life. It was going to be fun-having lunch with my new husband down town once in awhile. I could play and do my favorite thing in life, which is shopping.

I didn't have the opportunity to go to town often because I didn't like to drive in city traffic it scared and panicked me to drive in it. I only drove around the area I lived in. It will be a treat to hang out in an area I wasn't yet acquainted with and see different places in the city. Konn would pick me up during his lunch break and drive me to town. I'd shop and mess around until he was off work. Sometimes I'd slip up to his office and let him know I'd be waiting in a certain area. When some of his co-workers seen Konn and I together they teased us about being newly weds. I lit up all over. It was good to hear the word newly wed from someone other than me. Whenever I talked about us being newlyweds, he'd say get over it. It was exhilarating to see my husband in an executive position. I was overjoyed about the stuff I could buy and do now. Konn was going to be working steady now he can support me in a manner, which I intended to become accustomed to.

I bought him new clothes for work but he still needed a nice suit to wear for special meetings with the state departments. The job contract was connected to State programs for Y2K and he'd need a suit to attend some of the meetings the firm held with the state department. We went to one of the finer men's stores and purchased a distinguished gray suit. The store altered it to fit him to a T. We went to pick up the suit a week later. Konn tried the suit on to make sure altered adjustments were okay. Contemplating the boyish manner he was looking in the mirror as the sales clerk made sure it fit right I thought the color looked good on him and he looked handsome in the new suit. He lit up when I told him he looked great. At that moment I was very proud of my husband I loved him so. Konn said his new job was no big deal. But there was no mistaking he was happy about starting a new job. I was happy for him and for us. Sometimes I heard him repeat under his breath that he was so happy. He talked to him self a lot. Sometimes it was more than a whisper and I could hear what he was saying. The only thing is I didn't discern was that he was happy only for himself. He wasn't happy for me or that I was the woman by his side. He wasn't happy for us, as a couple or as man and wife.

I still didn't know I was not part of the overall long-range plan he kept locked in his personal vault. I was such a dope. I was so darn nice and he treated me like dirt and kicked the dust in my face.

I was simply the devoted sidekick always-telling Konn he was valuable in the sight of God. The talents he has with a computer were a gift from God too. He was worth the wages he should charge for his talents. For years he never charged very much for his services and he did quite a bit of work free of charge.

Konn often took me with him on his freelancing jobs. I noticed he would drive a total of 100 miles work four to five hours and charge $25.00. By the time he bought gas and ate it ended up costing him to go to work. He was intelligent but he didn't seem to know how to handle money or any given situation. He'd drive home on a flat tire then change it in the driveway and end up having to buy another tire.

When I became his wife he let me help with his business a little more. I started to charge customers $40.00 to drive 100 miles and $40.00 an hour for the work he did. Most of the calls the business received were to update and make changes to the program he wrote several years ago.

The customers didn't seem to care about the higher service charge. One lady told me he didn't send them a bill in over a year. They had no idea what to pay him. Hence they never paid him anything. They didn't know he'd never get around to sending them a bill and would continue to service the program with out charging for as long they called him. I did get a little perturbed they gave him nothing for his services even if he didn't send a bill. They knew he drove the distance and worked many hours.

Since we worked his business from our home there was very little overhead so after he procured a steady job we decided to continue some freelancing jobs as a sideline to make extra money. We agreed to screen calls and take on a few jobs at a time with some of the long-standing customers. We agreed that he couldn't take on too many jobs at a time for he'd be busy working at his new job and couldn't take time from the company paying for our bread and butter.

We firmly decided neither one of us could give his work number to people that called the freelance business. I didn't want any thing to interfere with his new job. Some customers asked me for his number but I told them we weren't giving it out. We used to tease about his business providing either feast or famine. One stipulation I put on marriage was he had to have a steady income coming in to support both of us.

My job in the freelance business was to handle calls, line up the work, write descriptions of the problem and make appointments. I set the fees we needed to charge for services rendered and kept track of money that came in and went out. I was willing and capable of doing my part to help earn extra dollars. Our agreement went by the wayside. He didn't bother to tell me he was passing out his work number allowing friends and customers to call him on his new job and was leaving his new job during the day to work freelance jobs. I approached him about the jobs he went to during business hours; He said his friend gave out his work number. He didn't tell me about the calls because I wouldn't let him do these particular jobs and he wanted to do them. I explained there's nothing wrong in wanting to do certain work but we had too many others lined up we needed to take care of first.

Eventually I was going to accept the jobs after he was finished with the ones that needed to be taken care of first for his time was limited. I need to know when he did extra work to keep track of money earned to have accurate tax records. Once again he agreed to let me handle lining up the jobs promising he won't leave his new job during work hours.

Just days after he started working full time things began to happen that made me leery of choices and decisions Konn made without including me. It appeared as if I couldn't trust or rely on my husband to make honest wholesome decisions and stick to them for both of our welfare.

The phone calls became an issue because I wasn't allowed to give his mother his business number. He didn't wish to be bothered with her calling him at work. He informed me he didn't want me to call him either and he wouldn't have time to call me.

It was peculiar he didn't ever ask how I learned some of the things he did and lies that emerged. After I seen the irrationality in his denials I wouldn't tell him how I knew he gave his number out not only to friends and freelance customers but to whoever sparked his fancy. I couldn't reveal calls I received from acquaintances telling me they seen Konn driving around town numerous times during the hours he should have been working.

The crap hit the fan shortly after he began working outside of our home. My husband advised me his newly acquired job was the kind of job he'd have to work long hours and give the company all of his time to further his career. He had his own key to the office rooms and could come and go any time he pleased. He was busy establishing himself in his new job and away from home practically all the time now. I was a lovesick newlywed I really missed him. We hung out together night and day for a year and a half and all of a sudden he was gone all the time. I thought his hours would be nine to five with maybe a little over time.

Since he was gone so much of the time in order to see him sometime during the day I'd get up at 3:30 am and fix his breakfast. I wanted to be with him before he left for work and waited up in the evening until twelve midnight to greet him when he came home. I centered my day on his hours making sure I was home when he was so we could catch a few minutes together. He was leaving home earlier and earlier each day for several months.

One morning at 3:45 I took the two dogs downstairs to let them out doors. I thought I had plenty of time to fix him a cup of coffee and some thing to eat. It never took long to let the dogs in and out so I waited downstairs by the door till they were ready to come back in. My husband stood at the top of the stairs and said I don't have time to wait for you to come upstairs I'm running late I have to leave right this minute and be to work at 4 am. I liked kissing him good by before he leaves in the morning. I'd walk him to the door and watch him as he drove down the street. He was in such a rush he took off before I made it back upstairs. Little did I know Konn had a destination but it wasn't related to being late for work or connected to his job in any way?

I ignored his request not to call and bother him during working hours. It took twenty minutes to arrive at his office so I waited half an hour before I called. When he didn't give me a chance to say I love you this morning being a die hard romantic I wanted to call him and sing the song 'I just called to say I love you.' I called back half an hour later he still wasn't at his desk so I sang the song into his answering machine. Before this morning I did seldom call him at work. I really didn't want to infringe on his work schedule. If something came up and I had to call I waited and called right before or after lunch hour.

This morning I was on a quest. I continued to call every half hour and he still wasn't at his desk. Around seven am his boss answered the phone from the reception area. I asked to speak to Konn. He said he wasn't there. The next time I called his boss answered again. He said Konn wasn't there yet. I asked if he had time to look throughout the fourth floor to see if he can find Konn and ask him to call home I need to talk to him right away. He said sure I'll look for him but I still don't think he's here I would have seen him get off the elevator. The elevators and restrooms were located in front of the reception area. No one could come in or go out without being noticed by the receptionist. Eight am he still hadn't called.

I called again. His boss answered and said Konn was not around he couldn't find him anywhere. Then his boss asked me why I was calling so early Konn never arrives at the office before 9 or 9:30 am every morning. This bit of information was a new daily bulletin on my husband's activities

I continued the half hour phone crusade on Konn's extension with no results. Around 9:30 the phone rang it was Konn. He said he liked the song message. I asked where he was when I called. He said in the bathroom. I called a little later and still couldn't reach you. I was in the kitchen getting a cup of coffee. I didn't tell him I called every half hour for five and a half hours or the information his boss related. I decided before I confront my husband I was going to investigate further. Konn vigilantly left home at 4 am every morning. I vigilantly called his extension every hour on the hour after he walked out the door. He was never there before 9 sometimes 10 a.m.. I didn't leave a message. As yet he has no idea I'm onto the sham he concocted and amused him self with every morning as he ran out the door smiling crookedly.

Some mornings he came back home at 10 or 11 am and took another bath after taking one before he left for work. I wondered why he came home to take another bath. He never said a word about anything he did at any given time. I ran errands and bummed around almost every morning. I'd come home and find the bathroom in a wet mess and grossly soiled shorts on the floor.

I speculated for several months as to what the heck is going on. As much as I try to fool myself into thinking nothing is wrong the outlandish alien does something more bizarre than the time before. I can't help but know the clues he leaves around tells me he is up to something shady but as yet I still want to believe the best. I called my friend and asked her expertise. How do you know if your husband is cheating? My husband had all the qualifications but I was mystified. He acts as if he could take making love or leave it and mostly he wanted to leave it. He had more excuses than Heinz had pickles. I'm becoming more alert to the phony deceitfulness.

I started to call his extension different times during the day and night. If he wasn't there I called the same time the next day. If he did happen to answer his phone I'd talk a few minutes. I'd ask him how his day was or if he thought he'd make it home for supper.

Besides disappearing five hours before work. He vanished about the same time every day for three and four hours at a time. He told me he had to work Saturday evenings but it wasn't the location he arrived at.

At the same time he wasn't showing up for work there were many other bogus behavior quirks taking precedent with Konn besides the vanishing acts. It was hard not to say anything yet. Especially when I was aware of the fabricating fables he told. Eventually Konn started to come home at seven or eight pm. sometimes he did actually have to work until wee small hours of the morning. That was far and few between though. There were times they did have dead lines that had to be met. But there many times he didn't have to work much past the hour of 5 pm and on Fridays most of the employees including Konn took off around 4 or 4:30 to meet in the hotel bar room. The employees had a nine to five scheduled job but they all had their own keys and could work whenever. I used to think Konn could do an entire days work in a few hours for there was no way he could miss so many hours and finish the programs they gave him to work on.

A few new items on his agenda were that he couldn't come home to have lunch with me as we planned for he had to have lunch with his co-workers and there would be times he'd have to take one of the women co-workers to lunch by himself to further his career. He wants me to know in case some one told me they seen him with a woman during working hours. Each new development was geared toward involvement with his co-workers. One day after he thought he established his luncheon dates with no hassles he informed me he wanted to go to the bars after work with his co-workers, unwind and talk shop. He said more business gets taken care of in bars after hours than in the office. He wants my blessings to visit divorced and single women co-workers homes to fix things that break down since it's the Christian thing to do because they didn't have anyone to help them. I asked if he wants me to buy him and the woman a handyman's book since he didn't know how to fix anything and never lifted a finger to try fixing things in his own home. Most of them earned from $40,000 to $70,000 a year same as he did and that was ample enough funds to hire someone to fix things. He knew the statement of entertaining women he's in contact with throughout the day would make me apprehensive.

I picked up on the way he liked to be the center of attention around women whether it was business or monkey business. He's demanding revising our lives at an incredibly fast pace. I didn't like the detailed descriptions he gave on the female co-workers appearance. One day he came home with a story on two gals he thought were pretty and essentially said he thought they liked him. I said if you're trying to make me jealous forget it. What makes you feel they would have anything to do with you? They both have children and are happily married to very handsome husbands that love them. Besides they are young enough to be your daughters. He was so mad he screamed bloody murder then left the house a few hours.

It is obvious the announcements he's making were geared to get past the trust he promised to build between us after he broke trust with our mutual friend promising he'd never look at another woman and spend the rest of his life building trust he carelessly broke. So far he made no effort to build anything but discord between us and continued to break trust on a daily basis.

As he plays the game of setting me up to make a thrust at freedom to act like Casanova using work related excuses my husband did nothing to make me feel secure, loved or desired. He rejected and neglected me numerous times and played no importance on having an intimate relationship. I don't know the full impact of what is going on yet but it's making me very nervous and insecure. He surprised me one evening by coming home to pick me up and taking me to have a drink with his co-workers in a bar they frequented after work. I heard the business that got taken care of. It had nothing to do with the office. I picked up on a conversation involving a married man working at the firm from out of town whose wife was not with him. He volunteered to play Sir Galahad and watch over a divorcee and a married women Saturday night as they went out drinking and make sure they get home safely. I heard the story on how a few of the married men went to a single divorcee's home one evening after work to fix her furnace.

It was obvious Konn was envious of the men that went to her home and he didn't get to go with them since it was in the evening and he had to come home after work. He was paving the way to try and visit her whether she needed her furnace fixed or not. He wanted to be part of the gang. I may not be the brightest person in the world and it may take a while to catch on but once I do I build from there and learn all I can about the subject I'm not to clear on. In Konn's love of himself and superiority he believes he has over everyone else he underestimated my intelligence. Which benefited me in overcoming the mind control along with his brutal resentment and contempt of who I am and what I stand for in God, morals and standards.

On the way home from the bar he said see nothing is wrong with going into bars after work with co-workers and then asked what I thought. I remarked I liked his co workers and thought they were very nice but I don't agree with married men going to bars with single women and vice versa. I'm not judging them if that's what they want to do it is their business and it's between them.

My sidekick was angry and said I was judgmental. He knew I was strong in my commitment not to partake in what others do simply to fit into their mold. I didn't want to live my life in the bar scene running with a mixed crowd of single and married people pursuing friendship with one another.

I'm a firm believer married people should seek a best friend relationship with their spouses. I think time after work hours should be given to spouses and family instead of spending it in a bar with coworkers after working and fellowshipping with one another all day long and some evenings.

I don't have to follow the gang if I don't want to and they don't have to follow me. They don't have to choose to live the way I want to live and I don't have to choose to live the way they want to live. I want my input into choices involving my life. That doesn't mean I don't like them it means I have the same right to make decisions as they do.

There is no doubt you knew where I stood on certain issues. I was giving both of us the option not to marry someone that didn't have the same standards and didn't want the same things. You knew I felt this way about the bar scene and the subject of single and married people of the opposite sex being best friends before we married. Especially since you had no qualms about chasing a married woman when you were a single man and made a move on her as if you were still single after committing to marry me.

There should have been no reservations I was not going to live in the same situation in marriage. I told you I didn't want to marry someone like you. You begged me to marry you, prayed and accepted God and now your doing a complete turn around asking me to go against principles I believe in. After declaring you're a Christian and you felt the same way I did in the pursuit to have me as your wife I am faced with seeing those words were nothing more than a deceptive confession.

He was getting by with plenty without me saying it is okay to live as a single man even though he is married. I won't give you my blessings or my permission to go into bars or to female's homes. You have the freedom to make decisions If you want to go I can't stop you but there is a price to pay in all we do. I didn't give in to all his demands or give him the green light to do whatever he wants. He kept telling me to get over thinking he had to build trust either I trust him or he wants a divorce, using the fact that I was now dependent on him to support me. I had already given up my income and wasn't trained to make the kind of money he could make. In his anger he smashed the keyboard to the computer and threw his keys across the room so hard it broke the glass in a picture on the wall.

Konn never accepted marriage is two people giving up certain things and certain freedoms with members of the opposite sex. It's one freedom both partners give up when they are committed to love one another in the holy sacraments of marriage. Freedom to do whatever we want is no longer an option. If someone wants the life of a single person they should not get married. We are accountable to one another in marriage and have given up a certain amount of freedom to do as we please. We are still free but not in the same way as a single person. We married as two people that became as one in the intimacy that should bind us together as a couple. Most significantly having respect for each other whether we are as two or as one.

Meanwhile, more of his secrets were exposed through carelessness. Sometimes he left clues on purpose to throw me off. It gave him an excuse to say I unjustly accused him of womanizing. Then the next time I confronted him with lies that surface in deception to hide sex related events he can scream he's innocent like he was the time before. It's all my imagination. I didn't see what I saw and I didn't hear what I heard. There was no way to talk things out with someone that changes everything they say, every word you say there by controlling even our conversations. It was a three-ring circus.

I started to give up and follow the leader of the games cleverly planned agenda to cause confusion. At times convincing me to believe he gave up pornography so I wouldn't bug him about it anymore. At the time he is asking me to give him the okay to live as a single man he's sneaking and hiding filthy porno magazines in various places, taping naughty videos in the front room while I'm sleeping. I didn't know exactly what was going on when I began to find soiled wash clothes in and under my bed all the time. It not only sounds disgusting it was disgusting. Especially since I liked cleanliness and would never leave anything soiled lying around anywhere.

For a long while I didn't say anything or ask him about the freaky things happening in the house after he moved in. His behavior was foreign to me. I didn't know what was going on. I never knew what men did with pornography. I thought they just looked at it and dreamed on. There were many signs indicating he is always up to something that didn't include me. The unusual behavior was constant and exhausting. He never took a break or time out.

The first thing Konn did when we woke at three am in the morning was to take a bath then jump back in bed and get under the covers while I fixed breakfast. Every time I walked in the bedroom to let him know breakfast was ready it startled him. He was so engrossed in what he was doing. I noticed he always had one hand under the covers and the other hand anxiously grabbed the remote. I thought he was flicking channels to see what was on TV. Some times I asked what are you watching so early. He'd say nothing just seeing what's on. After months of the odd behavior I decided to see what he was up to.

One morning I turned on the garbage disposal and left it running so he'd think I was still in the kitchen cooking his breakfast. He didn't hear me open the door until I was in the room. I saw his hand moving under the covers and his other hand squirmed real fast to snap the remote. This time I could see it was the VCR he clicked off. I picked up the control and said let's see what's on the VCR at 3:30 am that is so interesting. His face turned ashen gray as I clicked on the remote. The video showed nude sex acts and it was stilled to stay on the nude model engaged in sex. I didn't need the sky to fall on my head to know he was masturbating fantasizing visions of him self-engaged in sex with the nude model. I hate saying the word masturbate so I call it having sex with himself.

When I viewed what he was doing not only was I shocked I became a real wise cracking smart mouthed individual. With a pained voice I exclaimed I didn't know turning the garbage disposal on made you horny. If I had known that's what it took to turn you on to engage in sex with your wife I'd have turned the disposal on sooner. He didn't say anything, not a word. I'm in a serious dilemma. I was stunned, it was a low blow to learn why he doesn't want me sexually and he's warped in perversion and fornication with himself. I was distressed and disappointed at the reasoning behind why he didn't desire me and what he was doing to avoid an intimate relationship.

Although I was filled with many mixed emotions during this period in time I continued to make the decision to be as compassionate and understanding as I can be toward my husband. While I'm trying to be supportive and stand by his side he taught me other things about his character. He trained me to doubt him and taught me he had absolutely no morals, no standards or no boundaries. Things were unfolding that should not have been any part of our lives together. As far as that goes it shouldn't be a part of anyone's life. If he were Pinocchio his nose would reach clear to Australia or further.

I was upset he was using the job God blessed us with to further conniving deceptions and unstable conditions maliciously manifested to jeopardize our marriage and to dominate, influence and confound me from the beginning of our life together.

Some of the positive things I liked about my husband are that he let me do what ever I want and never asked where I spent a dime. I could buy what ever I want to. He had his check deposited to my account and he let me handle the money. I gave him a certain amount every week and during this time he handled his allowance carefully sometimes having funds left at the end of the week. He beamed when I told him how good he was with money. I was frivolous at times and never cared about the amount I spent. My positive attitude toward my husband was always short lived, each time I thought he did something good the purpose for his reasoning appeared and it was always negative. He was never sincere regarding anything? One week his check wasn't deposited in our account. He went to see the secretary to find out what happened. The State Revenue withheld his entire check and my honey bunny (our pet name for one another) had to admit he had debts up the yang yang. This was his reasoning for letting me handle the money and have freedom to spend what I wanted. It was a form of control I didn't recognize at the time.

He had a memory loss and forgot to tell me about the debts he had with the State Revenue Department and the Internal Revenue and $10,000 on three different credit cards. It turns out he owed the state $36,000 in back taxes since 1984 and owed the internal revenue $125,000 since 1984. He seemed to call the shots and nothing happened to him. Most people would have been thrown in jail and some people are probably still sitting in jail for owing less than the enormous sum Konn owed.

He gave me his debts as a surprise wedding present. I couldn't believe someone as intelligent as my husband had no idea how to handle anything. But then again how dumb was he to get by all these years and walk away from everything smelling like a rose. I showed him all he had to do for the last sixteen years to get out from under the tax burden he has was to hire a tax attorney. Which I did look for the best tax attorney I could find and worked with him.

I erased the $36,000 worth of debts he owed the state revenue for sixteen years before he met me. When I found out we could make an offer to the state I asked the attorney to propose a $2,500 settlement and the State Revenue accepted the offer. I used my savings to pay it and wiped out that debt first. I took care of two of the credit cards offering a settlement and they accepted. I did the task in love for my husband. I was going to work with the attorney on the I R S debt but he got stinking mean and love or no love I didn't finish taking care of it. During our divorce it came out that he really resented me handling the money but had no choice for the IRS would take all he made if it were in his name and maybe I wouldn't help him pay the debts he owed 16 years before he met me.

The truth is in all the time I knew him he never handled one problem from the time I started helping him before and during marriage. After our divorce he still called and asked me to help him figure out how to get his life together financially. The only thing I knew of that he ever took care of was his sex hang-ups and self- indulging in perversion that took over his mind and heart. It is apparent he didn't handle anything before he met me. His ex wife divorced him during the time he deceived her financially. When they were married Konn bought what was called penny stocks in the firm he worked for. The stocks cost him one penny at first and then 88 cents during the time he's writing a program for a new company just starting out. The firm eventually went public and stocks he purchased for one penny and 88 cents sold for $58.00 to $63.00 a stock in a private sale. He made big bucks and didn't tell his wife how big.

The IRS stepped in a few years later and took all their bank accounts, home, cabin cruiser, car and all they owned. Plus they took $200,000 worth of bonds belonging to his wife and a few bonds belonging to his daughter.

He didn't bother to tell his wife the enormous amount of money he really made on the sale of the stocks and didn't file on their income tax. He told her he made a certain amount and used a little of the money to buy a few things for their home. They were married sixteen years and his wife didn't realize he lied and deceived her in marriage until this time. He didn't know she and I became friends after she called me the first time and asked if I will take care of paying a credit card he owed and they stuck her for paying it off because she couldn't get a credit line until it was paid. I was curious about the mysteriousness of the man I married and as I became better acquainted with his ex wife I asked her a few questions about their marriage breaking up. She said he was gone so much of the time and she was so insecure she blindly trusted him up until they lost everything they owned. She said his behavior was perverted. I asked if she meant sexually and her reply was no I mean all his behavior. She didn't know he was into pornography and the sick habit he had of playing with himself all the time. She said she ran across a playboy magazine once and told him not to keep things like that in their home and that was the end of it.

He didn't tell her he hid a five-passenger cabin cruiser in another town or about $8,000 in bonds he stowed away. He cashed the bonds when we dated. I found a receipt in the clutter of his car. He took me to the town where he stashed the boat and showed it to me one day. He didn't pay the storage fee on it and he lost the boat too. I checked out a few facts with a brokerage firm to see if I could find out the dollar amount he made on the stocks he sold to see if he had money stashed somewhere but I never could get the actual figure because it was a private sale. The broker told me in order to owe the huge amount he owed the IRS he had to make over a million dollars when he sold the stocks in 1984.

He kept his double life secret until I uncovered it plus the many other things he subjected me to with all the personalities he displayed. I began to believe aside from God no one knows Konn Rodent the way his wife Rosie Rodent knows him. No one will know him in the same way I did because he is different with whomever he is with and can fool people for very long periods of time. My hunny bunny hubby was so unbelievable many people didn't believe and that was how he gets away with convincingly misleading most people to believe he is Mr. wonderful. Many just plain felt sorry for him because he extracts sympathy from everyone for his burn scars. I thought he felt being burned gave him an excuse to act horrendously and covers a multitude of sins.

I did end up seeing six counselors with my husband. Out of the six two of them seen through him and seen violence, untruth and the unreality he survives in. He called them quacks. One of the councilors said he could tell Konn was violent by his voice and his actions when he spoke to me. Further telling Konn he never allowed me to heal from one hurt before he piled another hurt upon me. The counselor said he wouldn't treat my husband because he could see he didn't want anyone's help. He won't accept Konn as a patient and work with him unless he identifies with wanting help and Konn would have to go to a violent seminar before he took him on as a patient. Konn attended one meeting and said he didn't belong there for he wasn't violent like the other men attending the class. He told the counselor I wouldn't let him tell the therapist when we argued so he wasn't going to attend any more classes. After learning I couldn't trust a word he said and the uncanny display to cover his tracks not only did I take time and money to check things out I went to my own private councilor.

I needed to learn how to deal with my husband's out of the ordinary behavior and learn about the addiction that took over every fiber of his being. I loved my husband. I want to know how to handle issues I knew nothing about. I thought maybe she could help me save my marriage. It was essential to find someone I can talk to, trust and show the bruises, under pants and other possessions I stumbled across belonging to other women along with the pornography items he concealed in just about every spot he can find.

Chapter Six

Control, Manipulation & Lunacy

One week after our wedding each time I disagreed whether it was daily or weekly my husband asked to be liberated. Whenever I didn't agree he grabbed his clothes out of the closet and drawers, threw them in his car and left. After he cooled down he came back home and hauled his clothes back in. The pattern of coming and going continued throughout our marriage.

Immediately after he started working his new job the fun and games became more rampant and prevalent. The firm he's employed by was family oriented. The management encouraged the employee's families to feel as if they were a part of the company and welcomed us to visit whenever we like. If his boss were nearby when I stepped out of the elevator he'd stop and talk or show me around and walk me to find Konn. Sometimes I waited at the reception desk and had him paged.

When I started to go to the office to have lunch with my husband I began to notice if women were around Konn pretended as if he didn't know who I was. Sometimes he'd introduce me to male co-workers, but never the women.

I was in love with my husband and at first I wasn't paying attention. I was in my own little world too. I'd talk to everyone whether I was introduced or not. I just tagged along behind the fast pace he walked. But I wasn't blind eventually I noticed the way he acted superior in public as though he were ashamed of me. It was beginning to bug me he looked at me one way and viewed every other woman in a different way.

One day I asked if a woman he was talking to in the elevator was a co-worker. He screamed, ranted and raved for days. Categorizing me into his mold saying I was born jealous and therefore I had it in me. I would always be jealous. One of the rare times we prayed together he said God. I hope Rosie's jealously doesn't break us up. He kept up the threats to leave and get a divorce anytime I asked whom he was talking to. I didn't just ask who the women were. I asked who the men were too when he failed to acknowledge I was part of his life.

After awhile if I was by his side when he stopped to talk to someone I made a point of asking who they were. I didn't care who it was. I cared about the way he treated me in front of others. However, I should give him credit for the one woman he did introduce me to before I took matters into my own hands. She was a Pastors wife. I thought oh boy he's finally introducing me to a female co-worker but as he introduced me he called me by his ex wife's name. He apologized immediately. I said it's an honest mistake it's okay. But I didn't say it was okay when he called me someone else's name when we were in bed. My daughter in law Sheri drove in from out of town to have lunch with us one day. She said what is the matter with your husband he doesn't treat you like your his wife. I was interested to hear more I asked what exactly did she mean. She said he acted indifferent as if he didn't like me. He definitely didn't act as though I were his new wife. I said he didn't mean to act that way he was preoccupied with his new job. As the days passed it became irritating my family and friends picked up on his disrespectful attitude. I paid closer attention and eventually rebelled at the inconsiderate manners of playing macho man right in front of me. Then tell me he did no such thing it was my jealous imagination.

The last time Sheri asked if we could to go to town to pick Konn up for lunch his boss spotted us as we stepped off the elevator and he started kidding around with us before he showed us where Konn was. He escorted us to the area Konn was working with a female co-worker. They sat in close proximity using the same computer laughing engrossed in conversation. They didn't notice us standing in front of the huge picture window watching them carry on.

His boss was a really nice person. He stayed by us and continued to talk. We were having our own good time. Sheri was very close to having another baby. She looked uncomfortable with her huge stomach. Her one-year-old daughter started fussing and the boss picked her up and started playing with her. Just then Konn looked up and spotted us. They quit laughing; a graven serious look came over his face. He said something to her then they got up and walked out of the room. She stared at me all the way down the hall until she reached her destination. My husband walked right by us heading for his office like he didn't know who we were.

I walked into his office to see how soon he'd be ready to go to lunch. The first thing I noticed when I entered his cubicle was my picture laying face down on his desk. I thought it was odd but I didn't say anything. I waited for him to finish whatever it was he was fiddling with on his desk.

After Konn was employed in an executive position One of the first things I said to my husband was how cool it was to be married to a big wheel now. Does that mean you want a picture of your wife to put on your desk? Yes of course I want to look up and see you smiling at me when I'm away from you all day. He acted as if he got a kick out of my enthusiasm over the good things happening in our new life. I was thrilled my picture would be on his desk as the woman he shared his life with. The other men plastered pictures on almost every spot they had in their cubicle offices. One of the guys in the office was a newly wed too and he had an 8x10-wedding picture on his desk with fancy things belonging to his wife placed around it.

It touched me to see how proud he was of his wife while telling me how fortunate he was to have her. I yearned to have the same affection and attention from my husband. I couldn't understand how he could act nonchalant towards me. It hurt so badly when he ignored me and acted like I was a pain in the butt. There was nothing I wouldn't have done for my husband. I picked up the picture and put it upright. The picture was only 3x5 nothing fancy just a simple photograph but it was my favorite. It was a picture of both Konn and I taken on Valentine's Day when we became engaged. It was the only engagement picture we had.

Konn was finally ready to go. We walked several blocks to my favorite restaurant. It used to be part of an old theater where a lot of the old stars put on live shows. After we were seated I asked Konn how things were going on the job. In a thundering loud voice in front of everyone seated in the restaurant he said he didn't care to discuss his job with me. I was appalled at the outburst in answer to a question geared at having light conversation. I looked into the glaring, flaring eyes that belonged to my mate. I was annoyed at the disrespect he displayed not only when were alone but in front of my family and in front of strangers no matter where we happen to be.

After the embarrassing out burst I acted demure and polite. Sheri was uncomfortable and my grandchild was frightened and hanging on to her mom for dear life. Several months of listening to Konn belt out verbally abusive lyrics have gone on long enough. I decided to give him something to yell about. Something I knew would tickle his funny bone and upset him immensely. In a sweet tone of voice I said; Konn who was the woman you were working with? It was your boss's idea to stand by the window and surprise you when you looked up. His voice was alarmingly loud as he answered. She flew in from another state and is training a few others and me. Adding that it was none of my business who she is.

I couldn't be budged. I was on a roll. Looking him right in the eye's I said I wondered who she was because as the two of you came out of the office you didn't say anything to your boss and whizzed right by all of us. Were you afraid I might acknowledge knowing what your name was in front of her? Both of you seemed to be having a good time together. Do you have any idea why this woman you were laughing with stared at me with a Mortimer Snerd look on her face craning her neck all the way down the hall? I wondered who you told her I was? In a quieter voice he said nobody. You got that right you have treated me, as if I'm nobody. My dear husband I am only your wife. I wanted to get along with my hubby. He was weird and confusing but he also had moments when he was nice and fun to be with. Sometimes he was totally opposite from the uncaring mean cruel bastard that manifested in his personality so much of the time. I didn't like to argue or be put in a position to defend myself all the time.

I yearned for us to enjoy our life as a couple, treat each other like it was our last minute together so I always forgave him and laid aside behavior he perpetrated that I didn't consider appropriate. All I could do was carry on and love him. We don't love people because their perfect.

The next few times I went to town with Konn he made a point of nervously running to his office. He left me standing with my mouth open wondering, why is he scurrying off so fast.

Sometimes after I was through shopping I'd take items I purchased to his office and leave them till it was time for him to give me a lift home. Most of the time I waited on another floor by the exit door. Some times I went up to get him so we could leave the office together hoping someone would catch on that I'm his wife.

Many times after he slithered off so fast I'd stop and talk to the co-workers having a smoke by the door leading to the mini mall. Then I'd wander over the skywalk overlooking city streets. It was a pretty view of the city I loved to look at no matter how many times I seen it. Konn acting nervous, sneaky and suspicious the minute he set foot inside the entrance door was a sure sign something was happening. I could only hope whatever it was is saner than some of the other things I observed and wouldn't be another maladjusted experience.

One particular day as we entered the building he started to scamper ahead of me I asked him to slow down so I can go with him to his desk to use his phone. I walked in his office the same moment he did and seen my picture lying face down on his desk again. Without a word Konn quickly put the picture upright. I was puzzled as to why it was face down on his desk again. This time it hurt my feelings. Each time I came to town he continued making a beeline to his desk the second we walked in the door. It took several months before I caught on to what was going on in the new soap opera, "A Day In The Life Of Konn Rodent."

I mooched a ride to town one day without telling Konn. I walked in his office unexpectedly. He was surprised to see me. He noticed the first thing I did was glance at my picture lying face down. I put it back up and a light flashed on, the mystery was over.

I knew for certain why Konn hastened hurriedly to his desk whenever I'm with him. He knew my picture was always lying face down and didn't want me to know so he hurried to put it back up before I walked into his office. He saw the hurt in my eyes and tears streaming down my face. He didn't say a word and neither did I? The entire episode became a matter as pointless and disturbing as all the rest of the crazy chapters in the land of loony stories. I participated in the droll activity and went to his office unexpectedly several times for the sole purpose of seeing if the picture was up. Each time I walked in it was face down and I put it back up.

The charades continued until several months later when I went to his office and Konn wasn't at his desk as I walked in. I picked up the picture lying upside down on his desk and threw it in his trashcan. Minutes later he saw me standing in the doorway by his office. He raced down the hall and as he approached me he glanced to see if I put the picture up. He looked all over the room then spotted the photo in the trashcan. He picked it up out of the trash and said what is this doing here. I told him I threw it in the trash where it belongs.

All the trouble you have gone to in the last four months to hide the fact my picture didn't merit being displayed in your office can only mean one thing: your ashamed of your wife. The picture belongs in the trashcan where you have already thrown me.

Just leave it the trash and you won't have to worry about hiding it anymore or run to your office to put the dang picture back up when I come to town. My picture was the only one in all the offices on this floor I seen lying face down and not just here but any office I've ever been in. Every one of your co-workers has pictures of families and spouses plastered on every inch of space. As I pass by their office they all ask me to stop so they can show me pictures of their families with love and admiration in their eyes describing each person in the photo. Your behavior sucks. This ridiculous caper was more than just a hideous evil trick. You pulled me into a cat and mouse game you were playing without me suspecting I was the bait.

He said the man sitting next to him kept putting my picture down to be funny. If that was the case thank you both for making me the butt of the entertainment in your office every day for the last four months. If the man next to you was messing with our picture wouldn't it have been much easier to tell him to knock it off immediately, don't ever touch my wife's picture it hurts her feelings to see her picture isn't up. There is no way to justify suspicious behavior you went to the trouble of displaying just to hide what you knew you were doing in your willingness to participate in the painful experience you put me through playing on my hurt. Why is it harder for my husband to appreciate me as the other person he's sharing his life with than it is to give up deceitful plans you constantly sanction to harm and enormously wound me? What makes matters worse you didn't say one word to ease the hurt you saw in my eyes and the tears I shed in this unprecedented horrible experience that was totally uncalled for.

Remember how excited I was to have a picture of us on your desk? Well Mr. executive now I don't care what you do with it. For all I care you can stick it where the sun doesn't shine. I'm sure it will fit there along with the name I'm giving you to match your behavior. I'm fed up with deception and lies. It was disheartening to see the degrees he went to in order to break my heart a little more each day. I didn't get an answer or an explanation for his participation in the inane joke. I sold out for a dozen roses and forgave him. But I entered the arena and joined the battle in the war of roses my husband declared on me. I was going to take matters into my own hand.

One day as Konn and I were walking down the hall to his office and a couple of women co-workers in one of the cubicles a few feet down from Konn's office turned to look at us I stopped and introduced myself to the women. I said hi I'm Konn's wife. I'm introducing myself because my husband never introduces me to women. They laughed and we said a few more words. After wards when they seen me we talked and joked around. My thoughts ran ramped as we walked to the car. Driving home I turned to Konn and said how dare you act as if I'm an embarrassment. Get real and look at yourself. Look where you were when we married and where you are today and maybe you can appreciate who I am. I was smart enough to know how to bail you out of predicaments you had in your life for sixteen years. Why can't you accept me? I was a cool person, I love Jesus and I'm good-natured with a sense of humor, kind and generous and a big plus I love my husband over everything he does but I hate what you do.

What could possibly motivate you to treat me as if you don't know who I am? I was always clean and neat and pretty. Sometimes prettier than anyone you look at and desire. I can't comprehend why you're ashamed of me in public or for that matter anywhere else. The only thing you have to be ashamed of Konn Rodent is yourself and the way you behave toward your wife in private and in public. (I'm your wife and that should mean something to you.)

Our life together was a game and everything intertwined in the playoffs are connected to obscenity. No one knew the games he invented better than he did. I caught on to a few but he knew when to make the changes, when to switch and go back to square one. The times I thought I was making progress and getting through to him was only because he let me think I was. Taking his clothes and leaving was a maneuver to purposely frighten and hurt me emotionally and have more of a hold over me. Dominating with the mental games he played. He knew it scared me not to know where he was and fear of never seeing him again stressed me out so bad I'd have an anxiety attack. I told him I never got over seeing my husband one minute and in the next minute Angels took him by the hand into the Promised Land. After that experience I like being in contact with my loved ones at different times through the day fearing something could happen and it might be the last time I'd ever see them. I was afraid I'd never get to talk to them again the same way I didn't get to talk to Franklin before he died. I never got over not having a chance to say goodbye or thank you I treasured your love and all the things we would say to our loved ones if we knew they were going to die in the next second.

It was cold and cruel to manipulate command with the very words I shared confidentially concerning my dearly departed loved one and use my expressions to condemn and beat me over the head with. He acted like a parrot using all I told him to glorify him self and throw my words back at me in a distorted method. Konn let me think he wanted me as his wife, a family and a home. After marriage he let me know in no uncertain terms he didn't want marriage to be the same way I did. He had his own dictionary. Had I known before I married him I'd have asked his definition of certain words mainly the word commitment? He didn't want me to know where he went or anything he does. I wanted to know where his destination is at four am and where he disappears to for hours at a time during work hours. I was going to find out one way or another.

Chapter Seven

Perversion Rears It's Ugly Face

Like all the rest of my dreams I said bye bye to thoughts I had of chasing each other around the kitchen table into the bedroom all the time or at least for the first twenty years of marriage. I thought we were going to have fun and be as spontaneous and spur of the moment with an intimate sex life as we we're in doing other things.

The whole concept behind the act of making love should have involved the bride and the groom and not just the groom seeking self-gratification from his own body. In quest of pleasure he derived from indecent sexual fantasies, wicked immorality, nude stripper prostitutes and all that pornography offers and promotes.

As my bridegroom aggressively sought individual satisfaction with him self he deliberately lied and led his new bride to believe he didn't like engaging in sex. He tried to withhold the intimate relationship that bonds and grows between a husband and a wife getting to know one another.

I'm astonished and stunned to learn my newly wed husband didn't want to show affection or share intimacy that should have been normal and natural between a husband and wife. Instead he turned the act of making love into one more power play to enhance the sick enjoyment he received rejecting his new bride knowing it was the ultimate hurt beyond anything he could have done to his wife. All the while he is taking care of his own personal sexual needs with himself he robbed us together as a married couple and robbed his wife of a harmonious, romantic, loving, caring and fulfilling time of getting to know each others needs as a couple in love that desire one another and maybe sometimes having intimacy be a giggly fun time. My husband never gave me a chance to show him all the love I wanted to shower on him. Nor did he give him self the option to see I could have been the best sex partner he'd ever hope to find. He never gave our marriage the opportunity to get off the ground. It was doomed from the start.

There were many unpleasant incidents that occurred during my husband's sadistic supremacy power play in this area. One of the first was the insecurity from the insult of the coldhearted rejection using intimacy to control and keep me confused so I would never know where I stood in our relationship. In my naïve makeup I had no idea what was really going on as my husband displays strange abnormally sick habits with our sex life. I didn't know the truth about the great imposter's mysterious motives yet or what the unexplained strategies were in the great white deception. Everything he did took me by surprise.

As the days went by the frustration and hurt grew. It was like living with a puzzle but none of the pieces fit. Konn's affection consisted of throwing a crumb at me now and then if I barked often enough. Naturally my reaction was to think it was my fault. Maybe there was something wrong with me. I felt unattractive, undesirable and unloved. It was always the center of trying even harder to please my husband thinking he'd eventually see what a great wife he had by his side and he would accept me. That never happened and my reaction to deny anything is wrong stepped in as I ignored all he did for a while. I went on more shopping sprees than I can count. But nothing could take the place of the hole I felt in my heart as he scorned and rejected me as his new bride, his wife and a woman.

Then I found a pair of someone's undies he hid and revenge began to rear its ugly head in my thoughts and behavior. I had to give this classic loony story a title. I call the experience; " The Mattress That Gave Birth to the Mystery Woman's Underpants." Why would a woman give her filthy underwear to my husband and why would he want them? Who knows the identity of the mysterious women? How long has he been carrying a pair of her undies in his pocket, in and out of the house and in his car? Only the shadow Konn Rodent knows!

I discovered the undies the day we arrived home around four am after we went to a football game out of town. We were tired and we took a nap after lunch. During the course of sleeping I rolled over and my hand rested on his pant's pocket. The moment my hand touched him he quickly rolled over and put the full weight of his body on my hand. He wouldn't let me move it out from under him. I shoved and yanked until I finally freed my hand. After living with his odd ways seven months now I wondered what uncanny and unbalanced act was taking precedent today. There's one thing I knew for sure I could count on it being something flaky.

I wanted to see what he'd do if I put my hand on his pocket again. Sure enough he pinned my hand under him again. We finally got up. All through the day whenever I looked at him his eyes darted back and forth. He looked like a cat that swallowed a canary. At one point during the day I noticed the mattress on the bed was off the springs and over to one side. I went in the bedroom to straighten it. As I pushed it back in place he bolted off the sofa and came running in to inquire what I was doing. In that very moment he gave himself away. Running that fast into the bedroom as I'm fixing the mattress meant only one thing he must have hidden something under it. I thought he bought a gift when we were out of town for one of the gals at work and didn't want me to know. I gave him the same innocent act all day he gave me for seven months. I pretended I didn't know he was up to something evil again. If he wanted to cover his tracks he should have taken time to straighten the mattress after he hid the undies. He kept me close to his side and made me go wherever he went through the day. He followed me every time I walked in the bedroom.

I played the game like a pro. He acted so suspicious I intentionally went in and out of the bedroom many times through out the day to see if he'd follow me. A couple times I acted like I was straitening sheets to see how fast he'd jump up and run into the room.

I went to bed early in the evening. He stayed right with me. He got up as usual at three am to bathe. The moment he went into the bathroom I got out of bed and raised the mattress and there was a pair of undies wadded up and shoved clear to the middle of our bed. Traumatized and shocked I couldn't believe my eyes. I picked the undies up, went downstairs, put them under the sofa, then quickly went back to bed and stayed there. I told him I didn't feel good and wasn't getting up to fix breakfast. I thought his behavior the previous day after he hid the panties was more than astounding. It was plain bizarre. Believing his new wife was too stupid to catch on to what he was up to and how delighted he comes across when he plays I've got a secret Rosie ha ha ha. It literally made me physically and emotionally sick. Maybe he was right, I was stupid, I got up every morning at three am to fix his breakfast with love. Making sure it was perfectly cooked, sometimes I served it to him in bed wanting to please him and in my desire to be a great wife for my husband.

He never gave a thought to the way I cared for him when no one else gave a damn if he ate or froze to death sleeping in his car. Broke and homeless and he had only me the lovesick fool. I looked at him with love and he looked at me as someone he could use for his own personal financial gain while he plays me for a fool. Heck so what if in the process he breaks my heart and leaves me penniless just so he has money to romp with strippers and pay them for sexual favors. Eventually I learned that was all that mattered to Konn. Rosie can go to hell. The very place he told me to go when he reached an income of $100,000 a year and didn't need me anymore. The tragedy of the whole affair is that I needed him but he didn't need me. The great lengths my husband went through to pry me out of bed as he tries to get the undies and go about his indistinct business showed me he's always aware of the motives he has for all his conduct. I want to see how far he would go not knowing I had the undies. Rosie are you going to take a bath? No Konn. I'll take one after you leave. That didn't work so he said I love it when you walk me to the door. Will you walk with me this morning? Okay Konn. I got out of bed and started to walk to the front door with him.

Half way to the door he turns around very quickly and heads back toward the bedroom saying I forgot my tobacco. I stayed right next to him and walked back into the room with him. He's having a hard time trying to figure out how he can get the undies back with me on his tail. He gave up, left for work and ten minutes later he's back. He knew I had a doctor's appointment so he said I came back to take you to the doctors honey. Konn you never cared when I went to the doctor or ever asked why I was going before or after I went. For that matter you've never asked how I feel. Why the concern now?

I'm calling my boss to tell him I'm taking my honey to the doctors. He starts to dial the phone and I put my hand on the receiver. Honey bunny I have the undies you tried to conceal under the mattress. I know you have your reasons for taking me to the doctor's. After we arrive at his office your going to tell me you forgot something at home. Then drive home grab the undies you hid under the mattress. Then you will stash the underpants in your car or in your pocket till the next time you want to play with them. Next you'll smile cunningly and tell your self how clever you are to put one over on your wife again.

The last step you were going to display in the deceiving scheme to fetch the mystery woman's undies you hid behind my back in front of my face is that you'll pick me up at the doctor's office with a smug superior look of secrecy in the questioning wonder your putting me through trying to understand why you don't desire me and why you have someone's undies to begin with. Now I find the reasons behind the sick fun you have all the time is always at my expense in one way or another.

Your behavior is so shockingly outrageous it paralyzes me. I can't even move a muscle or believe my very eyes because I could never comprehend any one can conceivably behave in the manner you conduct yourself. Therefore I don't know what your doing most of the time. The reasons I don't know what your up to most of the time is not because you're as clever as you think you are. It's because I can't conceive of anyone behaving in the disgraceful, sneaky deceiving method you constantly perform. All your activity can only be regarded with suspicion. I've never been exposed to anything you represent but I do know behavior that's contemptible and despicable and I'm not sure how to deal with any of it.

Your not only unprincipled sexually I believe all your behavior is perverted. The look on your face illustrated how much you enjoyed the game of hide and seek you played with me all day long after stashing someone's dirty undies under the mattress of our bed. It's a hoot to know you put one over on me and your dim-witted wife is sleeping on top of another woman's underpants. Do you really believe you don't have a problem with deviant traits your displaying daily? All the while your taking care of your sexual needs in a demented style you are acting as if I'm unaware of anything simply because I love you and I'm trying to please you. I have a news flash I can see and hear. Everything I confront you with is not my imagination. It is all truth and reality of behavior you implement toward yourself and toward me. I'm your wife that should mean something more to you than it does.

All these months you made me feel undesirable and rejected as your new bride. Vigorously delighting in the insulting negative response you choose to enact to avoid an intimate relationship. Your sexual preference is not only culminated with demeaning pornography, fantasies and playing with yourself now I find your doing something freakish with some body's dirty underwear. With all those notches in your belfry how can you have the nerve to act conceitedly haughty informing me that sex is two consenting adults and I don't know what passion is? I'm overwhelmed in the struggle to convince you with the intention of relaying your married to me; I'm your wife. I'm baffled you don't make love without an argument, leave the house, lock yourself in the bathroom and every other crazy humiliation purposely perpetrated to make me feel bad about myself amusing your self with all the devastating wicked iniquity you've displayed thus far.

I want to know why your carrying undies in your car and in your pocket and what you were going to do with them when you brought them into our home?

Obviously you wanted to keep the undies to go as far as you went to hide them and get them back out of your hiding place before you knew I found them. Acting superior and arrogant saying things to destroy me as your wife and a woman let alone as a human being. With all the peculiar behavior you display look in the mirror before you point at my faults or me.

The nonsense of refusing to be a husband saying your too old, too tired, you can't get it up, there is something wrong with me you should be able to just look at me and get an erection. I should get over being a newlywed and call me someone else's name in bed. It's not the right time to have sex no matter what time it is. Along with all the other crap you spewed out lusting and fantasizing about every woman you see and naked orgies you're indulging in watching porno videos. Along with the woman you're cheating sexually with and collecting undies from.

Where are you going when you leave home at four am and show up on the job five hours later? Where do you go when you vanish from your job all hours of the day, come home to take baths in the middle of the day and leave soiled shorts on the floor for me to pick up. It is like having another woman in bed when your fantasizing sex with them and now you bring your girlfriends undies home to play with too. This is the most torturous disturbing activity I was ever subjected to endure. Always telling the counselor I'm hallucinating because you don't do that anymore. Well you don't do it any less. Don't tell me everything is my fault and your not doing anything wrong. I should see the damn counselors. I was born jealous because I want my husband to quit acting like a freakish nerd with sexually addicted transgressions you keep denying and I keep finding. I'm sick of you taking the heat off yourself saying I'm sexually obsessed because I want some answers to your immoral foolhardy manners.

I think you better go to work your never getting the undies back. Get out of my sight. I don't want to talk to you let alone look at you. I can't believe you willfully choose to torment me with sexual abuse. I was miffed, sad, hurt, discouraged and brave all at one time. I finally got my sidekick to leave the house. Minutes later he's back saying the undies belong to his ex wife he forgot they were under the car seat. He was looking for a rag and shoved what he thought was a rag in his pocket. I didn't want you to see them so I put them under the mattress. I was going to throw them away. Husband you have not seen you're ex wife that remarried six years ago. Your telling me you had her undies six years in a car you owned less than one year. I checked under the seat two months ago after I found the sack of porn magazines you kept in your car and there were no panties under there at that time.

You didn't have a change of clothes when I began to help you but you held on to your wives stinky slinky undies. What planet are you from and how did you get here?

I'll go so far as to put it in this context. Let's say you had a pair of your ex wives undies over six years. As a married man why did you want to keep them? Why bring them in the house? Why go to all the trouble to hide them and get them back? Why didn't you at least take them back to the car instead of amusing yourself knowing it will hurt your wife to know you had them to begin with? There was plenty of time to dispose of them in the six years you say you had them and plenty of time to get rid of them during the day you tried to conceal them from me. Anything but the way you played this new sporting event.

The entire episode caused irreparable damage to our marriage, to me and to building trust? You have been teaching me not to trust you for so long; congratulations I'll never trust you again. I baited you the whole day. I didn't have to be an intellect to know you were up to no good. I never dreamed the secrecy you subsist in would turn out to be a pair of woman's dirty underwear with faded old ministration bloodstains on them. It's beyond shamefully revolting. I was shockingly ill and nauseous the second I found them I had to run to the downstairs bathroom and throw up. I played the game with you but it deeply affected me as I watched your reactions all day long. Playing the role of sicko say's you delight in what you're doing with all the lies you tell, the deception and sexual indecency with unbalanced immorality you display bounces back to me. The action of purposely putting undies in your pocket when you came into the house says you know why you wanted to keep the underwear belonging to your mystery women. I'm not playing your games now; I want to know the truth as to why you have them and whom they really belong to?

The extreme disturbing lengths my husband went too with the entire incident shows he knew he was doing something shady and knows the undies don't belong to his ex -wife. He knows the motive behind every lie he tells and every lie to cover that lie and the next lie and the next and the beat goes on and on.

The story of undies belonging to your ex should be mounted and sent to a liars club. We could win first prize. Konn said call and ask her if I helped move her and they fell in my car, you'll see I'm telling the truth. How did they get in the car you've owned less than a year? He never knew I met her and we talked from time to time. I did call her and I told her about the undies and the way Konn related how he acquired the panties and that he said they belonged to her. I think it's appropriate to guess what she said. I put the undies in a plastic bag and stuck them in my purse. I went to see my friends in the beauty shop. It was December 13, 1996. I waved the undies around like a flag and said see the Christmas present my husband gave me. Don't ask where you can buy a pair just like them I don't know where he purchased them. I called a friend to come over and showed the undies to her too. She got sick to her stomach and almost threw up.

As the day progressed I called him at work. Konn I took your clothes to a certain motel. I don't want you to come near me ever again. There is money and everything you own in the motel room. He said okay we don't get along anyway. That evening he broke down the door and came in saying you're my wife. I have every right to be here. I notice he's trembling and shaking. I listened then softened and said okay he can get his clothes and come back home. I was filled with apprehension and the hold he seemed to have on me grew stronger. Unhappiness was my middle name. Now I don't want him to touch me.

Konn told me he'd take a lie detector test to prove he is telling the truth. I called his bluff and lined one up. I checked into an investigative service and asked how to go about finding someone with equipment to give a lie detector test. They told me they knew someone out of town that would do it.

I told the detective my husband volunteered to take the test. I'd never have thought of asking him to take a lie detector test. Once he said it I grabbed hold of the humongous bluff. I want him to tell the truth so he has to deal with it. I can handle the truth but I can't fight ghosts. This was his way of trying to get me to accept his story. I never dreamed I would say okay let's do it.

The detective came ready to give the lie detector test. At the last minute Konn said he couldn't make it he had to work. I called the detective that drove 50 miles one way to come here. I told him Konn couldn't get off work. I lined the test up for another evening. He took my husband into a room where he set up the equipment and talked to him alone. After they talked awhile the detective called me into the room. He got out of taking the test by saying he worked a lot of hours and was really tired for he had very little sleep. For some reason the detective said he couldn't give the test if Konn didn't have any sleep.

I wondered if Konn knew the tiny little fact that if he was tired he didn't have to take the lie detector test for he knew how to say he would take one. He said Konn was telling fairytales. He went on to say my husband would answer a few questions I wrote out for him. But he won't answer the question of whom the undies belonged to, why he had them or where he went at four am and when he left work so many hours plus several other questions centered on lies he told. I wrote a few questions that would have shown when he was being truthful or deceitful. Konn got out of taking the lie detector test the same way he gets out of everything. He just doesn't do whatever it takes to get to the truth and reality of the depraved darkness in his behavior. Before we left the office I asked the detective to have the undies analyzed. He said forget it you two look like you love one another there are to many divorces so go home and get along with one another. If he messes up again throw him out. I didn't realize at the time what I was asking for was a DNA. I guess I was a little ahead of the times and used the word analyzes. I should've left the undies at the office. Years later I heard of a few cases where women had DNA test's on articles connected to their husbands cheating and they sued for plenty and sued the women their husband cheated with claiming the women took the affection that belonged to their wife.

After we left the detective's office and the lie detector test my husband squirmed out of following through with taking the liars test he copped a cold-hearted uncaring attitude about the entire affair. I was upset he didn't answer to anything after I called his bluff to get to the truth. We went to bed and I said if you don't tell me whom the undies belong to I'd take them to work and ask the girls whom they belong to. I don't know what he expected his hurt newly wed wife of seven months to say when her hopes and dreams were crushed.

He turned into a crazed animal tearing the room apart looking for the undies. I still had them in a plastic bag in my purse. I put my coat on and started to leave. I was getting in the car and he came bounding after me, grabbed me out of the car and started to hit me and wouldn't let me leave. I managed to get the garage door open and was going to walk over to my daughter's house next door. He came after me hitting, grabbing and pushing trying to find the pants and he wouldn't let go.

I fell and cut my knee and leg. I'm down on the ground bleeding, hurt and in pain trying to get up. He pulled my coat and all my clothes off. I stood stark naked outdoors in my front yard with the garage lights shining on me like a spotlight. I had to walk in the house naked, betrayed and dishonored.

I thanked God my daughter was sleeping downstairs on the other side of the house and didn't hear the ruckus and witness her mom walk in the house nude and bleeding. He walked in after me and still wouldn't let go. I took the undies out of my purse and put a match to them so he can't have them. He took them out to the patio and finished burning them on the grill. I was washing the blood off and called Konn to come in the bathroom to see the bruises, cuts and scratches he put all over my body. He said Rosie it was your fault. I hit you because you said you were going to take the undies to work and ask the girls whom they belonged to. Once again that was the real Konn Rodent. The despicable wretched man I married.

My body hurt from the bruises, cuts and scrapes. I'm in agony over all that took place in the course of three days. I can't stop crying or feeling nauseous. I thought of how brutal and violent he behaved. He was like a bulldozer wrecking havoc until he got what he wanted. He wasn't going to stop harming me until I gave him the undies back. The next morning I seriously thought of calling the police and ask what I should do. I wasn't thinking rationally. It isn't easy to function and know what to do when you're in a state of shock. I didn't know all the times I didn't react the name of my reaction was shock.

I called my husband at work and told him I was going to have him arrested for assault and battery. He came running home from work, smoothed things over and I gave in once more.

Till the day I die I will regret not calling the police and having him arrested the minute the violence occurred. I should have let him know from the start he can't manhandle and do whatever he wanted and get by with it. Konn talked me out of calling the police and he got by with assaulting me. And ended up getting by with all the rest of the ruthless behavior and performances after that.

I didn't tell my family Konn put me in harms way and hit me. I learned the hard way by staying with him after he displayed violence I was showing him I tolerated his behavior. I didn't even look at the way I protected him and set the course of action he would execute on me though out the rest of our marriage. I was living with the enemy in his campgrounds. As I witnessed outlandish aggressively vicious sadistic deeds I knew I needed an ally to help me cope with the unbalanced confusing dilemma. I didn't know which way to turn. It was hard to comprehend Konn's continual constant I love you, I hate you attitude. I didn't know if I was coming or going. He'd tell me twenty times a day he loved me but his other words and actions said I hate you. I was not aware I was walking around in trauma and shock most of the time. We were married only seven months the day I found the undies and the very day I looked for a councilor for myself. I recognized I needed help and I needed it badly.

Distraught, depressed and discouraged I prayed for God to lead me to the right person. I looked in the yellow pages to find a professional with experience. A counselor named Demi caught my eye. I chose her for the impressive criteria she advertised and her office was just a few blocks from my home.

It was my first encounter with my own private councilor. The first thing I did when I walked into her home was to wave the panties I found hidden in our bed. I tried to hand them to her and she said put those dirty panties away I don't want to touch them. We laughed and had an instant rapport. I went back three days later to show her the bruises. I continued to see her not only because I was befuddled but also I felt there was going to be a day I'd need an ally. I discerned I might need documented proof of his behavior someday. Immediately Demi was like finding an old friend. She became my confidante and support system. She was wonderful to me. I loved her kindness, sympathy, empathy and her. She saw the anguish on my face and the pain of a grief stricken heart struggling to hold onto my husband and our marriage.

Demi encouraged and cried with me. She taught me about the behavior I was being forced to deal with. She made me realize I was in an abusive, mentally disturbed relationship I continued to deny for several years.

She made me aware I was functioning in shock all the time. I never really got over anything that happened from day one because he didn't give me a chance to recoup from one hurt before he piled on another.

I continue to see her to this day. I'm not totally to the place I want to be at and haven't regained all the self-esteem I lost along the way. Knowing I needed a counselor was the first step to getting a grip on my life and toward understanding I was in a dysfunctional violent situation. I was being compulsively forced to deal with my husband's deviant behavior because he would do anything to benefit himself simply to hide his disturbing selfish demoralizing addiction. Before finding Demi I had already been to a few councilors Konn made me see with him under threats of divorcing me if I didn't go because I was jealous and was imagining things that pointed to his cheating. Down the line he had other objects belonging to women including a g-string.

He actually gave me an answer when I told him to go ahead and get the divorce he wanted for so long. He told me what he did with the undies. Probably only told me because he knew it would disturb me even further. It was an upsetting answer. I'd have been better off not knowing the answer.

The enitre time he's telling me he didn't like sex and didn't make an attempt to adhere intimately I now learn he held the unknown woman's underwear on his genitals as he self coddles his own body masturbating visionary sex with hundreds of women in the course of our marriage thus far. Why should this make me upset and jealous?

For a while Konn acted like Mr. good Guy. I'm still upset and cry all the time since finding dirty undies and witnessing the harmful dreadful aggression to get them from me. But the bottom line is I love my husband. I have to try. He was making an attempt to pay attention but I'm still skeptical. Now I'm worried he will catch a disease from his defective activities. I don't want him to touch me and I rejected the halfhearted advances he makes toward me now.

I actually believed Konn when he said he was sorry and will do all he can to do right by me. He started to bring me a rose every night, came home directly home after work and stayed with me all-evening. I begin to have hopes, dreams and plans again. But it turns out the good guy routine is filled with vile deception no matter how nice he acts. He didn't give up anything and continued with the addiction. He just became sneakier and more misleading. And continues to intentionally cause doubts and confusion. I believed him when I shouldn't have and I didn't believe him when I should have. This way he can get away with whatever he does, cry innocent when falsely accused and get away with perversion by focusing on the times I misjudged him.

Konn was so believable at times I'd let my guard down and swallow his stories whole. I believed him when all odds should have been against my believing him. I gave in and never realized it enabled him to see how far he could go with me and he went all the way.

Chapter Eight

Pornography and Councilors

My husband pressured, cajoled and repeatedly screeched Rosie you're jealous you think crazy either you see a counselor or I want a divorce. He kept up a quest to push me over the edge advocating a nervous breakdown to add the final touch to prevent the undertaking of all I tried to accomplish in relation to helping him face truth and reality. His only hope of keeping his sex secrets is to deplete my credibility so no one will believe me if I decide to tell the details on his dreadful behavior. He hated me for uncovering what he kept concealed from every one before me. No one ever held him accountable and responsible for his behavior until I came into his life. There were some things I couldn't shove under the rug. He wants me to stop questioning his addiction and disappearing phenomena's.

Konn attempted many different ways to get me to back off. He tried every way possible to make me believe everything is my imagination. He wants me to believe the lies dealing with his uncanny schemes. He was too clever to believe his own lies. I don't think I ever got across to anyone how intelligent he really is. Controlling his words before and after the fact and controlling my reaction and words adding doubt with manipulation to control. I don't think someone should be categorized as dumb just because they don't know how to fix a leaky faucet or change a tire. It took a lot more intelligence and remembrance to go to all the trouble to survive in the untruthful unreal world of deception he survives in than it takes to live in honesty and reality.

He had a motive to his madness only someone with the same mindset could know. I caught on to some of the foolishness through trial and error. If I was to survive in his loony land I had to figure out what he was up to but why he enacted the phenomena's will always be a mystery. Only Konn knew the reasons for the acts he committed but there was no rhyme or reason to act like the class bully or constantly harasses me with deceit or put fear in my heart. I wanted our marriage to work so I finally gave in and went with him to see the first counselor I ever encountered. At this stage of the game I thought it certainly couldn't hurt. He started the session by telling the therapist named Sam I was jealous and would not give him freedom to go into a certain divorcees house to fix her furnace. The other men got to help her. He said it was a Christian thing to do. I prevented him from being a Christian. Up to now the only person I knew of that he helped was himself.

After a few sessions it dawned on me. He wasn't getting anywhere with me in the request's and demands he made. The entire drive was to have the counselor help him obtain freedom to cavort with any women he wants to without my questioning him. He couldn't quite figure out how to get around me when I took a stand, voiced my opinion, confronted him and held him accountable for his behavior. He played it all so cool. I told both the counselor and Konn if she has so many men that know how to fix her furnace why does she need his help too? My husband needs to learn to fix his own furnace in his own house before he fixed others. I was glad I went with him to the few sessions I attended. They gave me more insight into his reasoning behind dragging me to a counselor.

My feelings and emotions hung out in the open whether I wanted them to or not. I was straight forward and honest knowing in order for us to have a good solid marriage and bring us closer together as a couple we had to have truth between us. My hubby's comments about me doing things with my friends made me feel anxious over doing anything with them anymore. Even having a friend bugged him. He said I hang out with my acquaintances why can't he hang out with his friends? You can Konn who are they anyway? You know my friends. You keep your friends hidden so I don't know who your friends are I haven't met one yet.

I told the therapist the circumstances connected to thoughts I had due to the sex problems and pornography material I kept finding. Konn merely said he didn't do that anymore and that was the end of it. Sam believed him. I listened to my spouse say whatever it took to catch someone on his lure one too many times. When Konn was done telling falsehoods he invited the counselor to pick him up at work and have lunch, so Sam could see he wasn't doing anything wrong. They went to lunch, and my partner was on his best behavior. At the next session the counselor said my husband was a great man. He could see why I didn't want my marriage to break up. Then he turned on me and said I had the problem because I didn't trust Konn. There was nothing wrong with his behavior. I had a bad attitude toward Konn wanting to further his career and my husband didn't look at women the entire time they were together. What could I say? Konn would persist in the lie and the therapist will believe it all. My partner knew all to well that he is an expert in dishonesty. He had plenty of experience deceiving everyone. I went a few more times then I refused to go.

Each time I went it was a repetition of accusations. It was more than I could swallow on a steady diet so I didn't go back. But I did listen to some things and followed the counselor's advice and backed off. I gave my husband as much room to do his own thing and as much of my trust as I could under the circumstances. The rest is history. Shortly after the visits to the councilor I found Konn's reality in a huge trash bag filled with lewd magazines on the floor in the back seat of his car. Early one morning we had to take his car to the mechanic to be fixed. It was so early the mechanic wouldn't be open for a few more hours. The mechanic told Konn to park his car in front of a locked fence door until he arrived and leave the car door unlocked and put the key under the mat on the floorboard.

I didn't have a set of keys to his car and he wouldn't let me in the car unless he was in it. The back seat of his car was trashed. Filled to the brim with junk he carried around. There were pieces of old computers, papers, dirty clothes and all sorts of debris and trash from fast food restaurants strewn everywhere. We left his car at the mechanics and I drove him to the bus stop dropped him off. I went back to see why he never let me in the car alone. He wouldn't let me use his key if I forgot something in the car he had to get it for me. I asked what was in the trash bag behind the seat and he said it was garbage. I looked in the bag and it was packed to the brim with vulgar wicked magazines. He was right the trash bag was filled with garbage.

I didn't attempt to go though the treasures of garbage in the back seat for it was astonishing. I thought something might be growing in the clutter it had been they're so long. I asked Konn, don't you worry someone will see all the stuff you carry in your car, think it's valuable and break in.

After a while I quit worrying about anyone breaking in thinking a thief might have been as astounded as I was looking at the litter piled to the roof of the car and wouldn't know where to start looking for something of value. A week later I told Konn I'd like to clean the car right away and trade it in on another one. He always put me off when I wanted to do anything with his car. This time I told him I would hire someone to open the door if he didn't do it for me. First thing I did in front of him was open the trash bag. Well what do we have here? Are you hiding my birthday gift? He almost lost it. But he didn't say a word.

I pulled one of the magazines out of the trash bag, opened it up and the pictures were a mixture of nudity engaged in grotesque sexual deviation and mixtures of males and females. I wanted to take the magazines to the councilor, throw the whole bag full on the floor and ask him to take a whiff and see what cheating and deception smells like.

I checked to see when he purchased them. Some were recent and some were years old. I didn't think to ask him to open the trunk to see what he was hiding in there. Wonder of wonders I thought he was trying to please me when he made a point of taking the huge trash bag filled with the magazines out to the curb right in front of my eyes because the trash truck would be by to pick up the garbage early the next morning. I was proud of Konn taking a step to throw the filth out of his life. I thanked him for respecting the way I feel about the magazines. I believed throwing the smutty material in the trash was a real breakthrough. He was so convincing. I wanted to think the best but it was foolish to consider he'd do something for our marriage and for us.

All the while I'm cleaning the car he made a fuss about me throwing away old papers and restaurant rubbish strewn on the floorboard. After awhile I was tired of picking up the mess and hauling sacks of trash to the curb I gave it up and called it a night. I took a bath and went to bed. Konn said he was going to stay up awhile. Little did I know after I fell asleep he went back outside, got the trash bag filled with magazines and stashed them. I took out more garbage after Konn left for work at 4 am. I noticed the sack with the sex material was gone. It was noticeable because he didn't set the sack of lewd material near the other sacks he put it over the side. I opened the other sacks to be sure he couldn't say I was hallucinating. There was no mistaking the magazines had vanished.

When he came home from work. I told him after he left in the morning I took out more trash and the sack of porno material was gone. What do you think happened to it? He said workers on the garbage trucks walk around, look through trash and keep what they want before throwing it in the compactor. The trucks were nowhere in sight until two hours after I took the rest of the garbage outside. Two years later I found the same trash bag filled with the same magazines he conned me into believing he threw away. It was trusting and gullible to consider he sincerely threw his seducing collection away. The porn he supposedly threw away to please me was stashed in the safest place he could find. He hid it right under my nose. I should say right above my head in my personal closet. He must have chuckled every time I opened my closet door. It was no fun living with a low down sneaky Pete slinking around plotting and planning his destiny without me. I found the trash bag on a day he drove me to the beauty shop. It was one of his favorite places to drive me. I had a weekly appointment and he could come back home uninterrupted and lose himself in the twilight zone of sexual visions.

Every time he brought me home from the beauty shop or other appointments there were spots of white flexes on the carpeting. I never thought too much about it. We had flocked ceilings I figured some of it came loose from time to time and fell to the floor. This went on over a period of two years before I caught on to his safe hiding place. I never opened the small attic door in my closet in all the years I lived here. I didn't open it until long after Konn moved in the house carting all his old baggage filled with every wicked, evil, worldly habit he could conceivably pack in his suitcase. Along with the discord and confusion he carries in his heart as he moved it all in to my home and turned our bedroom into a den of iniquity, adultery and fornication.

He was getting more careless than ever. Several things occurred prior to the morning I came across the hiding place and found the same pornography material for the second time. One thing he facilitated was that he dropped me off at the hairdressers but it was not the correct time for my appointment. I was two hours early. I didn't want to wait around that long and I asked one of the girls to drive me home.

I didn't have my house key so I rang the bell. Konn answered the door with the same familiar sneaky look on his face. I told him I got the time mixed up. I walked step for step with him into the bedroom I seen him pick up a pair of undies off the corner of the bed and scrunch them in his hand.

He walked into the bathroom unaware I was right behind him I stood and watched him as he shoved the undies down the front of his pants at the same time he's shoving his hands in his pants he's talking loudly saying he's going to run a bath. He turns and sees me standing right behind him inches away observing all he is doing. Slovenly hurrying to hide the undies he didn't get his entire shirt tucked in properly and it was half in and half out of his pants.

He didn't say a word and neither did I? The shock is traumatic. It took me two days before I asked him. Hey Konn what did you shove down the front of your pants in front of me. His reply to my seeing the disgusting drama is that he didn't remember doing any thing like that my mind was playing tricks on me again. After that encounter finding the trash bag he'd hidden for two years full of nudity was duck soup. One day when I came home from the beauty parlor I walked in the bedroom, my closet door was open and my silk bathrobe was lying on the floor. I took special care of the robe for my daughter in law bought it for me in China. I very seldom wore the robe and I don't leave my closet door open.

I looked up at the white specks on the floor and up at the ceiling and the attic door catches my eye. Suddenly I realized he's hidden some thing in the attic and the white flecks must be falling as he opens the attic door. I got a ladder and opened the little door.

I reached my hand in and felt something plastic. I still couldn't see what it was and the bag was so heavy I couldn't lift it up over the ledge. The ladder wouldn't fit close enough so I had to get on the tiny ledge in my closet. I stuck my head in the attic opening and there is the trash bag filled with the naughty magazines he wanted me to believe he threw away two years ago. Recognizing all that took place behind my back and before my face from day one and the way he turned out to be an alien weirdo in my life and in our bedroom threw me for a loop. I almost passed out before I got off the ladder.

A few weeks before finding the magazines in the attic I was getting his suitcase out of the trunk of his car and under the spare tire was a paper sack with six more putrid nudity books. I'd clean his car out every week when he arrived home after being 300 miles away from home all week and there would be receipts for playboy videos on the front seat and cigarette butts with lipstick in the ashtray that was clean when he left plus a long filthy false fingernail his friend lost in the car. I bought the car for Konn so I insisted on having a set of keys. I went in and out of his car whenever I pleased. It was ridiculous to be his wife and not be allowed to have a key to the car and the same privileges and access he had to all my things and all I had before I married him.

As I took the bag out of the attic I thought why should it surprise me he deceived me to believe he threw the magazines away such a long time ago. I was always so easily taken in and constantly surprised because my heart desperately wanted to believe good things about my husband. It was heart breaking to be taken in while he made a big deal of throwing the porn magazines away to please me. How he can condone all his behavior is beyond me.

I showed him what I found when he arrived home after being gone all week. He argued about something inane skipping over the issue and wouldn't discuss the topic. He said he didn't care if I found it. He had other options now and was meaner and haughtier than ever.

I think he set me up to find the trash bag for he had it safely hid in the same spot without my knowledge for the past two years. He was making a last ditch effort to have his devious thirst for chaotic freedom culminated. Minutes after I showed him the bag he got in his car and left. He called me and we fought long distance. He didn't come home for several weeks.

He quit acting like it bothered him if I found filthy porn items around. At this point he doesn't care what he says and does. For a while he made a halfhearted attempt to act like it bothered him when I found women's undergarments and all the perverted material. There was a time when he wouldn't reveal how he really felt and would not dare say some of the things he started to say. He was getting by with more and more.

After I found the sack of porn I started to rip the foul books into pieces so no one can ever set eyes on the batch of revolting obscenity. After tearing them awhile my arms started to hurt and there were so many more to rip up. I took the rottenest garbage I could find and poured it over the magazines in the enormous garbage sack.

I didn't take the trash bag outside until I seen the garbage truck pull up. I handed it to the workers and watched as they pitched the sack into the trash compactor. I needed to make sure the sinful material was where it belonged. Konn was out of state this morning.

He didn't ask what I did with his treasures. I volunteered to tell him I threw them in the trash and seen them destroyed in the compacter. He was more than angry and disturbed I threw his immoral collection away. His eyes continually blazed hate and his mouth voiced extreme dislike the rest of the time we were together.

Konn never spoke another word under a roar and changed my name to every filthy word in his private dictionary. He kept up a barrage of verbal abuse that would have affected a den of lions. He turned on me with a vengeance and kept it up until he left. He talks so loud and so fast he wouldn't let me say a word it made me so nervous I shook all over. He started barraging me with the jealously routine again.

I stopped trying to compete with getting a word in edgewise. He was belligerent and adamant in statements he made on jealousy. I wanted him to point his fingers back to himself for all the while he is envious of my friends, my family, and me, of finances I had through tragedy and whatever I did before I met him along with all I did while I'm with him. He was even envious of my vehicle and my home that I shared with him when he was homeless. He made comments about everything and anything that had to do with Rosie

ROSY LATUR

Rodent. He left no stone unturned. My jealousy consisted of wanting my husband to knock off the unnatural sex degeneration he revealed in many different ways. I was jealous of all my husband gave other women he should have given in love to his wife. I put all he did and other thoughts I had on hold. I didn't want a divorce. I wanted my husband. But seeing him do or say anything to feed his addiction shocked me into speechless oblivion. I wasn't sure which way to turn. I felt shoved into a corner. Divorce scared me more than he did. I didn't know how much longer I could watch the destruction as it was taking its toll. My dreams and plans were going down the toilet. I became physically ill so much of the time now.

Pornography was wherever my husband was. It was in his heart, in his behavior, his words, my life, our home, in the car. It was in every thing we owned. It felt like it was in the very air we breathed. Nothing felt clean and good and wholesome anymore. Perversion took over all we did or wherever we went. We fought over sex, women, his addiction, what it promoted and berserk behavior it provoked in one way or another. All we fought over can be summed up into one word 'immorality.' We never fought over money, where to go or what movie to see. Even if I had to cover my head through spooky movies he liked and I didn't. We didn't fight over where to eat, what to eat or what to buy. There was no time to fight over anything but sexual deviancy. It took every waking moment from both of us. I fought hard but to no avail. I carried my feelings of rejection with me wherever I went. I had thoughts of spitting in his eye every time he said I was the one that was obsessed.

It was competitive because it had a hold on my husband. It wasn't a fight about any one particular woman our fights were about the entire concept of the sex addiction and what it was doing to him and to me. How it took what belonged to me as his wife. When I told him I wanted the best for him he never knew I was talking about me. I was the best. I was always competing for his attention. I started to think I had to compete with everyone and everything. I had to look the best, be the best, funniest, cleanest, anything I could do to get him to look and see what he had in me and who I was. I want him to see how much I loved him and what he was missing and observe how willing I was help him. I thought if he could only perceive all he can have with me maybe he'd take a sharp turn in the road. Take a different route than the one he was traveling on and I wouldn't have to feel like a cigar butt he threw out the window as he speeds down the highway.

104

My spouse never accepted pornography related incidents took his honor, dignity and self-respect he accused me of taking from him whenever I confronted him with the way the addiction was destroying our marriage and us. I couldn't accept him being oblivious to the destruction his perverted preference was causing. If my husband's vocabulary and behavior toward me had included the word devotion I'd have stayed by his side forever. Devotion means fidelity, love, and ardor, faithful, constant and loyal. That say's it all. Without devotion saying I love you to someone is saying empty words. Devotion is a natural affection that goes hand in hand with truly loving someone. A natural affection that bonds and cements a couple in love so not even a blade of grass can fit between two people totally devoted to one another. The gift of love with devotion is for every man and women no matter what their faith is or if they have no faith. I think devotion is the key to happiness and the T.L.C. (tender loving care) in marriage.

I longed for my husband to love me. I wanted him to find the key and unlock the door to his heart then unlock the door between him and I. I needed him to see me standing on the other side, do what needed to be done to reach me, pull me toward him and hold me so close nothing can come between us. There was only one key that fit the door between us and it was on his key ring. I didn't have one that matched. I couldn't do it alone. It takes two to make a marriage work. I continued to hold on and believe it could happen until the night I heard what consoled him and secrets to the double life. The lies living within him was laid wide open and exposed whom the real Konn Rodent really is.

Chapter Nine

Deceptions & Womanizing

I was joining the ranks. I commenced to play his games the way any wife and any woman that is neglected, rejected, scorned, ridiculed, mocked, scoffed, taunted, put down, tormented, hit, bruised and cheated on would have played. "Down and dirty."

I acted like all was well in our own little ludicrous loony land but it wasn't. Having to deal with additional mendacious melodramas my husband endorsed daily I never got over the underpants catastrophe. It was the turning point in my attitude. It was piled on the top of the growing mountain of wounds and scars of painful grief that broke my heart during the last year and a half. My independent nature had been stifled. I wasn't going to sit back, do nothing and go through repeated aggravation. I'm determined to make my presence known as the wife of Konn Rodent. He can knock it off and be a loving husband that accepts me or he can get the heck out of my life.

I intended to play detective and find out who the underpants belong to one way or another. I want to uncover where Konn goes when he disappears, whom his friends are and whatever else I can find out about the inexplicable man I called my husband. I'm going to know who the alien is that hit me and unmercifully ripped my clothes off and showed no mercy or sorrow. My husband never wiped a tear from my eyes nor showed compassion in any given situation. I wanted to show him he couldn't ignore me or shove me around anymore. I'll have an opinion whether he wants to hear one or not. I'm taking authority as his wife whenever he pretends he doesn't know me. I decided to show him that it hurts when your partner teases and smart mouths everything.

I'll introduce myself to every woman he's in contact with through out the day whether it's at work or in his travels. I intend to nurture friendships with every female he works with. I established myself a few times when I told a few of them my husband doesn't introduce me to women. A few of the gals asked; why doesn't he, I'd reply," I don't Know." We'd laugh and it was the start of becoming friendly. I made up my mind he needs to learn to acknowledge me to every one whether they're wearing a skirt or trousers. After he seen the way I was moving in the midst of his world he tried to cut me out of he began to acknowledge me. I wasn't a happy camper I had to take a stand simply to have him recognize I was his wife. It was imperative he put his ring back on and act like a married man. All Konn did during the stand I took was become a little more cautious and craftier. Observing his behavior around females and the way he used what he learned about them to get next to whomever he is conning I believed he acted like the woman he tries to impress by taking on her personality. I think most women like Konn because it was like looking in a mirror and seeing themselves. Thinking back to the dating games I realized he took on my personality. No wonder I liked him he acted just like me.

We all like men to tell us were pretty and to fetch and carry and my husband was more than ready, agreeable and willing and able to do whatever it took. He was the only person I ever knew that could express details on a particular woman's looks in such an intricate description. I was tired of Don Juan Konn scoping out women. I told him if he doesn't stop staring and undressing them in visions when I am with him I will go up to the women right in front of him and tell them my husband is raping them with his eyes. By this time he knows I meant what I said.

At first I thought what he did in visions wasn't real. Just a figment of his imagination so when I went to see my counselor I used to tell her I thought the sex incidents were merely in his dreams and fantasies it wasn't like he was with someone in the flesh.

I realized to late that to fantasize sleeping with other women gratifying his sexual needs is the same as committing adultery. As he neglects his wife in his torturous ceremony every time he visualized women sexually whether it's women he's in contact with or walking down the street or in the form of pornography he is putting every one of the females he hallucinated between us. After a year and a half the number or women grew too numerous to count and could be another one for Ripley's Believe It Or Not.

One day a friend called to tell me to be sure and watch the Oprah talk show. There were four sexually addicted men and a doctor appearing that day. I didn't want to miss anything they said so I taped the program. The men talked about their addiction and how they sought help to overcome their problems. They said they didn't look at women as a person or as someone's mother, wife or grandmother but as body parts they could use to satisfy their sexual cravings. The only thing a woman meant to them was as a sex object. The men admitted they sought prostitutes too. They went on to say they did whatever it took to satisfy their lust and were never satisfied. They talked about the many ways their addiction; the lies and deception damaged their family. Two of the men's wives stayed with their husband and two of the men were divorced. All their words pierced my heart. Living with my husband I was witnessing the very things they were saying.

For a while I didn't know where he was coming from or what I was seeing when he got a crazed look on his face watching women. Of course he denied the way he stared at females.

My husband wouldn't admit he had a problem and couldn't be helped until he recognizes he needs help. He was not willing to give up his enjoyable addiction. I told him about the program and he wouldn't watch it or listen to what the men had to say. He flipped and did the usual about face pointing his finger at me and said it was my problem. Knowing he had sex with himself while he ignored me was a festering sore point that stayed with me all the time. We fought about it constantly. I was so insecure I did fear if he continued to fantasize he'd eventually want the real thing.

At one time I thought he cared about losing me but it was only because he wasn't ready to leave yet. I thought he had a certain amount of stability with me he didn't have before. He knew the job he was working on only lasted two years or until they finished the Y2K update so he hung on to me awhile longer. He constantly and continually kept blaming me for his sex hang up and all that transpired. Every time something gross turned up linked to his addiction he'd say Rosie, everything with you is sex, sex, sex that's all you talk about, your crazy. You're the one that needs help let's go to a therapist. We ended up seeing another counselor and it's a repeat performance.

I heard a theory on something in our brain called endorphins. It is supposedly the pleasure mechanism where visionary fantasies take place. It appears the endorphins store the imaginary sex visions that can kick on and begin to take over. Nothing else matters accept the craving for sexual pleasure. A few female co workers commented on the way my hubby walked the halls every five minutes talking to him self and the numerous times he left the building all through the day. Several gals continued to tell me every time he stared at them for long periods of time without saying a word. Some women worked on the same projects with him in the small cubicle offices. They had to stand or sit very close and lean over him to share the computer and it must have driven him buggier than he already was.

If the theory on endorphins is true as heavily addicted as Konn is and as much as my honey bunny was into satisfying him self with fantasies the endorphins could possibly have kicked in and might have become uncontrollable for him to be in such close contact with women all day long.

I began to think Konn couldn't contain himself and probably had to walk the halls and leave work all those hours and go somewhere to partake in sex. Fantasizing the 60 women he worked with all day is a big job for anyone especially someone that couldn't take care of one woman.

Konn's co- workers liked me. They invited me to everything that went on within the firm. The employees got together almost every day for lunch and held special lunches for all the employees once a month and on all the holidays. They'd call me at home to invite me and tell me to bring Italian food. I made them laugh and became the center of attention whenever I was around. They always had something going on. There was the annual Christmas party and dance. The night after Konn physically harmed me to get the undies back I sold out my self-worth to go to the Christmas party with him because I wanted to dance with my husband. I wore a long sleeve, up to the neck dress to cover the bruises.

The entire staff welcomed me with open arms whenever they seen me. I had the freedom to walk the entire 4th floor, which was an honor because most of the visitors had to be escorted. One of the bosses referred to me as being one of them. Sometimes I went shopping and went on coffee breaks with some of the office gals. Some employees came and went according to their children's schedule. They could pick up their children no matter what time it was and take them where they needed to go. Sometimes they brought their children back to work to wait for them. The employees were always fellowshipping.

Whenever any female told me how lucky I was to have Konn as my husband, he is such a good guy and so much fun to be around and all the nice things he did for them. I didn't care who it was I'd tell them he was okay if you like a mean husband that brings used undies home for his wife to find and hits her to get them back. He doesn't have any idea when he's acting suave and debonair in front of them they heard he is a jerk and they aren't buying what he has to sell anymore.

I was upset and unhappy he treated other women nice and desired them sexually while he scorned and rejected me. I felt like all he gave them in a nice kind manner belonged to me as his wife. I went down town once or twice a week now. I talked on the phone with some of the girls during the week. I learned what went on in the work place. I took breaks and talked with his co-workers in the lobby of the hotel or on the third floor balcony when they went to have a cigarette.

A few co workers went so far as to e mail my husband and told him they thought I was wonderful but of course they knew he was already aware of what a nice wife he had. I almost fell over when he showed me a copy of the kind things they said of me. I wondered why my husband couldn't grasp that I was as cool as his co-workers felt I was.

I met so many people and heard the scuttlebutt that went on with the workers and in the office. Plus I had the fringe benefit to hear some things my hubby was up to.

It seemed like a fun place to work. Sometimes I wondered how they got anything done they were always doing something else. If I told the gals there was a great sale in a certain shop in the mall they ran right down to the store and shopped.

One of the girls hired a stripper during a surprise office party they gave one of the guys that was leaving. Never having been a part of the business world I did wonder about some of the things I seen and heard that went on in the office and between co-workers.

One co-worker became a close confidante. She took phone calls in the office during the day and transferred calls to the extensions. She knew the business people connected to the state office that worked on the projects with the firm. She confided that a few calls he received weren't business calls and Konn hurriedly took off whenever he got those calls. Several times she said Konn's line was busy and asked if they'd like to leave a number. Then she gave me the numbers. She was right they were not business associated. I couldn't say anything to Konn or she would have lost her job. We acted congenial to one another in front of Konn but we didn't let him know we were close friends. Along with losing her job he probably would have sued her or worse.

One day we arranged to meet for coffee before letting my hubby know I was in town. I went downtown to see my friend and thought I'd live dangerously and go upstairs to the office area and pick her up. My husband wasn't back to work from where ever he escaped to during working hours. Just as were ready to leave we spotted him and ducked into one of the cubicles. When he was close to turning the corner leading to his office we seen him make a u turn and head back down the hallway toward the vicinity we were hiding in. He walked up and down the hall several minutes talking to himself under his breath. His lips were moving a mile a minute. He looked goofy. We waited till he was done strolling the hallway and turned the corner to his office. We raced out of our hiding space and went down to the coffee shop. The hallway section is very long and one of several hallways situated on the entire floor. The hallway he roams back and forth on is located in front of the receptionist desk where co-workers gather and chitchat. She said he walked up and down the hallway all the time and Konn made her feel uncomfortable when he would stop, stand in front of her desk with his hands under his chin and stare at her for long periods of time without speaking a word.

Not all women liked Konn's mannerisms and were wise enough to know he was shrewd. One of the woman said she wasn't real sure what he was doing when female employees were in the storeroom getting supplies for he'd stop walking, stand in the doorway grinning and gawking and never said anything to either of them. He didn't stop to chat or just say hi and continue walking the hallway; he just stood there like a geek. I told her he is visioning having sex with them. In other wards he is raping them without their knowledge or consent. After I told her he is into pornography she avoided him like the plague. She asked one of the girls if he made her feel funny when he stared at her and she said no he's okay he's just friendly.

I believed all she told me for several times I saw him gazing at females as he stood in the doorway of their office room. He'd be so engrossed in undressing the women he didn't notice me standing near by watching him make a fool of himself in fantasyland. I'd study his mannerisms while he's gaping and wait to see how long it took until he turned around and saw me taking in his peculiar performance. When he does finally spot me scrutinizing his weird facade he just meanders over to where I'm standing like Duh!

One time we took a friend to lunch and said good-bye to him near the elevator area. As he walked away he almost fell down craning his neck trying to see up the dress of a girl standing on a chair trying to reach something on a shelf in the reception vicinity. He managed to catch himself before stumbling clear to the floor and he glanced over at us to see if we were watching the comedy of his actions but he didn't say a word. We giggled all the way down the elevator.

But nothing he ever did was really funny my insides were always churning. What else could I do? Sometimes I just had to laugh to keep my sanity. God's word say's "Laughter does the heart good like a medicine."

As I observed him walking back and forth in the hallway mumbling to him self I recalled the daily routine he has of talking to himself all the time no matter where he is. Sometimes he talks under his breath but you can see his lips moving. His voice changes often during the times he's talking to his invisible friend. Sometimes it is a whisper but you could make out what he was saying and at times it was very loud. I tried to ignore it as much as I conceivably could. I never saw anyone talk to him or herself as if they were carrying on a conversation with another person. It was so out of the ordinary sometimes it fascinated me. I couldn't help but listen to what he was saying wondering whom the heck he is talking to.

Sometimes he talked real loud especially when he was in the bathroom with the doors locked. I don't know who he thinks is in there with him. On several different occasions, I heard him say f- -k you to whomever he imagined was in there with him. Then he'd answer himself. At least I think it was his imagination. Who knows? I don't. Only he knows whatever or whomever he is speaking too for it was real to him.

A few times several of my friends told me they seen him in the car having a conversation with himself gesturing with his hands as if there is someone actually in the car with him. They were perplexed and wondered what he was doing. He looked so intent talking as though he was discussing something important. Thinking it was unusual and humorous we laughed and imitated him talking and answering our selves saying silly things in the way we seen him entertaining him self.

It might not have been so funny if we knew why he had the odd habit or whom he is really talking to. The strangeness of the habit looked so funny I wasn't sure if he was aware he is doing it in such a noticeable way.

I began to feel disloyal cracking jokes regarding his characteristics. I didn't really want people to see him look deranged and talk to himself. I stopped making fun of him. I thought if I told my husband I could hear him talking to him self all the time he'd be more careful about doing it. He said what is the matter with you Rosie I don't do that.

He didn't accept what I said. So hence whenever he talked to himself out loud. I'd ask him what did you say? Are you talking to me or is there someone in the bathroom with you? He stopped some of it and watched it a little closer but continued to have conversations with his unseen buddy.Sometimes he would be clear on the other side of the house in another room and I'd hear him say loud and clear I love you Rosie my honey bunny. I'd think it was so darn cute. I used to love the childlike quality he seemed to have at times. As time went by the childlike quality disappeared completely. After a while all I seen was a monster with ugly cruel, brutal flaring nostrils, glaring evil eyes that cut me into pieces with fiery arrows that spewed forth venom shooting from the top of my head, to my toes and into my heart, Into my spirit wounding and scaring every inch of me. It seemed my world and my existence was in the hands of Konn Rodent the monster mash man.

One morning my partner put on his suit and said he had to work with state people that day. Later in the morning I thought it would be a good day to dress up, ride downtown with a friend and surprise him. After he's done working maybe we could go to dinner and catch a movie. My friend and I went to lunch at my favorite restaurant. At 1:30 pm she drove me to the building where Konn worked.

I went upstairs to his office and his computer was off. I looked for his boss and asked him if he knew where Konn was. He walked with me and together we looked all over but he was not there. We checked the state sign out book and he hadn't signed out. I went to the third floor balcony where some of the workers were having a cigarette. I talked with them but kept my eye on the door two floors down. From the third floor balcony you can see just about every thing down on the lobby floor. After three hours I spotted my husband coming in the front door. I remarked to his co-workers there's my hubby coming in the door. He walked into the lobby hooked a left and must have gone to the restroom situated in the direction he was headed. Then he went back out a different door to the side of the lobby located next to the gift shop. Strangely enough he walked clear around the building outside and came in the back entrance. When he walked directly underneath the balcony where I was seated right above him I leaned over the balcony and said hey Konn, what's happening? I startled him and he hurried to the balcony.

He was nervous. I said hi I've been waiting three hours to talk to you. Where have you been? He said he had a meeting at the state building with Dominic. I checked upstairs and you didn't sign the state ledger. Signing out was one strict rule employees had to abide by if they were going to the state office. So where did you go? He didn't answer and wouldn't talk to me.

He walked over and engaged in conversation with a few workers. When they started toward the elevators he went with them. I followed and asked him if he'd talk to me a moment before going upstairs. I told him I wanted him to prove he was at the state building. He got a serious look on his face didn't speak a word and scampered away.

Usually when he disappeared from work he went in his car. It seemed odd he was either walking or someone picked him up and dropped him off in front. I went down the hall into an office and asked if could use the phone. I called Dominic and asked to speak to Konn Rodent. He said I haven't seen him all day he wasn't scheduled to work at the state today. I called his extension and asked him to meet me downstairs and he came down. I said Konn where did you go this morning when you left home at 4 am showed up on the job at 9 am. Left work at 11 am went back to work at 1 pm, left work again at 1:15 pm and came back at 4 pm?

Konn you were not at the state, where were you the last three and one half hours? You've been leaving home at four am every morning saying you have to hurry, get to your job and then show up five hours later. I want some answers here and now. I want to know where you go at four am and where you vanish for hours and where you were the last four hours? He said we will talk about this later and went back to work.

At this time we have been married ten months and its two months after the milestone undie occurrence. When he was through for the day he came down to the balcony floor where I was waiting for him. His excuse for leaving during working hours is that he went for a walk just like his co-worker Bob does. I said Bob walks fifteen minutes and he's back on the job. You were missing a total of 11 hours just today. How do you get by with taking off work anytime you want for that many hours? He said he wasn't doing anything wrong. Just walking and before work he drives around then parks in the parking lot and listens to the radio to unwind before going into work. He gave absolutely no answers and that's the end of the issue. This is the baloney I'm not taking anymore. He got by without being accountable for his actions for 53 years.

But sadly in the long run I did end up taking it and much more. In his cleverness to conceal where he really went he said you didn't see me come in the front door. I came in the back door. You only think I came in the front. I said others seen you come in at the same time I did. That evening he said let's go for a ride. He drove me back to the building and enacted his version of all the deceiving untruthfulness he told during the day.

My husband tried to add bewilderment to the matter at hand so he doesn't have to answer for his behavior. He was avoiding the truth and reality by focusing on his entrance to steer clear of the real topic of where he went all those hours. He went so far as to have me sit on the third floor in the same spot I was sitting earlier; he came in the back door and walked under the balcony. He looked up at me and said that's what happened you didn't see me come in the front way.

Konn said people that work on computers need to get away for a little while to clear their head. Well Konn you must have a lot of clearing to do since your gone all the time. Is it fair to vanish into thin air for hours during the time the firm pays for your services? No answer. He stayed with his story. The only comment he'd make was on which door he came in.

It really distressed me when he treated me as if I was a blithering idiot. There was no mistaking Konn coming in the front door. I'd know my husband anywhere. I'd recognize that half baldhead and 6 ft body a mile away. I'm familiar with the way he pushes his hair from one side of his head to the other to cover the hairpiece he wears as he walks in out of the wind. I knew the exact clothes he wore that morning and the gold rim glasses he wears. I bought the suit, shoes, shirt and tie he had on.

I'm familiar with every hair he had left on his head, every scar and mole on his body. There was no mistaking I knew without a doubt Konn walked in the front door. What I don't know is where he went and whom he was with and did the underwear he hid under the mattress belong to the person he sees when he leaves his job during the day?

The presentation he illustrated to convince me I didn't see what I saw in his bid to make the door he came in the focal point and the answer to his problem to skip over the truth was not stupid, it is very clever. Not giving an answer to anything is not dumb he just walks away from everything as if the wind will blow it all away. Having no remorse it doesn't matter if the problem gets blown away or not for he simply doesn't care.

Sometimes I wanted to ignore everything and walk away without a care in the world too but it wasn't real. No one that cares and has a conscience can just walk away. I hired a detective to follow him one morning. I got the idea from lining up the lie detector test that bombed out. He said Konn drove clear to the opposite side of town of the location where the firm he works at is located. The address he drove by at four am was Veronica's house and after he drove a few more blocks he ended up ditching the detective and was nowhere to be found. They checked the parking lot several times over a period of hours and he wasn't there until after nine am. I couldn't tell him I hired a detective to follow him thus I can't confront him on the deceiving stories he tells concerning his whereabouts.

I felt guilty I had him followed. I never did anything like that in my life. I didn't want to check on him every time he is caught in the quagmire of dishonesty. I didn't know how to live with a person that never tells the truth and I'm not able to trust anything they say. I didn't have any peace. It was one calamity after another. I wanted to get back at him. I purposely started to call him at work all the time. I checked up on him to see if he was working and I'd tease him and say anything I could to irate him if he was away from his desk for long periods of time. I learned he couldn't take being teased. He can dish it out but he can't handle it when someone scoops it back to him.

When his voice mail came on I left snotty messages like hi honey whose undies are you bringing home tonight? I found the porn magazines you hid in the car. Who are the unlucky women your fooling around with today? He'd start to cry on the phone and get shook up and come running home to smooth things over.

It was a phenomenon he didn't say he wanted a divorce when I started to act up and he'd try to appease me. Most of the time my reactions to all he did to hurt me was simply to tease him cause I knew he didn't like it any better than I liked all the brutal perverted behavior he portrayed toward me.

I didn't start calling and teasing him until months after the undies dilemma and after a year of continually disappearing, ignoring me and twisting all I said. I began to call several months after he made which door he came in the answer to all his vanishing acts. He tried to pretend he was at work one of the nights he stayed away from home. He put a co-worker on the phone and wants him to say he seen Konn working all night. The co-worker said he didn't see Konn and he wasn't going to lie for him. I was embarrassed he tried to have someone delude me to cover his tracks. Apparently the man he put on the phone did work all night and Konn did go to his office in the early morning. He left work and gave me a copy of the time the automatic door logged him in when he opened it. He knew the person he asked to lie for him was working at that time. Konn checked in but he also left shortly after he logged in. I was perturbed he stayed away from home all night again. I took his clothes, put them in a box, wrote his name on the box and called a cab. I paid the driver in advance, had him take the boxes to the fourth floor offices and drop them off by the reception desk.

I called the receptionist and asked if the boxes arrived and she said yes. I asked what my husband did when he seen them and she said nothing he just went about his business.

She commented on how cold she thought he acted when she told him he had boxes waiting in the lobby for him to pick up. He immediately went to the secretary and signed a form to stop his next check from being deposited into my bank account. This was one of the rare times Konn didn't have much money on him having spent it all the night before when he stayed away from home all night. He borrowed a few dollars from one of the guys and went to a co-workers home to spend the night. He called the next day. I told him I'd meet him outside of our church and I'd give him a couple of hundred dollars. He said he wanted to come home but I said no. Even telling me his friends said he belonged with his wife didn't sway me at the time.

My reaction did bother me and I felt bad I went so far as to humiliate him by sending his things to work. At the time all I could think about was he stayed out all night again and the way he violated, humiliated and physically harmed me. I kept thinking he spent the night he left with who ever the undies belonged to and he can take his clothes and live with her. She can wash them and keep him clean.

He sought out a couple that counseled us one time after I made him leave because he can't figure out how to get back in the house. They were both pastors I knew quite a while before we went to them for counseling. They knew the evening he went to see them alone the words he spoke of me were false. After running me down he asked them how he can get me to talk to him. After they conversed with Konn both pastors astonished me when they said they would never recommend someone get a divorce but they believe in this case I should get a divorce right away because Konn was bad news. They wouldn't divulge the conversation that took place between them and Konn.

The next evening my hubby left a message on my answering machine. His voice cracked and sounded despondent. He merely said I want to come home but the sound of his voice got to me. I felt sorry for him. The next time he called I told him okay in a few days if he behaves and acts decent. Before he is allowed to come back home we need to study a few verses in the bible on immoral and deceitful behavior. I was not going to condone or live with it anymore.

I thought he might have been a little concerned at this time because he realized he doesn't want us to split up. I didn't recognize he was afraid of being out there alone again with no home or money because the job he is on was winding down and would soon end. I let him come home and he told me I embarrassed him in front of his co-workers but still doesn't acknowledge embarrassment he puts me through in front of every one all the time. He refuses to accept the reality to the factual truth that if he had done nothing there would be nothing to react to. I wouldn't have to react to finding his girlfriends undies and cheating or to his deviant addiction and all it promotes in sexual perversion. Nor would I have to ask where he went during the hours he vanished or tell him it's embarrassing when he pretends he doesn't know I'm his wife.

He won't give an inch or grasp the concept; if he treated his wife with loving kindness, honor and devotion I wouldn't have anything to say about daily calculated ill treatment and uncalled for violent predicaments. To this day Konn really believes he did nothing to aggravate the situations building into mountainous predicaments. He told me I shouldn't have reacted to anything. Maybe I shouldn't have reacted but his nasty cruelty went past the point of no return. I was tired of the violent disgusting acts he pulls off in front of my loved ones and me. I won't take it anymore without handing it back and he can see how it feels to put the BS he hands me back in his corner.

Chapter Ten

Twisting Reality, Self Mutilations & Suicide Attempts

I began to take a stand and confront my husband on his extremely peculiar mannerisms and the lies that start to unfold in the unnatural perversion he has a hang up with. Konn carelessly left clues for his neglected bride to find. It wasn't easy being the first person in his life to challenge his demeaning conduct. He was never told no or held accountable or asked to take responsibility for his words and actions. I conveyed to Konn that he couldn't do what ever he wants in our marriage. Freedom to be with other women was a "no no." We are partners and accountable to each other. So when I began to ask questions he couldn't take it and our home turned into a sci-fi thriller.

My partner commenced to add another scene to the horrendous dramas. Konn started mutilating him self whenever I inquired any thing dealing with his behavior. No matter what I asked he did something to physically hurt himself. Even a simple question to engage him in a conversation like where did you have lunch today was cause for Konn to go into a tailspin, throw hyperventilating tantrums and beat on his head and body.

I persisted trying to talk things over in a calm manner. I felt talking things out together and letting your partner know where your coming from is part of intimacy. I'd have done whatever I could possibly do to help matters. Part of the reason I accused him of lusting after other women and having a girlfriend was because my husband didn't accept anything I said. He refused to care or understand lying deception and withholding or disregarding the intimate sex life we should be having also included sharing our innermost feelings with each other. My spouse was taking away my feelings when he refused to grasp the full meaning having undies in his possession was the start of the accusations plus the fact all his behavior points to sexual promiscuity with someone other than the woman he married. He never thought any of this was cause to ask questions or accuse him and continued to say I was born jealous. I continued to accuse him every time he did something strange and unusual; which was all the time.

I once contemplated if he asked me for a pair of my undies I might have given him a pair thinking he finally did something intimately connected to me. He wanted nothing to do with me sexually nor did he act like I'm the woman that slept in the same bed with him night after night and woke up with every morning. When I told him I wasn't going to take being unwanted and neglected anymore he'd slap his own face over and over and beat on his head. All the time he's hitting himself he keeps repeating he is a bad man. He beat him self in the head so hard with a hairbrush he broke it in half just as my daughter walked up the stairs. She couldn't believe what she was seeing.

He changed the dramatic drama and started to claim he doesn't want to live without me but still continues to scream and display volatile behavior. Constantly saying in repeated combination I'm sorry, I love you; I hate you till it made me dizzy trying to figure out which emotion he was conveying.

One evening he continued yelling and I asked him if he would please talk in a quiet voice. Pleading let's work out whatever is bothering him. I begged him not to scare the children again. Marty and Francis cry and become so frightened. I took my first finger and gently placed it on his lips and said sh sh please don't yell. The gesture was in the same manner I put my finger to my lips to shush the children in church or at the movie. He slapped me so hard I saw stars then he dialed 911, told them I hit him and I'm abusing him. He ran out of the house got in his car and be-bopped down the street to avoid the next scene. When the police came I told them the story he told on the phone was not true, he ran off and wasn't here. They started to look in my closets. They said sometimes a spouse hides the other one. They were going to go through the entire house searching everywhere for the innocent victim that was the real abuser and guilty as sin.

I begged the officers to believe me and not to go downstairs and wake my daughter. They could see my house was spotless and in order and believed I was sincere. They were very kind and they stopped searching. After the police left Konn called and asked if he could come home. I said yes. When he came home he justified his actions by insisting he hit me because I hit him in the face first. Thereby taking away the truth of his actions and the pain I suffered over the fact he hit me with the same hand I held on our wedding night.

Twisting the whole affair of what really took place showed he was capable of saying or doing anything to exonerate his erratic methods. It was becoming very scary. He hit me very hard then twisted and changed everything to fit the need he seemed to have to make me the scapegoat of the foreign alien course of action he induced. All I endeavored to do was prevent his loud boisterous voice from waking the children. When my daughter heard the noise she'd come running up the stairs and I'd tell her to go back to bed the argument was between my husband and I. Through all the adversity I took my husband's side. I realized it had to stop for sometimes I was to blame for waking her thinking I could get him to listen I tried to talk over him and all that did was wake her up. After a short period of time I stopped raising my voice he didn't listen anyway. I felt terrible when I learned Francis was calling her sister at two in the morning. She'd be crying and telling her sister she was afraid he was harming me.

Her dad never raised his voice, never mistreated her mother or subjected the children to the despicable display Konn was causing her to suffer. Francis was never exposed to anything but love.

Most of our arguments took place in the middle of the night. If I had an especially bad day dealing with Konn's behavior and decide to avoid a hassle and not confront him I'd lay awake reliving things that happened during the day. I tossed and turned and sighed and he'd wake up and say what's the matter. I'd say nothing. Acting concerned eventually he cajoled me into confiding what was troubling me. I yearned for him to care about our life together so I fell into the design of the patterns more and more. I'd give in and tell him what was bothering me. No matter what it was whether it related to him or not he'd jump out of bed screaming, get dressed and leave. What ever was disturbing me at the time became another fight and offends me even more. His concern was just another ploy to get me to keep my mouth shut and never speak of anything no matter how small or large the problem was. As time went by when I was restless I avoided telling him why I was sighing and went into the next room. If he was going to be nutty it was going to be before two am. However, I wasn't going to let up on holding him accountable and responsible.

He was okay if all we talked about was a movie or a book we read. Eventually the insane behavior he displayed worked to his advantage because I left him alone. I stopped questioning and confronting him. I didn't want to deal with his denials or see my children terrified anymore. He not only disturbed my daughter Francis and I, he was terrorizing my granddaughter too. Her bedroom is located in the same area as our bedroom with only a thin wall between our duplex separating both bedrooms.

He shrieked so loud and threateningly my granddaughter woke up petrified and frightened. She ran downstairs and woke her parents saying Konn is hurting her grandma. Then her parents call me and I say it's nothing; I upset my husband, it's okay now he's calming down. After Konn vigorously yelled he wants a divorce slamming the door as he leaves and frightening my children so many times I began to tell him to get out when he starts screaming and acting kooky. He can rent a room a few nights or until he cooled off. He used to take off and spend the night somewhere anytime he wants to anyway so he gave me the idea to have him leave and rent a motel room when he acts irate and horrible. When I made him leave he'd call home crying hysterically, I want to come home I miss you so much. Sometimes he sounded so pathetic I said okay. But sometimes I said no just stay where you are until you learn to behave when you're here. I'm not going to let you distress and alarm the children or me anymore. Konn didn't seem to care as my husband he was part of a family. We were not on an island alone. The children were in his life too. I knew they'd never accept him as their step dad or any kind of relative. But they would have accepted him as my husband after we were married if he had treated me right.

The children were kind to Konn. They didn't like him doing naughty things to their mom and causing disarray to all our lives. I was over whelmed with depression and sorrow of all the things happening in so many lives. To all the people I love and the family God blessed me with.

I was so busy cleaning up Konn's messes; checking up on him and trying my darndest to please him I didn't have time for my family anymore. I wasn't there for them in the same way I had always been. After awhile they were upset with the psychotic behavior he displayed and they didn't want him to join us in any more family get together. I told them it would hurt Konn if I told him he wasn't invited to family celebrations. My loyalty went to my husband. I told my family if he wasn't welcome I wasn't coming either. In order for my children to have me join them they had to accept Konn being with me. So they did and they were always congenial towards him for my sake.

Angel and Rick told him our homes were joint property and when he breaks something in our home he was destroying part of their assets too. After he kicked the door down for the third time they wouldn't let Konn come home until he went for counseling. He kicked them down with such enraged violence I had to replace three doors. My son in law warned Konn not to destroy anything else. It didn't do any good for the children to force him to go to a councilor. He only went to see the councilor so he could come back home and torment me some more. I stood by his side and went with him but once again he turned the reason he's seeing the counselor back around to me.

I already learned through trial and error my husband couldn't be helped if it isn't his idea to seek help for him self. He reminded me of a cat running around in circles chasing his tail. When he can't reach it running around in circles one way he turns around and chases it the other way and never really catches his tail completely, he just keeps going around in circles. For over two years now I tried to reason with him, pray with him, went to therapists with him and whatever else he wanted me to do. Nothing worked. At this point in our marriage I didn't care what he said or if he got loud and vicious I'd simply tell him to get out. Doing his about face he started to get shook up when I told him to leave. He cried on the phone and came running home from work to smooth things over. It would be okay for a few days or if I was lucky possibly a week.

One morning he was in a rage. He threw the key to the house on the counter and said he is never coming back. Sheri happened to drive to town with my three grandchildren. We decided to have lunch across the street from our home. It was raining and Konn had no way to get in the house so I left a note on the door telling him where I was. No matter how much we fought or what he said or did he always came back. I thought it would be okay to tell him where I was for he liked Sheri and the children and he surely wouldn't act up in front of them. When he was trying to make an impact with my family we took them to quite a few places of interest. He doted on the children showing them things and buying whatever souvenirs they wanted.

My children and I were in the restaurant having lunch. He came over to where were seated with a look of hostility. He didn't say hello to anyone. He said I want my key. I tried to act like nothing was wrong. I'll find it later okay why don't you sit with us, have a cup of coffee or bite to eat and visit with the children then we'll go to the house together. He ignored the family and assertively demanded I give him the key back. I said no. I was perturbed for I was kind enough to tell him where I was so he wouldn't have to stand out in the rain. He could act sane in front of my family. Besides he threw a fit threatening to leave if I don't do what he tells me. He knows by this time I'm not taking all he dishes out anymore. I'm rebelling against every deceiving demented word he speaks.

Sheri asked me to give him the key. I said no he could sit with us and be civil. He left the restaurant, went over to our house and kicked the front door in, dead bolt and all. There were pieces of chipped wood everywhere. Sheri and the children were coming in the house with me. We didn't see the door was kicked in until we reached it. They became frightened when they seen the mess. The carpenter estimated the damage to be around $2,000.

Now the rest of my grandchildren are not allowed to come to my home without their parents. Sheri was the last one to cut me off from seeing my grand children. I had no idea why living in the dark twilight zone with Konn that I wasn't really fearful of him yet. When the children left he wept and carried on. I asked why he couldn't just sit down with us at the restaurant. I wouldn't have told you where we were if I thought you were going to act like a maniac again. I can't turn the other cheek anymore. My youngest grand children were present during the violent upheaval. They are one, two and five years old and drove 125 miles to see me.

Don't try to justify breaking down the door again because I wouldn't give you the key the minute you thought I should and consequently felt it was a call to be violent. I wanted to talk with you before giving you the key.

The commitment of marriage means we both need to work at things together. You can't continue to terrorize my children and me. There's nothing more to hold onto. I make an effort to reason with you all the time Konn thinking I can rationalize everything no matter how violent and tense the situation is but I was wrong to continue living in domestic disturbances. Go get the divorce you asked me to give you every week since we said our wedding vows.

You've used the word divorce so often to emotionally black mail me knowing I don't believe in divorce. I can't stand the sadistic look on your face each time you make me feel inadequate and insecure. I'm tired of hearing the same threats over and over. I just wanted you to think about why I had the key to begin with. All the controversy taking precedent between us centers on the great lengths you continually sanction to hide your sexual preference. You threatened to leave for so long; now I want you to leave. Your addiction is not only costing me the price of my emotions it is driving a wedge between my family and me.

By now I'm so mixed up I know some of the confusion started to come from me. I tried to do the tough love thing having him leave and then when he's gone a day or two I couldn't stand being without him and I want him to come home and try again. I had to have him with me under any circumstances. I just can't let go. Then he'd do something cruel or crazy and I threw him out again. When I took a stand and said get out he would try to hold things together and I pulled the other way. When he tore our life asunder I held

126

things together and he pulled the other way. I was frazzled after the children left. I said let's end the wretchedness. Do me a favor get out of my life and get your divorce.

My husband went in the kitchen, took a butcher knife out of the drawer and started cutting on his wrists. I become hysterical and had all I could do trying to get the knife away. I'm five feet to his six feet and I'm not very strong. I couldn't get the knife away from him. I didn't know he only scratched the surface of his skin for he was dripping blood all over. Suddenly he bolted out the door with the knife. He was walking down the street in the rain holding the bloody knife. Angel and Rick were coming home and seen him walking in the rain with the knife. They brought him in the house and tried to calm and comfort him.

When they came in I was washing blood out of the sink crying and feeling really sorry for telling him to get a divorce. After I took a stand and turned the tables I knew the word divorce coming from me would shake him up but I was furious when he kicked in the door and after I came across more filthy junk hidden in the house. Never the less I stood by him and told the children it was my fault he was shook up. I shouldn't have told him to get a divorce.

I don't know what I was thinking of to continually protect his behavior except that I'd feel guilty and remorseful I hurt him with my words. It was ungodly to retaliate no matter what he did I was responsible for my behavior. I couldn't take it when he mutilated and hurt him self. My heart went out to him while he was sitting on the kitchen stool with a tearstained face; blood on his clothing, he looked so forlorn and desperate. I felt like I was looking at a ten year old that had no one to help him with the hurt and pain he must have felt at that moment. Angel was moved by his appearance and she put her arm around him and tried to reassure and console him.

I strived to let him know how sorry I was that I hurt him. I couldn't stop crying and wanted to do whatever it took to make it up. Then he'd end up doing something wicked and I'd end up taking more abuse. For a while I thought of how much I loved and wanted to be with my husband so I'd ignore his strange habits and deception. Then the egotistical attitude kicks in. I find something gross he hid and I can't deal with it another moment. I'd confront him and hold him responsible for his behavior. He would wail and sob, hyperventilate, throw himself on the floor, hit himself and say what a bad person he was.

I didn't know what else to do after the nightmarish ill treatment but let him know if he continues to mistreat me he's going to get it thrown back at him. Every time I lashed out and said things I shouldn't have like calling him a sob pervert and a cold uncaring cruel bastard I ended up hurting myself

I'd stand up to him then break down in tears and sorrow. I'd think it was my fault and wonder how I could have possibly said something in a certain way that made him feel he needed to go through the motions to commit suicide and hurt himself. I couldn't take my wishy washy behavior anymore than I could take his. I just want to die every time he hurt himself when all I tried to do was get to the truth of the matter at hand hoping he'd see the seriousness of the situations he persistently committed against both of us. I didn't want to hurt him in anyway. I loved my husband I only want him to recognize he needs professional help and his behavior affected me just like mine affected him.

I went to see my councilor. She said he was not going to kill himself he was using the act of suicide to control the situation he found himself in after he kicked the door in and each time he is caught in his own deception. He made decisions to do as he chooses in his addiction and in his marriage. Every time I told her the experiences I went through each week she said Rosie, he needs specialized help. His behavior is mentally disturbed. I don't know how I'd have held onto my sanity if I didn't have my councilor keeping things in perspective. Even then I didn't grasp the full meaning of all she was trying to warn me of by staying in an abusive relationship. I had so many things to tell her every week. His behavior was getting more out of hand with each passing day.

Just the same after the latest spectacle I didn't say the word divorce to him for a very long time. I couldn't go through the suicide ordeal with out losing it myself. Besides I really hated the word divorce. I didn't really want one. However, I continued to tell him to leave every time he went berserk. I was so exhausted physically, emotionally and mentally. At times I think I was as goofy as my husband. I couldn't deal with anything anymore.

Konn wore glasses and we had to replace them three times in one month. He twisted and broke all three pairs and threw them at me. The last pair he broke was one after noon when he came home for lunch and started arguing. It was frustrating to have to replace another pair of glasses and I raised my voice too.

It wasn't a heated argument but I want him to recognize I wasn't happy about the way he kept breaking his glasses. He was always so loud I wanted to be heard too. He went in the other room and I'm talking loud so he can hear me in the next room and he called 911. He came back in the room and handed me the phone and said 911 is on the other line. I thought he was kidding. I said hello and they said what's going on we hear a loud voice. I said nothing is wrong really, we are merely having a disagreement. All the same they came to the house but not before he took off so he didn't have to face them. I told them I don't know why he called 911. They said I should tell him he could be arrested if he calls again when there isn't a real need to call 911.

The fact he called 911 several times scared me more than his bullying tactics. It was one more thing I never lived with before. I don't know why I didn't think to call 911 when he pulled the suicide stunt. It happened so fast my first reaction was to try to get the knife from him.

Nevertheless before it was all said and done I ended up having to call 911 soon after the last false alarm he turned in shortly after we returned home from a bus trip to at an amusement park. Walking to the bus when it was time to leave I needed to use the rest room. It was located close to a swimming area. When I was coming out of the restroom door Konn was standing a little ways down leaning against the building and staring intently at the young girls in bikinis. Merely staring in their direction wouldn't have been an issue? It was the way he gawked at several very young girls that got up and had to walk past him on their way to the restroom. He wasn't paying any attention to whether or not I was coming out the door so I stepped back in the restroom so he couldn't see me but I could see him. I was curious to see how far he will go ogling them. As one of girls got up and walked toward the restroom he acted mesmerized as his head turned with every step she took until she was out of sight. He didn't see me standing just inside the open doorway. His eyes went back to the other girls in bikinis until another one headed for the restroom. This time I stood in the doorway and as she reached where I was standing he spotted me. I said did you like her more than the bikini babe that came in the door a few seconds before her? I wasn't staring what is the matter with you I never look at anyone but my wife. I love you honey.

He had a habit of holding onto me when he was caught with his hand in the cookie jar and he knew I was agitated. I had a habit of not wanting him to touch me after it was. When we got on the bus he tried to hold my hand and I pulled it away. He put his arm around me and I took it off. When he held onto my hand or held me in his arms in public it was not an endearing kind of hold. It was a hold that said he owns me and can do whatever he wants which includes holding me and he will do it whether I want him to or not.

Konn didn't just hold my hand or hold me when he did something sick and odd. He held onto me all the time. He always put his arm around me when we watched TV or went to a movie. He held my hand all the time. Whenever we walked, in the store, in restaurants, in church. He grabbed my hand the moment we got in the car and held it until we reached our destination whether we drove five or 500 miles he never let loose of my hand. He holds onto me regardless if he is angry in the car or staring at women in church or in restaurants or wherever we are. The only time he didn't hold my hand was when he first started his new job and acted like he didn't know me in front of female co-workers. But after I let everyone know I was his wife he held my hand when we walked down the halls in his office and in the elevator. The funny thing is when we parted I missed him holding my hand and holding me.

We got home from the trip and I didn't say anything more till the next day. I couldn't keep my big mouth shut. I said Konn why did you stare so intently at the girls wearing bikinis? Don't you think some of the girls you were staring at were a little young? Talking about the young girls he stared at in bikinis may seem like a nit picky thing but I was talking about the whole ball of wax. It just never ends I can't go anywhere without seeing the look of desire in your eyes for everyone but me. It doesn't seem to matter what age they are. It is violating to them and to me. I can't take being the pitiful rejected wife. I waited so long for you to show some sort of sign that you desire me. The only sign you give is to constantly make a mockery out of our so-called intimate marriage at the same time you desire every woman that tickles your fancy. Every time I see you look that way at females it hurts more than it irritates me. I'm really talking about all the women you make a show of letting me know you want to have sex with and don't want me unless I initiate the first move. Even then you put me down and start a fight to degrade, humiliate and take a little more of my dignity from me.

I'm fed up with your endless infidelity and mannerism that is not now and never has been acceptable. It's driving me into an emotional breakdown and repetitively destroying both of us. Everything that happens between us is associated to women and the sex compulsion you don't admit having and refuse to get help. I can't take the way the abusive rejections are affecting me. Were like two pieces of sand paper rubbing each other the wrong way. I can't get over one incident and there is another one ready to rub me raw.

Will you please consider getting help for the problem that keeps getting in the way of us having a normal natural fun time getting to know one another before it's to late? He took a huge antique ashtray threw it in the bathroom sink. It made a loud clashing noise shattering glass everywhere. He grabbed a piece of glass and started to cut his wrists. My daughter happened to be home. She heard the crash and came running up the stairs I told her to call 911. The second she dialed the number he ran out the door and left in the car speeding and squealing rubber all the way down our residential street like a frantic mad man. 911 came and I showed them broken glass everywhere in the bathroom and blood that dripped all over after he cut himself. I asked the policemen what could I do to help him?

I asked them to pick him up and take him somewhere that will give him the kind of treatment he seems to need. They said it would be better if he turns himself in because it can be rough to involve the police in a forcible mental treatment case.

They left and my partner came back. Once again I felt sorry for him. It was all so crushing to see him harm himself then watch him leave and equally upsetting for me to let him come back. I asked him to check into a program at one of the local hospitals. I said I'd stand by him and do whatever it took. At that moment I realized asking him to do something normal when he doesn't comprehend normal is as ridiculous as the drama that just took place. At this point I'm beginning to wonder what normal actually is anymore. I lost sight of so many things I held dear.

My councilor said he was using the act of harming himself to manipulate me again. He is not going to really hurt or kill himself. She said I have to realize once and for all that my husband is repeatedly trying to push me into a nervous breakdown. If I didn't watch it he would succeed. I took cutting on his wrists seriously no matter if his wound was only a scratch or what his motives were. I was disheartened and I couldn't shake it. He knew it hurt me when he hurt himself and it was one of the way's he used to put me back in my place of doom and gloom and keep me there.

Demi was a comfort. I don't know what I'd have done without her guidance. She said this is what he is doing to you when he say's I love you. She pinched my arm and kept repeating I love you at the same time. As she continues saying I love you while squeezing the pinch more intensely the pressure on my arm became more painful. That is what I love you means to Konn. She was so right. Konn telling his attorney I heard voices and had mental problems and that I took prescription drugs everyday confirms my partner really was purposely causing emotional trauma to shove me into a serious nervous breakdown.

No matter how many times my councilor told me my hubby wanted to push me over the edge I couldn't fully comprehend or accept my spouse would go that far to hurt me. I kept hoping and holding onto what I thought were good things I liked about him. When he spoke twisted illusions of me to his attorney he actually was describing his mother. In reality his mother had numerous breakdowns and several drug over doses. She was in and out of drug rehabs until a physiatrist diagnosed her as having a chemical imbalance. She had to take pills every day the rest of her life to keep it under control. As long as she took her pills she was okay.

I heard she overdosed the same night Konn married his first wife. I was told her emotional breakdowns started when she was eighteen years old but I can't verify the story. It was hard to believe she had emotional mental problems because throughout the entire time I knew her she was a sweet elderly lady and never showed a sign she had a chemical imbalance. She was a really nice person. She loved Jesus and was a very devout church going lady. I included her in our life all the time. She loved me for being with her son. His mother's chemical imbalance along with Konn's nutty behavior was one of the reasons I asked Konn to have the same chemical test he refused to take. He lived with his mother's mental instability all his life and tried to do the same thing to me that was part of the environment he grew up with merely to hide the addiction that took control of his entire being and to get rid of me so he'd come out smelling like a rose. His parents were separated so his father was not around all the time. Konn said his mom wouldn't give his dad a divorce and they remained separated until his dad passed away when Konn was sixteen.

I was kind of stunned when his sister Skyler told me so many stories about her family just a few minutes after meeting me as her new sister in law for the first time. I was taken aback when the first thing she told me was that she hated her father and went on to say he was a mean violent drunk and a womanizer. Konn didn't see his dad that way. He saw his father as the parent he loved, the one that took him fishing and did things with him. His father was the parent he wanted to stay with and resented his mother because she wouldn't let him live with his dad. She told me both her mother and Konn lied and manipulated and her brother was never told no. He was allowed to do whatever he wanted with no restrictions. She said he was lazy and never did a hard day's work in his life. She remarked that Konn would stay with anyone that would let him move in with them.

Skyler asked me if Konn was still violent? That question got to me and I spilled my guts. We both said we wouldn't tell anyone the things we said. I thought it strange she blurted her family's history just like that to a new sister in law whom she didn't know. I thought we were comrades after our first meeting and all we shared. She also blurted out negatives things about her brother to my daughter the first time they met. I never told Konn the things she told me in confidence. It seems futile now to keep the confidences we shared back then. I want everything that happened out in the open. I'm not hiding anything anymore.

I liked Skyler right away and I thought she liked me too. I was happy to have a sister in law and all of Konn's family as part of my family too. She made me feel like she wanted to be close with me and to feel free to confide in her anytime. So I did call her and told her some of Konn's antics. Later on I was to learn our camaraderie relationship was not what it appeared to be when she turned on me during her mother's illness, death and funeral. In the meantime at this point Konn and I are still together. I'm still trying to hold onto my husband. It doesn't get any better it gets far worse. But I can't let go just yet. I love my husband and I don't want to be without him. All his antics worked in his favor because I stopped questioning and fighting with him. I want my marriage to work so now I remain docile. Konn persisted to view me as someone in his life he is superior to and elevates himself by demeaning me even more after I let him come back home without seeking treatment after the last suicide attempt.

He treats me as a person that's smaller, helpless and defenseless, He acted like I was merely in his life as someone he can torment while he towers over me blaring in my face making me feel trapped in a cage in his domain. It was unnecessary since at any time the sow could have just left and stayed with his piggy. He could avoid the theatrics to come back home instead of beating me down to his level to accept his rules. I was never going to give in to accept immorality of the adulterous pigpen he played in with his own personal stripper and friends.

Chapter Eleven

A New Job & A New Loony Tune

After Konn attempted to cut his wrists a second time I stopped asking questions regarding anything including the weather and he calmed down a while. We were kind of getting along without too much controversy in the last few months although nothing pertaining to his addiction ever changed.

I decided whether the suicide attempt was to obtain more power over me or not I backed off. I went further into denial. I did what he wanted, followed him around like a puppy dog and kept my mouth shut. Instead of his wife I was an obedient pet he patted on the head once in a while.

The job on the Y2K project was coming to a close. Some of the people working with Konn already procured another job. A friend of mine called and told me her husband landed a good high paying job with a company located in the downtown area. I asked Konn if he would put his application in at the same place my friend's husband acquired a job. I thought it would be smart to find a job as soon as he can for in another month he'd be out of work. There were jobs in a bigger city fifty miles away but I didn't want him to drive out of town. He said there were job opportunities available in a bigger city that paid big wages. I thought we could get the same wages in our hometown. It took two weeks before he got around to applying for the job. He got an interview right away and was hired on the spot. He wanted to talk with me first before he gave a firm yes.

I learned from the first job he landed with Konn's ability we could name his wage. I told Konn to put $65,000 as the starting wage and ask for several thousand a year in raises. He was hesitant he thought it was to high a wage to ask. I said let's fleece the Lord. In other words we'd pray together and ask God for the $65,000 wage. If it was offered to him then we know it is the job he is supposed to have.

The next day the supervisor called my husband and offered Konn the job with a starting salary of $65,000. The exact amount we prayed for. Plus he will get a raise of $3,000 a year, bonuses, expenses accounts, matching 401k funds, Health insurance covering every type of doctor and we pay only $5.00 for every visit and every prescription plus it had dental and eye insurance included. The firm provided a fully paid life insurance policy worth $100,000 and we took out an additional $75,000 policy that only cost $36.00 a month. He was offered sick leave and one month paid vacation a year with more vacation time after he's there one year plus opportunity to invest in the firm and advancement careers. We hit pay dirt. The only thing Konn didn't tell me was the job would mean traveling to other states all the time. He knew I wouldn't like that part of the job. It kind of threw me because my friend's job was in town. Nevertheless the company encouraged wives to go with their husbands and their expenses were paid too. We could stay at the best hotels. The expense account included coming home every weekend.

We were excited about the income and benefits. I wasn't thrilled about never knowing where the job would be located. It could be 3,000 miles away or 300 miles. My daughter was still living at home and although she was in college the thought of being away from her was tremendously weighing on my heart. I had a little income still coming in from interest in the savings I had before Konn so between both of us we pulled in around $6,000 a month. Konn's new supervisor wants him to be available in a week. Oddly enough they didn't have any place to send Konn two more months but the checks came in weekly. He was paid two months wages for doing nothing.

Then the call came and he was sent to work in a state 300 miles away. He wanted me to travel with him and I did for a while. We stayed at a fine hotel. I'd go shopping during the day and goof off till he got off work. The town he worked in was ten miles from the hotel. He drove back to the hotel to pick me up for lunch every day. We drove home Friday evening and went back Sunday afternoon. I washed clothes and did chores that need to be done after being gone all week then I packed the suitcases and we were on the road again.

Konn took his mom to buy groceries and whatever she needed to have done. She didn't like us being out of town but she didn't say too much and accepted whatever Konn did. She once told me her Konnie never did anything wrong. We kept the pace up for six weeks and then boom. The two-month honeymoon of getting along was over and we're at each other's throats once again. Konn threw my things out in the hotel hallway and kicked me out of the room because he didn't like something I said about President Clinton and Monica. I pounded on the door real loud till he opened it. Needless to say I didn't travel with him the next week. We called each other all day long. He came home on the weekend and asked me to go back with him the next week but I didn't travel with him yet again for several months. The fighting raged on long distance. We called and hung up on one another. Sometimes while I was talking to him he threw the receiver in the trashcan near his desk. Our phone bills were $ 200 a month. Konn was enjoying the road trips and liked living in a motel room. He was making it real plain he is glad to be away from home alone.

I started nagging him to tell his boss he wants to work in our hometown. I had vibes about the changes taking place in his attitude while he's traveling by him self. When he came home for the weekend if we disagreed over the least little thing he began to take off after he's home only a few hours. He was cussing all the time now saying f- -k you and other choice words he started to call me. Sometimes he deliberately didn't come home for three weeks at a time. Then when he decides to call and ask if I'd like him to come home I taunted him with things I knew he'd whine about. Sure come on home your probably wore out after being away three weeks. I'd ask what he has been up to? I bet you can't wait to get home and make love to your wife. He'd get flustered and cry and carry on. I knew he was not doing without anything his cold heart desired sexually and taking care of him self watching the playboy channel in his motel room but as yet I wasn't aware he was hanging out in strip joints.

After not seeing me for long periods of time when he did come home he didn't say hi honey, how are you? Or I'm so glad to see you I missed you. Instead the moment he walks in the door I'm subjected to the same tired old speech, the same loud ranting and raving about being impotent and he can't perform and needs Viagra. What motivates you to come in the door whining about Viagra after our long estrangement? We both know the reason you want to take the drug but why is it the first thing you articulate the second you see me. His answer is to turn on the tears and tell me he can't help it if he can't perform without the drug and I shouldn't make fun of him because he needs to take Viagra to enhance our sex life and he's doing it for me. I'm certain the purpose for wanting the drug has nothing to do with enhancing intimacy with your wife; I'll be 300 miles away when the so-called Viagra kicks in. I can't help myself when he leaves himself wide open. I jump right in, make smart remarks and he turns right around and leaves once again.

One evening he came in blaring so loud after a lengthy departure and I asked him to hold it down Francis had a friend visiting downstairs and he got louder. I could hear them giggling at things he's screaming about impotency.

They usually ignore him but they came upstairs and said they didn't want to hear about his sex life. He ignored them and kept it up till I told him to take off and don't bother to come home on the weekend again.

He left and before too long were back to calling back and forth squabbling and trying to settle I don't even know what anymore. He didn't think anything of driving 300 miles back and forth sometimes three and four times in the same day. That was 600 miles round trip. He was like the roadrunner. Sometimes he drove almost 2,000 miles a day. Many times he made the trips trying to smooth things over between us to keep a hold on me I was slipping away once more. At times I'd say come back home and let's talk and he'd drive the 300 miles back and forth without blinking an eye. I decided to go with him one week after he made a pitch on missing and wanting me with him. I never learn because in my heart I want to be with him. I never did approve of the single lifestyle he wanted to live as a married man. All the same here he is living it and loving every minute. He was slipping further away from me too.

I'd start to fear a final breakup between us and I'd resign myself to try again so one weekend I went with him when I was just getting over a bout with bronchitis and I wasn't feeling too whippy. When I stopped traveling with my husband he began to stay in a motel instead of the hotel.

I felt weak and woozy after the long drive so I climbed in bed. I turned on the TV and the Bill and Monica fiasco that got worldwide attention was on. Konn was watching a TV in the other room. I wasn't paying any attention to him and I hadn't said a word. I watched the show a few minutes; suddenly with no warning whatsoever he's in my face shrieking that he knows I think he's guilty of doing the same things they say on the news concerning the sexual encounter that took place in the white house and I was to get out. So I did.

I called a cab and sat with my bags in the lobby sicker than a dog waiting for the cab to arrive. He came in the lobby and asked me to stay. I said no. The cab arrived and I rode the 300 miles home in it. I didn't care if it was going to cost $200 I wasn't going to listen to him ramble and roar.

I called my daughter Angel from the motel lobby to let her know I was taking a cab home and to open the screen door so I can get in the house. She was angry I had to be on the road two am in the morning. She knew how sick I was before I left and how badly I wanted to be with my husband to work things out. She called Konn at the motel and had my friend call him too. I would have stopped them both had I known they were going to call Konn. I didn't want them to interfere. I knew his conversation would be filled with lies and this was between Konn and I. I only wanted her to make sure I could get in the house when I arrived home. He told my daughter he never loved her mother and didn't want me for his wife amongst other things and told my friend the same story. Angel told me all he said the next day. I called and confronted Konn and he denied everything. I asked him if he'd like to come home to talk and he came. My daughter confronted him in front of me and he denied saying any thing to her. I believed my daughter. I already knew he was going to deny what he told her. But I want us together and things between us to be okay at any cost no matter what he said. My life became a bewildering dilemma. One minute I want to be with him and the next minute I didn't.

Nothing between my husband and I made any sense to me or to anyone else. The only one our life made sense to was my husband because he called the shots. He led a double life for so long he had his motives down to an art. He seemed to enjoy the upheavals between us. I didn't know his secrets were far more disturbing than anything I learned of him thus far.

I was a glutton for punishment. When I felt better I tried to go with him one more time. As we're driving down the highway 55 miles an hour he kept screaming. I felt like a prisoner when he yelled in the car it was ear shattering and I couldn't get away from it. I told him to shut up or I'd jump out of the car, he reached over to the passenger side where I'm sitting, opened the car door pushed on me arm and told me to jump. My life was in his hands. I was gullible enough to trust him to keep me out of harms way even after he put me there most of the time. I believe he'd tell my children fabrications of the truth if anything happened to me.

I cried until he brought me back home. There was a short time when he was a little more careful about some things he said knowing if he said certain things he'd push me too far. And there was a time he seemed a tiny bit worried if I discovered immoral items. But that's all past history. Nowadays he didn't care if I find stuff belonging to other woman and sexually explicit things. His words consisted of superior smugness as he remarks so what if he has women's undies and pornography material. He didn't give me a ten minute break the vocal battering was nonstop.

He wasn't concerned if I knew he left work early or if he's in his motel room taping and watching sex videos wearing his little thing off playing with himself. He acted like it was his pride and joy like he was the only one that had one of those things. I used to wish it would fall off when he was fooling with it or wish he'd hook up with Lorena Bobitt if you can remember back that far to know why she was in the news.

He knew what he was doing when he came home tuckered out and said he couldn't perform sexually and so did I. One evening after a tiring tirade of denials I couldn't believe the way I reacted. I said Konn you're supposed to be my husband in every way that includes sexually and your not leaving until you behave like a husband and take care of my needs too. Half the time I didn't mean most of the words I spoke. I was testing the waters again trying to see where I stood in the scheme of things. I wept all the time. It was all so embarrassing to think of the things I said and the things he said and the way he behaved every time he came home. He had long-established a talent for telling incorrigible lies so it was beyond me why I took the precarious betraying words he said to heart.

One evening he came to town and called to ask if he could come home. I said no go see your waitress friend that told me you were flirting with her. He said okay if that's the way you want it and he hung up. The next morning I was talking on the telephone to a friend, the doorbell rang and I told her to hold on. I laid the phone down on the sofa and forgot she was on the other end. When I seen it was Konn I didn't say a word I just closed the door. I kept the screen door locked so he couldn't use his key. He screamed so loud I opened the front door again but I wouldn't open the screen door. Bellowing shrilly he held a piece of paper in his hand and said it was a note from the waitress telling me he wasn't the one that flirted with her. And here's a receipt to prove I was at a motel alone last night so unlock the door and let me in. I forgot my friend was still on the phone while he's yelling. My friend Sarah thought he was hurting me and called the police.

I was stunned when I seen the police walking up to the door. I asked why they were here I didn't call them. They said my friend called and asked them to check on me because she could hear Konn screaming on the other end of the phone line and was worried he was hurting me. Konn believed I called them even after the police told him I didn't. They said perhaps Konn should leave until things cooled down. He left and I didn't hear from him all weekend. I ended up calling him long distance Monday morning when I knew he'd be at work but he hung up when he heard my voice.

I didn't hear from him for a few weeks. The next weekend he pulled in the drive. I went outside to talk to him, opened the car door and there's an enormously long filthy painted false fingernail on the car seat. I picked it up and said maybe your girlfriend would like to have this back. He merely said your always snooping through my car looking for things. I told him to get lost and went back in the house. He took off.

I gave up, filed for a divorce and had the papers served on him while he's at work. I didn't want a divorce but I was purely falling apart. I don't believe I knew what I was doing anymore either. I didn't see or talk to him for about a month. Then once again we began calling one another. The state of affairs was as insane as everything else we did. I was so distraught and annoyed I involved his daughter in our affairs this time by having her and her husband come and get his clothes so he doesn't have to come near me. He barraged me with letters and phone calls begging me to get his clothes back and I did. I shouldn't have involved them. My reasoning for involving them was surrounded around the many times he subjected my family to his crazed actions without blinking an eye. I thought it was time his family knew too. He kept asking me to drop the divorce telling me how much he loved me and wanted to spend the rest of his life with me. No matter how much he pleaded I persisted in going ahead with severing ties.

We incessantly fought long distance. Needless to say once again there was the calm before the storm. The day before my birthday he drove 300 miles to come home and talk then drove 300 miles back to work. That evening he drove 300 miles back home put a dozen roses and a love letter in the door and drove the 300 miles back to work. It was seven am when he arrived at his motel room after the night's road trips. He called and told me to look out the front door. There were a dozen roses in a vase to the side of the door and a letter was placed between the tiny bars on the door. In the letter he asked me yet again to drop the divorce. I was touched when I seen the flowers knowing he drove all those miles to say happy birthday. He drove back again in the evening and we celebrated my birthday together. Once more I sold out for a dozen roses and dropped the divorce. In spite of everything I observed in his uncanny behavior I still didn't fathom just how dark he could be.

He finally got his boss to locate him in our hometown so he wouldn't have to travel anymore and we could work on our marriage. He came home the end of November 1998. I was glad his traveling days were over.

He didn't have to work the entire month of December because it was his paid vacation time. Then his firm didn't have any work lined up for him to do in town until February. The company gave him three months off and the checks continued to come in weekly. I've never heard of anyone having a cushy job that paid over $5,000 a month to stay home and do nothing. Not that I was complaining I spent every dime of it.

I will never know why he asked me to drop the divorce pleading with me to work on a new beginning. He turned on me like an incensed tyrant more vindictive than before I filed. Only now there were no good days in between the fury of hell and the wrath of Konn Rodent's wickedness. His behavior was unbearable. I learned first hand we will tolerate all we can until we can tolerate it no more.

In all the time I found evidence he's cheating and the whole nine yards he's making life miserable I still didn't think of him as someone that might be a steady participant partaking of the strip club scene. I didn't know in his travels to and from his job out of town he had been frequenting strip clubs and frolicking sexually with strippers while coming down on me like gangbusters. My friends tried to tell me the first time I found the pair of undies that they could only belong to a hooker but I just couldn't believe it. I'd stand up for him and say he wouldn't do that he's not that bad. He doesn't drink or do drugs. He told me he was approached by a prostitute only one time in his whole life and told her to get lost. He said he never went to a prostitute nor would he ever have anything to do with them. I chose to believe his absurd tale. They said can't you see he does everything cold sober. No I couldn't see I loved my husband much too much to believe the very worst.

I lived in denial for what seemed like an eternity trying to hold things together. Listening to deceiving falsehoods of unreality I was living in an unreal world too.

I never knew where he was coming from everything about him was misguided unnatural reasoning. He would say I said something I didn't say or deny what he said to me and always told me I didn't see what I saw or hear what I heard. Konn distorted whatever both of us said in our conversations. He twisted and mangled the words into something totally whacked out and different than what was really said. He made our life so hard when it could have been so easy. We had plenty of money and a nice place to live with every thing we needed. We bought and did whatever we wanted within a $5,000 to $6,000 a month budget.

I loved him so much I desperately had the need to think that just maybe I'm wrong about things I seen and heard. Maybe while I'm dealing with his addiction I might be bum raping him and he really could be innocent. It was the way I survived in my own safe world for the outcome of believing other wise was too much to cope with.

Experts have proven sex addiction and pornography nurtures abnormal perversion and violent abusive behavior. After awhile lewd sexual fantasy

142

visions are not enough never satisfied with one level the addict goes into another level of depravity so imbedded in the mind nothing else matters and nothing else exists. The sex addiction took complete control of my husband. He lived for the addiction from early morning until he fell asleep and for all I know in his sleep. He did call me by someone else's name from time to time. He fantasized sex with every woman he was in contact with. For all I know every women in outer space. The only women I know of that he didn't envision having sex with was his wife.

I kept telling my councilor Demi I want my husband to accept me. I practically lived for his acceptance. It was the focal point of the way I tried to please him. Even if all he gave me were crumbs of affection it put a smile on my face and made my day. My councilor explained an abused person is always seeking acceptance from the abuser. I kept looking for him to recognize I sought after his approval in the worst way. I thought if I had his acceptance and approval he'd acknowledge what he was doing to both of us. I yearned for my husband to take me in his arms and ask how he can make it all up to me.

Chapter Twelve

Exploitation, Deception & Violence

I'm one of the people that didn't understand why some women stayed in abusive relationships. Why they took appalling treatment their husband commits and forces on the innocent spouse that just wanted their love and acceptance. They simply wanted to please their spouse. I never really knew what it felt like to be in the over powering burden of living with someone that doesn't care who they hurt. Then feel justified as if they had the right to do whatever they want with no regard toward putting their spouse in harms way. My husband proceeded to act as if he had a right to do whatever he wishes to degrade, hurt and take my self-worth from me. The final decision to let go began to manifest. Trying to please Konn I learned the hard way no one deserves to be treated inhumanly or aggressively brutal just to please his or her partner in a relationship.

One evening he was outdoors screaming he wants his dignity back. I didn't know what he meant. I thought he was screeching in relation to my not letting him come back home. He kept his secret trashy lifestyle hidden for years. His ex wife lived with him 14 years and didn't realize he was hooked on pornography and sexually addicted. Here I come along and say hey Konn what the heck are you doing?

Konn was infuriated and harbored resentment toward me for uncovering his secrets and for the stand I took against immorality and for throwing away filthy magazines he collected for years. He became more indignant each time I called his bluff and spoke to him in regard to real over unreal, fact over fiction, accountability and responsibility. My councilor said my husband felt I attacked his character and took his honor when I didn't let him get by with dishonest shams and wanted answers to his strange mannerisms to cover the lies he tells on habits he tries to hide that I discover and confront him with.

My spouse didn't see he took his own honor and was taking mine right along with his by exposing me to untruthfulness and erroneous abuse and at the same time demanding I say he is innocent of everything he knew he was doing.

Having the problem within him self he was making me part of the whole scenario. I wasn't taking his self-respect he simply refused to recognize the addiction was taking any semblance of honor he might have ever had.

He put his heart and soul in the effort to scrupulously destroy my dignity trying to hush-hush what was in his closet for years. I was sick of the selfish attitude of not caring about anyone but his own self worth, He didn't give a hoot if he stole someone else's self respect but he didn't want anyone to take his. I recognized to late blaming and belittling me for his behavior was solely to make him self-look good and cover up the real issues. He proved where his heart was the second he knew I wasn't going to permit him to set foot inside the door unless he sought help for his problems.

Subsisting with my husband was an eye opener to all that is immoral, indecent and offensive. He was a scoundrel and there is no way to represent a scoundrel unless you are one. I believe a scoundrel is someone that has no heart, honor or dignity. He gave quite a performance in exits and entrances. Impersonating a man with no remorse or conscience. Except it was not an act. Each time he started a brawl and left I virtually walked around in circles, filled with stress, fear, anxiety and worry. Even though most of the time his behavior said I hate you Rosie I still wanted to believe he loved me. He pulled me toward him and pushed me away, told me I love you, I hate you. Left home then came back. Instead of marrying him I should have just bought him a yo-yo. I felt like one most of the time.

My husband's last exodus from home took place Sunday morning May 16,1999. I'm sure he thought he could come home like he always did. His game his rules, act like a loon, have a memory lapse and forget where he spent the weekend. Leaving for the umpteenth time claiming he's never coming back. All he took was his VCR and video's. He didn't take a change of clothes or his computer, which he always lugged in and out. Taking just a VCR and video tapes was telling me he is set on fantasizing women whether in fantasies or in the flesh. There was no doubt as he left he had plans to have sex that didn't include his wife for the last time.

He proceeded to get in the car, drove down the street, turned the car around and came back a few minutes later. A smirking sarcastic grin plastered on his face he went directly in the house got his alarm clock, gave me a knowing look, a hi ho silver and away he went to find his friend Tonto.

Two days later he called and asked if I'd like to have breakfast and talk over our marriage. Rosie, I'll come back home if you go to a councilor concerning accusations you make in regards to my being with other women. He put it back on me for leaving, for being a cheating ratfink. I responded there is nothing to talk about we don't truly have a marriage, we have a headache.

Konn informing me he'd come home if I went go to a councilor was only part of scheming episodes he utilized to justify things he alone is responsible for. I wasn't agreeable to see a councilor with him one more time and give him the satisfaction of shredding me to pieces in the fabricated perverted method he spoke of my personality holding me answerable for his problems. He persistently said I was the only problem he had.

I made up my mind he can go to a councilor for himself acknowledge his part instead of focusing on me while ignoring his psychotic barnyard behavior. All the after affects subsequent to the facts are only because he is caught in the middle of the web he wove. After he was away a few days he wrote six pages of defiling accusatory, slam dunk letters and put them in the screen door. He might have thought the letters were beautiful love letters and maybe to him they were. He wrote them for several weeks accusing me of every thing he ever said or did, claiming his virtuousness. To this day still believes he is the innocent victimized husband and I did the things to him that he did to him self.

If I told him I wouldn't read the letters, he'd cry and carry on as if he didn't plan the entire episode of leaving. It was apparent Konn wants to come home at this point in our misguided mendacious relationship as a guise to some other mentally disturbed plan he will eventually pull out of his hat. When he left Sunday I ardently urged Konn not to leave. I told him it's to hard to get it back together when you go and come back day's later. We have to start all over again. There has to be a finish line. Ignoring my pleas to stay he walked off smiling with no consideration or concern laughing as he got into the car and drove down the street. His heart didn't melt at the sight of my tears and stress he initiated before heartlessly driving away.

I didn't always ask my hubby to stay and there were times I told him to go. But sooner or later we always managed to get back together. But the events that took place culminated to the degree they were boiling over and no matter how much I want to be with my husband, there was no going back. It was the end of our emotional toxic melodrama.

The entire scene was blatantly obvious and purposely staged. First start a hassle, cause apprehension, upset my family, leave, come back home, act as if he did nothing wrong and condemn me for all of it. The routine is the same pattern he programs in his computerized brain and performs over and over when he has an itch to depart from home to participate in sexual orgies. I don't accept the sexual addiction he desired is a disease or an illness. I looked at it as a willful decision. He decided to keep the harmful addiction as the most important possession he holds on to for dear life above God, wife, family, dignity, honor, integrity and every thing else in his warped world. It was all so tiring and uncalled for.

Early Saturday morning May 15.1999 was the last time I allowed him to act out his version of " let's see if I can get by with the blackmail my wife trick again." He made threats to leave if I didn't sign a document he wrote, claiming he didn't have to pay me support if I divorced him.

No one will ever have an answer I can accept as to why he pursued having me drop the divorce, move back in with me and then spend the time he's with me after I cancelled severing ties to distribute everything in his power to force me to file for divorce again. Konn worked out the strategy he would use to fly the coop and wallow in a pigpen saturated in degeneration in a house of ill repute that operates under the façade of a gentleman's strip clubs. I believe men participating in the scurvy demeaning activity within the walls of a strip club should by no means be called gentlemen.

Trying to force me to sign the absurd document was annoying. I refused to sign it. I decided to confront him with a tape I accidentally left on the tape player as I recorded a song I wrote. At the same time I was playing the piano and recording music he was working on the computer. The computer is located close to the piano and tape player.

I was absorbed in what I was doing and I got up from the piano and went into another room and forgot I left the tape on. When I played the tape to hear how the music sounded there was more than the sound of music on the tape. I could hear my husband talking to someone in his cutesy voice. I thought of the way he smiled and his sickening sweet voice telling me oh don't leave I like it when you play the piano. He was clearly getting a thrill out of a sadistic game of having me near at the same time he's communicating with his girlfriend on the computer in front of my face behind my back. Some of the pieces to the puzzle started to fit in place. The picture shows he met someone during the time he was on road trips working out of town. He led me to believe the extra trips he made were to talk things over. Crying and pleading with me to please drop the divorce and give him another chance he will make everything up to me.

I recalled the many times he drove back and forth out of town and the times he wasn't on the job. The many unaccounted hours in between the time he left work, drove the 300 miles and reached home long after the time he should have arrived home. Along with the times he didn't come home for two and three weeks and other suspicious behavior. The tape was revealing some of the trips he made were not just to see me after all.

I've never felt very mature nor have I ever known what it means when someone says to act your age. I used to say how does someone my age act? It was childish at this stage in the game to consider the man I married would eventually do right by me. Konn entered into our relationship and marriage based on lies and it ended in the same fraud and trickery.

I prayed and dreamed we could have a harmonious loving marriage. After I read the letter he wrote testifying if I dropped the divorce we'd have a new beginning, he loved me and wants to live the rest of his life with me I was hopeful once more as I visualized us living happily ever after. I can't explain why I decided to keep that letter I threw all the others away.

It was hard for people that have a tough time forgiving others to believe how vulnerable I am and how easy it is for me to forgive people even before I was a Christian. There's no way I would have dropped the divorce I filed the first time if I had not believed the promising pledges to renew his commitment to treat me properly and respect who I was. I wanted that new beginning, my husband and our marriage the way I envisioned it was going to be right from the start. Starting all over again meant I had to lay down the distrust and trust him no matter how many times he broke it before. If we're going to have a new beginning I'm going to go all the way and really try harder.

Directly after I dropped the divorce he burst my bubble so fast I didn't know what hit me. The moment he moved back home I couldn't believe my ears when he told me he never loved me and he didn't love me now; I was not the woman meant for him and he definitely didn't want to be married to me. The exact words he denied telling my daughter and friend the year before. One day when he was being especially obnoxious repeatedly saying I was not the woman meant for him I confronted him on the subject of cheating. I played him the cassette tape with the slimy conversation he was having with his new friend on the computer microphone. Konn said he was talking to the dog. He became violently angry and begins to intimidate me as he tries to brutally take the tape away from me.

I tried to leave the house but he won't let me out the front door. He followed me to the garage and prevented me from opening the garage door too. Screaming at the top of his lungs he proceeds to dent the entire hood of my car banging it over and over again with his fist. At the same time he's wrecking my car he's forcefully holding my arm with the other hand. I tried to push him away but I didn't have the strength to break free of his insatiable strength while he's menacingly holding me captive. This was the first time I was truly terrified and in fear of the intensely violent out bursts. When I finally squirmed out of the gripping hold he had on my arm I managed to open the garage door. As he continued to beat on the hood of my car I hurried over to my daughter's house next door. I went in and asked her to keep the tape for me. It was a mistake to go to her house for she was always fearful of my husband's venomous loudness and cruelty. Shortly after I arrived at her home he followed me and stood at her front door lamenting and blaring loudly. She was shook up and told him to go home. He did leave then but he was livid.

It was the first time I asked for her protection from the onslaught of his terror and directly involved her while he's still in the midst of enacting one of his tirades in full force. I apologized to Angel and told her I shouldn't have dragged her into the craziness. I was shaking with fear and didn't know what to do. I didn't want to call the police. The police were called to our house so many times. I detested having to live this way. I never lived with police calls and police driving up and down my street all the time keeping an eye on our home because of the domestic disturbances that began shortly after Konn moved in.

When I walked back into our house he bellowed piercingly I hate you more than I ever hated anything or anyone in my life. You can't prove a thing with that tape I wasn't talking to a woman I was talking to the dog. I kept quiet. I didn't remind him of all the sneaky shrewdness and betraying infidelity that took place during the course of marriage. Nor did I say anything about lies and deception coming through his entire demeanor.

Nor did I remind him of the horrible incidents that occurred in just the last six months since he asked for another chance to restore our marriage. There were the phone calls he received on our second phone line he said I didn't hear and of course the undies he said I didn't see him grab off our bed and shove down the front of his pants when I came home unexpectedly.

As his uproar droned on I didn't mention all the times he ran downstairs to the computer the second we came into the house after we were gone a few hours or the way he clicked the computer to something other than what he was doing the minute I walked into the room. I didn't tell him I learned the computer can be used just like a telephone and I was aware he and his friend were calling each other all the time. But I really didn't catch on for several months that he was using the computer in different ways to contact her. During this time I knew nothing about computers many different ways of communicating with anyone anywhere in any state or in the world. I stayed upstairs most all the time. But after all the suspicion he exhibited one day when he scooted downstairs the second we walked in the house I followed him down to the computer. Demonstrating another tirade he said I was spying on him. He got that right I was spying.

When his job ended out of town and he moved back home the first thing on his agenda was to update his computer into someone else's computer and search out their programs and data. Nor did I know you could talk through the microphone connected to the speakers until I heard the a funny sound that evidently was a signal alerting him to answer a call and then heard him talking in the familiar sugary voice he uses to delude woman.

I thought it was out of the ordinary when he started to work on the computer day and night until five in the morning. He rarely came out of his office area. I asked why he was working all hours of the day? He replied he is working on a bible program and writing his own version of introductions to the gospels.

He told me he could only connect his computer to the mainframe of the computer associated to his job so he can work from home at times. I didn't question computer talk. I didn't know anything about them. However, after my husband left I experimented with his machine a few weeks. I called my son and he gave me detailed instructions on how to connect Konn's hardware into his computer 125 miles away. I linked into my son's computer within minutes with no experience whatsoever.

In the meantime before attempting to find out what he was up to on his computer Konn's still here awhile longer hollering how blameless he is, how much he hated me and he's leaving forever. I continued to be quiet and didn't say a word about the nights and weeks he stayed away from home with no explanations. It took too much effort to talk about all the distrust and reality of everything he executed that showed his involvement, as a womanizing pig was real. He'd never be exonerated or innocent of all the activities he endorsed and corrupted my life with.

I didn't say anything about him calling me a whore and a fucking bitch and other filthy words he swore in my ears ever since the day he tricked me into letting him come back home. I merely stood there shaking inside listening to the ravings of a madman. After I cancelled the divorce I was determined to do all I could to salvage our marriage. I did an about face months ago and concentrated on working things out peacefully no matter what he said or did. I never told him to leave anymore. Instead I kept asking him not to leave. Remarking time and again that I didn't want to spend one more night away from him or ever be apart again. My silence didn't appease him he told me I had to go back over to my daughter's house and get the tape immediately or he's going to break everything in the house. I went to my daughter's and got the tape. I regretted my decision to play the tape for Konn because of all the uncalled for disaster that took place after wards. I should have known if I confronted him with solid evidence he would link the incident to being other than what it really was and distort it to his advantage in deceiving refutations.

My husband was working on his computer when I came back in. I went downstairs to show him I had the tape back. I put it in my pocket and went back upstairs thinking that would calm him down. Instead he followed me upstairs and forcefully tried to take the tape from me.

My fear dissipated when he forced his weight on me again I became stubborn. I wasn't going to give him the cassette. I knew he wanted to use it to make me look ridiculous bending the truth once more trying to make him self-look like the virtuous victim by playing it to our friends and family as he tells them he was talking to the dog or the newspaper boy or Godzilla. He wouldn't let go of me so I yanked the tape out of my pocket and ripped it to shreds. That did it; he was beyond anger he was boiling over. His face was crimson red he started to jump up and down on the floor in the front room. Over and over again he jumped up and came down thunderously. The rumbling shook our house and rattled things on all the shelves.

My daughter called from next door and said her home was shaking and rumbling and she heard loud noises that sounded like earth tremors. She thought there was an earthquake and ran outside to see what was going on. She couldn't grasp the situation anymore than I could.

I was shook up but I tried to quiet her down. Surprisingly I still protected Konn. I told her I didn't know what she heard. I didn't tell her the earthquake was my husband stomping and jumping up and down with all the force he could disperse. Nor did I tell her he was rough and wouldn't let me out of the house and trashed the hood of my car. All she knew was that we argued over a cassette tape he wants to get his hands on. When I was through talking on the phone I noticed he's crying and proclaiming his innocence muttering that I tore up his evidence; while he's picking up little pieces of cassette tape and putting them in a container. He put the bits and pieces on his desk. His voice must have hurt from all the clamoring and yelling he did for he quieted down.

After the tape production I apologized to Konn for upsetting him. I felt there must have been something in me that needed fixing too cause I loved him. I still cried with him and for him and for myself. The sight of him weeping over the tape being torn to shreds made me sad even though I know his motives are connected to crazy. Apologizing to my husband for his behavior in the foolish immorally dishonest situations was pathetic because he knew what he was doing and every lie he told. By turning it all on me he never answered for anything. I did the answering for both of us.

I felt pity for him. He didn't allow him self to see the dark mania in all he does to deceive him self and mislead and hoodwink me. He didn't get it; if he would not lie, cheat and try to find new ways to hide a secret double life in his perverted addiction there would be nothing to deny, nothing to argue about and nothing to prove.

In all probability we could have had a loving relationship. I was willing to give him all the love welled up inside me that he stifled for so long. It's beyond me why he wishes to upset the apple cart and bruise the apple so many times. I wanted us to live in harmony and love, play and have happy times. My entire life consisted of sharing myself with people I loved. I wanted to treat my loved ones as though it was my last day, my last minute on earth. Say I love you to my husband, my family and friends while I could still tell them. My family and I had camaraderie. We had so many fun times together and always there for one another.

My daughter Francis was living in her own apartment shortly after I dropped the divorce. She thought if she moved it might be better for my husband and I to have time together without someone living with us. Although I was down in the dumps that she was moving out of the house and I wept for days missing her presence the prospect of being alone in the house was giving me ideas. I thought of fixing candlelit dinners every night. I could walk around the house in sexy nightgowns if I want to. I couldn't do that before because there were always children around. With just the two of us alone in the house I planned on doing all I could to have our time together be an adventurous romantic encounter. The minute she moved It was evident her presence in the house held him down to a semblance of some order.

Konn really laid into me; he was cruder, meaner, louder and more abusive. A new put down remark he added to the same words he's consistently shouting of his not loving me I'm not the woman for him is that he needs someone that will encourage him. That remark struck a chord after encouraging and saving his behind from poverty, paying debts he didn't tell me he had since 1984, helping care for his mother, loving and taking excellent care of all his needs while taking punishment he dished out that I didn't deserve. I couldn't help the thoughts flashing through my mind. I wanted him to go beat his head in, do his dramatic temper tantrums, throw him self on the floor and hold his breath and cut his wrists in front of his new friends in the same way he did those awful things in my presence. The diabolical words matched the evil looks he shot my way as he became more depraved and atrocious each day. It was impossible to have peace where there was none. Konn wouldn't accept there are enough problems in the day without creating more. He yelled non-stop the entire six months we were supposed to be building on promises he made to renew our relationship.

No matter what he said or did or what ever took place between us I still strongly believed the only thing that counts when we are on this earth is to strive to live the way God intended us too and give Jesus the glory for all he did and all he does for his children. I'm not a fanatic I simply love God and tried to live by "the golden rule" do unto others, as we would have them do unto us. But it was getting harder and harder to display the golden rule unto Konn.

The day my daughter was moving into her own apartment his mother became quite ill and kept calling Konn to take her to the hospital. I was helping Francis and she was already at the apartment waiting for the men still carting her furniture out of our house so I couldn't leave just yet. The last call his mom made was at five pm but Konn still won't go see what's wrong. I didn't know why Konn wouldn't take off and tend to his mother without me. He took her to the hospital with out me before. I couldn't budge him from the computer. I kept urging him to go see what's wrong with her. He insisted on waiting for me. I didn't know till I seen a transaction log he was programming his girl friend into the new hardware while mom was asking him to help her. I was between a rock and a hard place he wouldn't go and I couldn't leave yet. He knew she didn't feel well the day before and stopped in to check on her after work but he said the nurse was there and mom was feeling better. Several hours later there was a call from 911 saying they took his mom to the hospital. As soon as the furniture mover's left I said let's go

154

see what is going on with mom. We went to the hospital and they had her on a stretcher by the nurse's station she didn't look very well.

We hung around a while and decided to come home until they moved her into her own room. I asked the staff to have the doctor call the minute they knew what was going on with her and we'd come back. Even though we knew it would be a long wait before they had her situated in a room I felt bad we didn't stay with her longer. We took her to the hospital many times and sometimes it wasn't an emergency. She wanted us to take her to the emergency room because the hospital staff tended to her quicker than if she waited for a doctor's appointment. When we left the hospital I told Konn moms really ill it looks serious. It was late when the doctor called and said she was situated in a room. I asked about seeing her and he told me it would be best to wait until morning. Mom called early the next morning and told me she has Leukemia and had only one week to live. My first thought was to ask if she'd like to pray and ask Jesus into her heart and she said yes. We talked and prayed awhile. It was the last meaningful conversation we had. She passed away a week later exactly to the day she predicated.

I loved his mother and her dying just like that hit me hard. It wasn't easy to relate how I felt to Konn or his immediate family. I felt a coldness I couldn't fathom or penetrate so I kept most of my thoughts and feelings on how grief stricken I really felt about losing his mom to myself. Mom in law and I chatted with one another almost every day.

My husband's sister Skyler didn't want a service before the burial. I asked if we could have just a small service because mom loved God and we talked about Jesus quite a bit. Her church and pastor meant a great deal to her. Konn and I both agree we'd like her pastor to say a few words and include a little music. We should give people that loved her a chance to pay their last respects. Skyler told me it was up to the immediate family to decide and I was to stop horning in on something that's none of my business. The harsh words took me by surprise. I tried to back off and let Konn handle the situation. I was aware of all the sorrow Skyler had undergone in the last year and grief she must be going through due to her own husbands death within a week or two of her mother's departing. I thought of how exhausted she must feel and yet she kept a vigil at her mom's bedside rarely leaving the hospital.

I guess I did think as Konn's wife and befriending mom I was part of the family and it was my business too. I wasn't trying to disrupt anything. I merely made a suggestion for what it was worth but it's apparent it wasn't worth a thing to anyone except his daughter Mandy. Mandy was sweet and we liked one another. She knew after I married her dad I rallied around his family, helped care for her grandma and pulled her and husband John into our lives. We got to know one another pretty well during the times I planned family things through the year that Mandy, John, mom, Konn and I could all do together.

Mandy was her Grandmother's pride and joy. She said her grandma loved her music and she's going to play her instrument at the funeral no matter what. I said okay then I'll do something for mom too for she liked visiting the church Konn and I attend whenever I was a part of performing special music. After Mandy was unwavering in her appeal to play music Konn backed up his daughter's request. He wasn't her birth father. Mandy was Konn's first wife's daughter and he adopted her when she was five. It was evident Skyler was perturbed with me after Konn and I didn't back down on providing a small service. Skyler gave in and accepted the pastor saying a few words but she definitely didn't want any music. Regardless of her demands Mandy played her violin. I played guitar and asked people attending the service to join in and sing the choruses to 'Amazing Grace.' Konn said he was glad we honored his mom. He shed a few tears at the hospital and during the funeral but after wards I never seen him shed a tear in her memory and he never spoke of her nor once say he missed his mom.

Subsequent to the funeral I never seen him grieve or talk under a roar. His sister took care of all the arrangements to disperse mom's things and rightly so. She did a great deal for her mom and took care of her financially a good many years. Skyler's children loved grandma and they were very close to her too. His sister called and asked if Konn could come over in the evening she wanted to talk to him and needed his help with a few things. Skyler made a point of saying she didn't want me to come with him. I said sure thing let me know later on if there is anything I can do to help.

I felt strong vibes in Skyler's attitude toward me from the time she arrived. Something concerning me was irritating her. If she called and asked me to give Konn a message, she'd say can't your husband come to the hospital straight from work without picking you up first. I said Konn is picking me up and we're having lunch together afterward. She insultingly remarked we could both stand to skip lunch.

I was mystified as to why she acted so cold we had been friends since we met. Once again I felt defensive. I didn't think I was interfering when I stayed near my husband at his dying mother's bed trying to be a comfort to him.

Skyler had no idea no matter how many catastrophes were between Konn and I, there were times when he leaned on me in any given situation dealing with crisis and times he held onto me and didn't let me out of his sight and there were times I leaned on him.

I knew she was upset with me after I gave my opinion on the funeral arrangements however I didn't have any idea why she was upset with me from the time she arrived or why she continued to make a point to rudely exclude me. She looked with disdain whenever she seen Konn and I hanging close to one another. It didn't help matters when she said I kept close tabs on my husband and didn't let Konn out of my sight.

It was none of her business if I kept tabs on Konn. I had every right and every reason in the book to keep tabs on my wandering husband. She should have noticed Konn wanted me with him. We we're comforting each other for a change instead of fussing with one another.

I could understand Skyler wanting to see her brother alone. I'm sure they had a lot to talk about since they hadn't talked in length or in depth for many years, if ever. Konn was twelve years younger than her and was seven years old when she moved away. When I met Skyler she seemed detached from seeking a close relationship with her brother. The stories she told to both my daughter and me concerning her brother the first second we met led me to believe she didn't think too highly of Konn. However I did realize sometimes a death in a family draws people closer. I was glad she wanted to spend some time with her brother. I just didn't like the overbearing controlling remarks she made shoving me away from the first real closeness my husband and I had in a very long time. I'm not sure she realized I picked up on snide comments she made since she came to town and took charge. I chose to overlook them and act congenial regardless because of the circumstance. But it doesn't mean I didn't notice she's making all the decisions excluding her brother's wishes in the arrangements.

The strange thing is I was seeing some of the same similar traits in Skyler surface that I seen Konn execute each time he bulldozed his weight to control having his way. That evening Konn went over to talk to her and came home fuming. I asked what was wrong; he glared furiously and fiercely blew his top. I couldn't make out what he was hollering about but I discerned I was the target. I left the screaming mime in the front room and went to bed. He was calm when he went to see her so I wondered what in the world set him off and triggered him to revert back to his old self three days after his mom's death and so soon after the funeral. Especially when he exhibited the same behavior the next day and every day after that until he left. The next day Mandy went to the apartment to pick up things her grandma wanted her to have. Mom must have known she wasn't going to leave the hospital she put names on certain things she wants members of her family to have. She loved all her grandchildren so much and was so proud of them. Her eyes lit up when she spoke of them.

Skyler was going to leave the next day and I wanted us to part on a friendly basis so I called and asked if she'd like to have lunch with me. She seemed a little friendlier and accepted my invitation. I met her at the restaurant thinking it would be good to spend a little time with her before she left. The minute she arrived and sat down I knew in no uncertain terms the vibes I felt the entire time were warranted. In a harsh voice the first thing she said was I have no respect for you Rosie. What's wrong Skyler? She said I don't respect someone that tries to turn a child against their father. It's not fair to Konn to tell Mandy things about his conduct. Her words took me aback, a picture of all his demeaning behavior in front of my children clicked in my mind and tears gushed down my cheeks in buckets. I couldn't speak for several minutes. When I got my bearings I looked straight into her eyes Skyler; how fair is it for Konn to act like a frenzied brutal maniac in front of my children? How fair is it for my children to see Konn violently terrorize and abuse their mother right in front of their eyes. Is it fair for her dad to put fear in my children's heart as he frightens both my daughters and twelve-year-old granddaughter?

I didn't have to reveal anything to Mandy concerning her dad. She was smart enough to know something was up. She lived with him since she was a child of five and seen firsthand the after math of his behavior and path of destruction he's capable of long before I came into his life. Perhaps his conduct wasn't in the same criteria or context or as violently inane in his first marriage as it's been toward my family and me but just the same Mandy's mother divorced Konn after living with him fourteen years. There had to be drastic reasons to end a marriage that lasted that many years.

I love Mandy and John and befriended his daughter and son in law along with your mother. I included all of them in both our lives when they became my family too. Her dad rarely contacted her, if at all before I pulled her and John into his life to spend quality time together. I wanted Konn to have the benefit of being with his daughter and son in law as much as he can. You know Skyler irregardless of your new found love for your brother and your distaste for me I wish to remind you I'm the person that made your brother take care of his mother after you all made the decision to have your son fly

158

into town and put your brother out of mom's apartment and change locks so Konn can't get back in. As his sister you didn't seem to have any concern for your bother when you threw him out to live in the streets with no money, no food or a change of clothes and no place to sleep except in his car. Your son called and told me he left an envelope for Konn in my door. I didn't know what was going on or what to think of Konn's predicament.

I'm the person that showed your brother love and took care of him after you discarded him and he had no one to turn to. I stood beside him and helped care for both your brother and your mother, the family you left behind and you've been treating me disdainfully and as if I'm a stranger acting like I'm not a part of the Rodent family. After all the years of alienating Konn all of a sudden he is your brother and at long last decided to tell him you love him. My heart ached for Konn as he said Rosie; my sister told me she loved me the other evening. I was sad and happy for him at the same time for he must have lived his whole life not knowing how you felt toward him. I was overjoyed you told him you love him. But he's not just your bother he's also my husband regardless of our problems I love him too. I don't exactly know where you're coming from or why you suddenly feel Konn needs you to protect him to hide the truth of reality and responsibility of his behavior toward himself and his wife. No knows better than you Skyler before he met me every single member of your family including his daughter and ex wife knew Konn's strange and violent behavior started to manifest long before I came into his life.

Konn involved my family and in my quest to learn if his past was filled with the same mania he's displaying and his daughter happens to learn her dad is up to his old tricks and mistreating his wife and family in the process then that's to darn bad. I'm the one he's harming. How fair is that to my family or me? Mandy merely said she knew Konn was acting up. Does that give you cause to announce disrespect toward me or give you the right to butt in on thing's you know nothing about? Did it make you feel good to humiliate me at the funeral parlor when you told me to stop horning in on family business in front of my husband, your daughter, son in law and the funeral director? I'm not embarrassing you in front of anyone I'm saying butt out in private. You may feel all the love in the world for your brother now but you haven't been around him most of his life and don't really know anything about him or what he's capable of even though you knew he was capable of violence and manipulation when he was a child. I'm taking your words to mean no matter what he does to others or if he physically harms or kills me you don't want to hear the gory details because he's your brother and it's not fair for his wife to turn to his family. It's not fair of me to ask his family to lend a hand or to help him recognize he needs professional care or a chemical imbalance test or whatever he needs before he does injure himself or someone else beyond repair. What does that say?

I believe there will be no end to what he'll do now that he feels his sister will be there for him to exonerate his actions anytime he decides to use you for his own selfish purposes. I will not hide the truth from Mandy or anyone else. Nor will I protect his actions by keeping any of his behavior a secret any longer from neither my family nor his.

Telling me it's not fair for his daughter to know what she knew all along for many years say's it doesn't matter or make any difference to either you or Konn if my family sees and knows the truth of his bizarre behavior that even Konn knows is not acceptable to God, his wife, her family or any one else. Just as long as his family doesn't know about it everything will be honky dory. Well it doesn't work that way.

So I said a few things about my husband. If he had done nothing I'd have had nothing to say but regardless of all that happened I'm also the one that stood up for him many times when I shouldn't have because it was protecting behavior I didn't agree with. Mandy knows without a doubt I love her dad and she looks at the overall picture. She seen me pitch in, help him back on his feet, provide him with a loving home and saw how much nicer his life has been since he met me. If that doesn't command respect then so be it. I love your brother and all his family nevertheless there's nothing I can do if you or any other member of your family choose not to give the same love back to me. You initiated a close relationship with me from the beginning. I remember how amazed I was at all you told me about your father, mother & brother in the first ten minutes we met. Then encouraged me to feel free to call and confide in my new sister in law. Tears continued to stream from my eyes with ever word I spoke.

Skyler merely said oh I made you cry then went on to remark Rosie, I've just buried my husband and my mother and I've changed. I don't ever want you to call me or tell me anything about my brother again. He's the only member of my family I have left. If he abuses you throw his clothes out on the front lawn and get a divorce. Skyler, I'm sorry for your loss and for everything else. I know it's been hard on you losing your husband and mother so close together. Please believe that I didn't intend to make waves. But I have emotions and feelings same as you do. I've lost a husband too I know

160

how it feels. I'd like you to know I simply said what I think of the cold calculating comments you've been voicing on your perception of what I've been through in all I'm subjected to subsist in under your brother's abominable cruelty. I don't harbor anything against you in the stand I've taken in defense of the onslaught of insults you've made toward me since you hit town. I'm sorry if I misunderstood your friendliness and your confiding in me the minute we met as a cue for me to feel you wished to be my friend and confidante too. I liked having you for my sister in law because you were connected to the man I loved and married. I wanted all of Konn's family to like me. I turned to you because you gave me permission to trust you and directed me to believe you were there for me. Nonetheless, there is one thing you can count on concerning our conversation I'll never call you for any reason or under any circumstance.

After our discussion on the family was out of the way we made small talk a few minutes then ended our conversation. That evening as Skyler was getting ready to leave she was amiable and hugged me good-bye. I felt it was the last time we would ever see one another and it was. I thought going through a death in the family would draw my husband and I closer together and he'd need me to comfort him but it was just the opposite.

My spouse never once turned to me after she died. He turned on me and away from me. Despite the fact his mom never said no to her son nor held him accountable for any of his actions I realized her presence held him at bay and kept him around for 53 years even though the entire time he's doing things for her he resented being saddled with staying in this area to take care of her. He told me he didn't like his mother he tolerated her and resented her for making him responsible for her welfare and she wouldn't move out of state to live with Skyler.

After the funeral and private discussion with his sister he never uttered another decent word shrieking non-stop night and day; I want to be rid of you, I'm going to leave; you whore, I want us to separate bitch plus other verbally unfit words. He stayed on a green light of go and the light never changed to a red stop. He was incorrigible and uncontrollable. It's unmistakable now that his mother is not around to hamper his choices and decisions he's preparing to dump our marriage.

During this time I became physically ill and immobile for months. I couldn't lie flat on the bed so I slept in the recliner. My daughter came over and fixed me tea and toast to make sure I ate. Konn totally ignored my illness and I ignored him as much as I possibly could but his voice was unavoidable as it permeated throughout the house spewing forth-wretched venomous malice. I made up my mind if he takes off one more time love or no love he is gone forever. I still resigned to do what I can to prevent splitting up but I was at my breaking point.

I took him back so many times I don't blame him for not believing me when I said, I don't want you to go, if you leave me one more time I am never taking you back. Please stay and let's work this out together. As Konn was making his exit, stage left I was the distressed pathetic wife asking her husband not to leave, our anniversary is next week. Let's plan something. He remarked Rosie I tried for three years to get along with you it can't be done. I did everything I could. I treated you like Jesus would have treated you and better than that. If you don't sign the document I wrote I'm going forever and that is final. As I listened to him blaspheming God I thought 'WOW' those are heavy-duty words he used comparing him self to Jesus. All His words and behavior destroyed everything I thought I'd have when I said yes Konn I'll marry you. But when he spoke of my Lord and Savior in the context of his deeds toward me I swear I thought the whole house sparked and crackled

How well I know everything can change before the completion of blinking an eye. I'd been through it before when my husband died with no warning. Konn gave signs and warning signals during the time he was planning to desert and betray me. But it still seemed like every thing was happening so fast. I was already feeling lonely and alone. It didn't help matters when he called five hours later and said I'll come home if you sign the document I wrote. I told him signing a paper wouldn't help anything. It takes two people wanting the same things. Konn do you remember I advocated the theory of two hearts beating as one sharing everything a couple should share together to make a marriage work. It also takes truth, decency, faithfulness, devotion, love, kindness, sex and intimacy you withheld and used to control me. We don't have a marriage to save anymore.

Sad to say my words cut me as deeply as his words did for I had to put him out of my life but I couldn't cut him out of my heart. I don't wish to be a part of the confusion anymore. I don't want to speculate why he tries to come back when he makes it plain he doesn't want to be with me when he's home? I don't want to see the two faces of Konn looking fierce one minute and in the next look like he's a lost lonely little boy and the innocent victim after he purposely perpetrated emotional upheaval and abuse every time I turn around.

I will no longer allow my husband to tell me everything is my fault and he's blameless. I can't let him erase all the emotional and mental pain he inflicts on my heart, soul and mind like it never happened. I can't stand the abusive put downs and ridicule spewing forth in venomous hurt that tears me to shreds. I can no longer tolerate pain and suffering he instills treating me as if I am of little consequence in the scheme of things. I mattered to my family and to myself. My husband is the only person I don't matter to. Letting him back would have been one more level of control. I wasn't going to say it was okay to come home once again just to cheat and mistreat me because he got by with it for so long. I was tired of checking out his lies to see which one was truth or fiction. This time his leaving has to be the last hurrah.

Chapter Thirteen

The Last Hurrah

As I watched my husband drive away I felt I was tearing in two; one piece of me rode away with him, the other piece stood still. I attached myself to him and he became a part of me. I had soul ties with Konn even though he didn't have them with me.

It was like a death, buried gone forever. Different yet the same feeling I had when my husband died. In a moment the same thing was happening all over again. The difference was Franklin didn't have a choice when he died. Konn had a choice. It was his decision to kill and bury our marriage in the death of our relationship. I felt like I didn't have a choice. He took it from me as he drove away and through out our marriage. I used to think people had a choice when they filed for a divorce. I thought they still had an opportunity while they're still alive to reconcile and work at possibly going back together. I learned not all divorces are choice some are forced. I felt forced to end it whether I wanted to or not.

Telling my husband he can never come back if he left meant I had to stand behind the words this time even though I didn't want to. I become conscious of how impossible it is to hold on to someone that doesn't want to be held. As I stood weeping, watching my husband's cold-hearted departure something struck me in a fearful way and sent shivers up my spine. I was not imagining pleasure he derived from sadistic disturbing actions he displayed. His love was in his demeanor as he drove down the driveway laughing at the hurt and anguish I felt as he disloyally discards me just like that.

Recognition of all that happened in the past few years hovered in my thoughts. In that instant Konn became scary. The enormity of his actions sunk in. I don't have an explanation as to why I wasn't afraid of him sooner. For the first time I understood there is a reason he never showed remorse, never showed natural affection nor accepted reasonability nor acknowledged his behavior blaring his actions are someone else's fault. I recollected the times he held me against my will and wouldn't let me out the door. The way he abused and hit me and said it was my fault and I finally believed he's capable of displaying serious life threatening harm to any one that gets in his way. I can't believe the way I shrugged off most everything he did and took him back in the name of love. This time it was different. He had gone way beyond cruelty for so long and made no pretense of anything nice or kind after we reconciled.

I finally grasped the meaning behind some of the deeds he displayed. If he can act as if everything he does is okay and does not see anything wrong with any of his behavior there would be no end to what he has up his sleeve with my name written on it. No end to what he was capable of doing to harm me more than he had already done. The moment of his departure I began to see Konn as a danger and dangerous. Each time he came home his behavior was worse than the time before. I was not afraid of him before the last outburst. Nor did I fear him when others said he could harm me in a violent life threatening way. He was my husband and I didn't want to believe he would go that far and I still don't know how far he would go.

The rages in his behavior become aggressively more brutal. The focal point of being afraid of what he would do if I let him come back home one more time was within the cold glaring evil taunting devilish looks that came over his face as he swaggered to the car sniggering at my dilemma. The unrighteous procedure was that of a man with no principles. All his activities were rooted in self-indulgence and self-love. In conclusion I recognized he has no intention of doing right by me, our marriage or anything or anyone else in this lifetime.

Most importantly I felt he wasn't going to do right for himself. I believe there is only one way he can or will ever accept anything. First and foremost he still needs to recognize the need to have Jesus as his Savior and truly surrender his life unto God without the deception to use the word Christian to further his own selfish motives.

I wonder if Konn knew God could distinguish a sincere conversion from an insincere one. I was the one that didn't know he wasn't sincere when he took me as his bride. What better cover up could he have than to hide his secret life behind a Christian wife and sit honorably in church with her by his side? I learned not everyone sitting in a church knows and accepts God and what they hear from the pulpit they leave in the pews as they walk out the church doors.

He was up to his old tricks seven days after his dramatic departure he put a letter and a dozen roses in the door. It was May 24,1999 the day of our anniversary. The letter said Rosie it's our anniversary. I suppose your not going to call and wish me happy anniversary.

In my heart I wish you would say something that will make me come back home. I left because you accuse me of lusting after other women. I'm not coming back to that. It was the same extreme excuse he used before he left to engage in the corrupt orgies. My perplexing husband left showing no emotion the week before our anniversary as I begged him to remain by my side. It's so unbelievable after torturing me months on end, the grand departure and now he wants me to eat crow and ask him to come home. Must have slipped his mind I asked him to stay and plan something special. He didn't know I had something planned for quite while as a special surprise to our so-called new beginning.

I arranged to astonish him with a trip to Scotland for his anniversary present. Scurrying away the week before I didn't have a chance to tell him he was going to have the opportunity to track ancestry in Scotland.

Its inconceivable he shows no regret nor was he saying he's sorry he's simply pursuing me after slanderously squashing me like a bug under his feet. His foot was coming down slowly on every inch of me a little at a time before fully squashing and spattering me all over the place. I can still see him driving down the road happy as a lark as he left me to lose all I worked toward. Losing my marriage, my husband, dashing all my dreams and hopes along with loss of finances I had before him as well as insurance and finances I'd lose from his income too.

I was the one that had to face the unknown future alone with no husband or money to live on. He's now earning around $100,000 a year after earning nothing before me. I didn't know until a few day's after discarding me he's giving every dime of our income to strippers he plays with and has one particular stripper he is deeply involved with. I do wish whomever he winds up with good luck she will need it some day.

My husband didn't give a darn about our anniversary and didn't care he was forsaking me. He merely used our anniversary as a focal point to come back home. He didn't know his mission to come home this time was going to be mission impossible. I can't tolerate him spending several days in vulgar passions while he acts as though he is the chaste virtuous victim trapped in the dreadful position he put me in.

I'm in the throes of despair at all he did to humiliate, violate and dishonor me with heartbreaking sexual indignity and the fanatical behavior purposely perpetrated, fulfilling his sexual delusions. Deliberately maliciously delighting him self in the process of destroying my already faltering insecurities as he steals my self-esteem. It was too tough to keep pretending all was okay in front of others wearing the same mask of unreality Konn wore. He cheated me out of a husband that should have loved and cared for me in the same way I did for him.

The last two days we spent together will live in my infamy. The alarming disruptive anger culminated my decision not to let him in my home again. It started the evening before he left. I put my arm around him as I was sleeping. He woke me up and jumped out of bed growling.

He woke me up so rudely all I could think of was all the times he turns angry and the extremes he went too making sex an issue if my hand touched him in the night. It didn't matter if I touched him accidentally in my sleep or if I was awake or if I just held him as he lies next to me. He'd get upset and throw my hand off and loudly state it wasn't the right time of day to have sex no matter what time it was. It didn't occur to him people sleeping together can't help but touch one another sometime in the night and it doesn't mean they want to indulge in sex.

It was too much to contend with the devastation of knowing he didn't want me to touch him and he didn't want to touch me. As yet I don't realize how deeply this act of coldness was to affect me until I learned he paid strippers to touch him and he paid to touch them.

Needless to say he got in a few more licks before flying off into the wild blue yonder and intentionally accomplished one of the most dishonorable defiling acts of indecency he knew would injure my heart beyond repair. Shattering and crushing any last shred of self worth I might have held onto. It was the night he told me he only talked about impotency so he wouldn't have to make love to me. Further stating that right from the start he never wanted me as a woman or as his wife. After he made the remarks I didn't want to cope with reality either. I wanted to be just like him and live in another world all my own.

I recalled coming down hard on myself thinking maybe everything is my fault when he continually said he was impotent so often. I began to feel compassionate and tried to console my husband saying its okay honey, don't be distressed I'm your wife I'll help you. All the time I'm reaching out to my husband and he's crying impotent I'm still unaware during his violating outbursts he is deviously performing with strippers. But even after I discovered the truth and seen for myself what he did with strippers prostituting their bodies in a private room all the remarks he made in bed haunted me for years.

When he first started shouting the idiotic don't touch me I hate you touching me routine. I asked Konn do you mean to tell me you disliked me touching you for three years and you're just now telling me in that tone of voice. My husband said that's right I never liked you touching any part of me I should be able to get an erection just by looking at you and that doesn't happen. Adding insult to injury he says's something's wrong with you Rosie and with our marriage if I can't look at you and be turned on. I want us to separate. I definitely want my own place. Subsequently following my husband's thunderously loud screaming not to touch him he would storm out of the house and leave for a few days then call home crying and moaning that he really wants to come back because he loves me and he misses sleeping with me and feeling my warm body next to his. Unbelievable!

After I finished reading the anniversary letter he put in the screen door and threw away the roses he left with it I gave him my last childish ornery salute. There was a radio station playing oldie songs and taking requests. I called the station and asked to dedicate a song to Konn and Rosie on their special anniversary. I'd like to request Connie Francis singing, "Who's Sorry Now." The radio announcer said hey Konn I hear you have a special anniversary today. This song is especially for you Konn Rodent from your wife Rosie. I taped every word the announcer said and the song. I put the tape in a small box with a set of his car keys, my wedding and engagement ring.

I sat down and wrote the infamous letter repeating all the sweet beautiful last words my husband Konn Rodent screamed in my ears for 190 days nonstop.

I started the letter with; Dear Konn, Why are you writing me letters and sending me roses, wishing me happy anniversary and asking to come back after your orgy is over? Why should I permit you to come home to persistently break my heart and eardrums hollering Rosie: I never loved you, I don't love you now. I hate you, your not the women meant for me sick bitch your the only whore I ever knew. There's something wrong with you Rosie I don't get an erection when I look at you. I'm impotent I need Viagra. I don't like having sex with you. I don't want you for my wife. I want my freedom you fucking bitch. Those are your words Konn. I can't stand to hear them one more time. How in the world can you continue to say you love me and want to come back home to be with me after all that? There's no further doubt you mean it when you say you don't want me to touch you. I wanted to believe you were just angry and didn't mean what you were saying so I overlooked most of your speech but I finally believe you meant every foul word you ever spoke to me through out our marriage. I intend to give you the divorce you so desperately ache for. Leave me alone and stop putting letters and roses in the door? I ended the letter with a thank you my dear husband for your devoted loyalty and all the beautiful kind words you gave me to remember you by. Thanks for the memories; all the horrific abuse and all you did to make my life a living hell.

You must be proud of your self for being the most wonderful loving husband in the world. Did you feel dignified and honorable treating me like dirt and kicking the dust in my face? Thank you for giving me underpants that belonged to other woman. I appreciate all the time you took to tell me you were impotent while at the same time you were committing adultery. It made me happy to see you overcame impotency when you took off weeks at a time and were able to perform sexually with your self and stripper friends.

It was such a pleasure to accommodate you in the violent displays of cruel brutality until you had the financial gain you used me to acquire. It was nice of you to permit me to live in the perversion and the loony bin you existed in long before you met me and brought all of your alien habits into my life and home. I was aware of sadistic pleasure you received knowing how bewildered I was when I caught you performing sexually with yourself visioning nude women that sexually took the place of your wife. It made me sick to see the pleasure you derived at my discomfort dealing with sex issues you enforced on me. You knew I didn't talk about sexual things nor even said the word sex before you came into my territory.

It has been a privilege and I'm ever so grateful to have been a part of entertaining you with all the enjoyment you received and delighted in knowing how very unhappy I was after months of uncovering your aggravating sexual preference and all the lies and deception you displayed to hide it. The laughter you received calculating how troubled I was to the fact that you didn't want me during the entire marriage war you declared between us for no apparent reason. All your behavior toward me should give you sadistic pleasure for the rest of your life. That is the last present you'll receive from me.

PS:...One more thing I played with your computer and found a transaction log you forgot to delete. It showed a list of times your girlfriend called on the voice mail that you told me we didn't have. It was nice of you to put me on fax talk so I wouldn't catch on. The transaction log shows the hours she called through the day coincide with a list of times you wrote down and left sitting on the dresser. I asked you what the hours stood for and you cleverly told me I didn't see anything.

Not giving me an answer as to what the times represented I tried to find an answer. I remember the time you giggled unmercifully as you seen me look in a TV guide knowing I thought it was a list of times naughty movies were coming on you wanted to tape while I slept. Just as you did many times before while acting like I'm too stupid to catch on. Did you think it was cute to play hide and seek running downstairs like a chicken with it's head cut off to the computer at different times through the day and the moment we walked in the house. I figured out the way the two of you communicated through the microphone on the computer. Just because I didn't say anything I did see all the times you hurriedly clicked the computer to something other than what you were really doing when I walked in the room. The anger you displayed was uncalled for when I came down to read a book on the sofa just to be near you for a little while. I know now I'd have been in the way when you received her signal on voice mail.

It was wonderful of you to verbally abuse and curse me the entire time your fraudulently cheating and talking cutie pie sweet to your girl friend. There are too many things to write concerning several pair of undies you acquired and held onto, the double life with all the women you committed adultery and fornication with.

Including all the behavior you committed in ambiguous treachery that wasn't tolerable or acceptable from the time I heard you say the words "I do and you certainly didn't."

I put the letter in the box and wrapped it in fancy paper. I went to the florist's, ordered three black roses to represent our three-year anniversary and tied the box to a black balloon. I wrote happy anniversary on a sympathy card and placed it in the cardholder in the middle of the flowers. I had the flower shop deliver the flowers with the box tied to the black balloon delivered to Konn at the minute motel where he was staying. My friend gave me the idea and slightly instigated the radio prank. I never would have thought of retaliating in that particular way for I never listen to the radio. I was ticked off and thought it would be a cool prank. I'm not blaming her I was solely responsible for my behavior and chose to retaliate. I could have thought of a lot of tricks to pull off all on my own but this one sounded like a classic. It seemed to go along with breaking my heart; dumping me one week before our anniversary then giving me roses and letters falsely accusing me and mixed with black mail saying he would not come home unless I saw a councilor for my problems. Along with the threat of signing the paper he wrote to exonerate paying any support if I file for divorce. Then confuse and twist all his behavior by sending letters telling me how much you love me and beg to come home.

Nevertheless later on I felt sad when I thought about retailing toward Konn in a way I knew would be shunning his efforts. I wished I wouldn't have done anything in retaliation and regretted sending the flowers and the box. The only thing I didn't regret was the letter. I meant every word I wrote but I could of had it delivered another way.

I knew he'd stay in the motel room all day waiting to hear from me and it would hurt him if I answer in the snotty way I replied to his gesture of roses in the door. I admit I want him to feel the same painful agony I felt as he left and I stood tearfully outside the door asking him not to leave. Yet I ended up feeling awful I behaved immature to a serious situation. It bothered me to hurt anyone but I couldn't help myself I did want to hurt him for hurting me so many times. Deep down I didn't exactly want revenge either I wanted justice and there didn't seem to be any. My emotions were shattered. I want him to come home I don't want him to come home. He made it obvious it was only a matter of time before he'd make his final move. At the rate we were going I didn't know if I could live through any more sorrow. My heart felt like a vise grip was holding it in place. I continued to be physically ill for a long time before he ran out the door to pursue stripper's full time. He never left home with out his computer. The fact that he left it home showed he would try to come back after the callous departure. The minute he read the letter I wrote and seen I was messing with his computer he was on the phone. He can't handle it when I uncover misguided information he uses to pull the wool over my eyes. I hung up the phone.

The computer didn't belong exclusively to Konn. I bought the computer when he didn't have a dime in his pocket. I never touched it before this time. I was afraid I might mess something up he might need for his job. I didn't even know how to turn a computer on. He was quite upset and fuming I messed around with the computer that had all his data and information not intended for me to see.

The logs showed both fax talk and voice mail transactions. He made sure my name and number showed. Of course he protected her name and id number by having it blocked from view on voice mail but the duration of calls was long enough to leave messages. The calls on voice mail stopped the exact day he left home.

I wasn't trying to prove anything I was just trying to live in truth and reality. I didn't need to prove a thing he proved it all by his little old self. I perceived when he was up to something through suspicious theatrics. I dislike going through the ordeal of having to prove things and it upset me immensely when he gave me no choice.

I knew when a woman other than his wife was in his life. I regretted not digging further and finding out exactly who she was when he was still here. But I didn't exactly know how to go about seeking information on someone until after he left then I became quite good at playing private detective.

Minutes after I hung up the phone Konn drove to my son in laws house and tried to draw Rick into our affairs. He's a computer technician too and understands computer lingo. He knew Rick couldn't confirm communication that took place on the transaction log with no id or name on the voice mail. Konn knew only too well my son in law didn't know what was going on in the latest battle of our private war. All he knew was the damage he seen done to our property. He didn't know all the destructive harm Konn did toward me physically, psychologically, emotionally, vocally, spiritually and sexually. My children only knew what I told them when I protected Konn. They knew what they heard and witnessed in some of his behavior. They didn't know all that went on behind closed doors. I was afraid to tell them.

My daughter called and was frantic. She said get over here right away. The neighbors can see and hear Konn wailing and yelling out in the yard. I learned later the neighbors heard and seen plenty all along.

In my rush to help her I opened the garage door from inside I was going to run under the door while it was closing so Konn couldn't get in the house. The door hit my back; I went flying out of the garage, fell to my knees on the cement, gashed my leg and tore one knee wide open. I was bleeding all over the place.

After all the ill treatment it was mind-boggling that I could feel so bad about Konn's distress. I forgot about the pain in my leg and tried to calm my husband. I felt sorry for him when he looked so pitiful and despondent, tears flowing down his face wanting to come home and have me take care of him. I had all I could do to let him go. Why did he have to behave so wretched before he left and now look as though he's falling apart?

Once again in my eyes he was like a child with no one to turn to, nowhere to go. I wanted to wrap my arms around him and never let go. I patted his arm and told him don't cry it's going to be okay. He asked if he could come home. I said no, I can't ever let you come back.

Konn was so believable and I loved him so much I almost weakened and went with him to the motel. I had to keep focusing on his cheating and the decision he made to leave laughing at my pleas and tears one week before our anniversary. He played on my sympathy like it's my fault he's out in the cold. I never did get it whenever I seen him look hurt and downtrodden I melted and felt like maybe it was my fault and I'd feel so bad and guilty. Even though sometimes minutes before the baby face actions I see his face contort and he comes down on me with violent ruthlessness and the fury of demonic influence.

I told him if he left quietly I'd call him at the motel. He kept insisting my son in law call him. I asked my son in law call him. After the sad scene that took place outdoors he told Rick he didn't want to be with me. I was the one that kept calling and pestering him. He apologized and told Rick he was sorry for scaring his daughter. I kept my word anyway and called him later. I didn't want him to come back manipulating another disturbance in the neighborhood. Just a few minutes after he apologized to Rick for scaring his family he changed his story and told me he didn't do anything to scare my granddaughter and wanted to come back home.

Not acknowledging he scared Marty when he spoke to me and acknowledging he scared her when he apologized to Rick is only one of the many twisted issues I didn't want to deal with anymore. When he arrived at Angel and Rick's home his piercing loudness frightened my twelve-year-old granddaughter and she thought he was going to kill her and all her family. She ran into the bathroom screaming and crying and locked the door. She was afraid of Konn's behavior after hearing him holler at me so many times.

If I asked him to be quiet and talk calmly so he won't upset and frighten her and the other children he got louder and plain didn't care she was just a child or that there is a teen-ager sleeping downstairs.

Both my daughters and granddaughter had dreams he was going to kill all of us. Francis said she dreamed he came to her apartment covered with blood and told her he killed all of us and she was next. I thought it was extreme but their dreams were real to them as they vividly described them. I blamed myself and wondered what kind of mother was I for putting them through the ordeal of fear.

At this time I still hadn't told my children he ripped my clothes off, hit and tormented me with mind control nor did they know about all the abusively vile language and verbal attacks. I wasn't happy he was involving my children in the deception of his innocence. They didn't know the way he played games but I knew only to well and I knew exactly how he was playing this game play by play. I didn't understand all his motives at any given time. He didn't want to be with me yet he would go to great lengths trying to come back home. He had to be desperate to go to my children's home to win their support to get to me in his thrust to come back home.

It's time for me to stop protecting him and protect my children and myself from the onslaught he is capable of when he isn't crying and looking pathetic. He scared my daughter and granddaughter for the last time.

I had to do something to stop the madness for their sake. I wasn't strong enough to do anything for myself. I was too much in love no matter what he did. But I loved my family too they were part of my life.

I filed for divorce a second time, put a protection order on Konn and changed my phone number in one day. He never set foot in our yard again. It took a long while for my children to feel safe again. It was a long way's from being over with for me. Konn and I were to have one more episode as ex husband and wife without my family's knowledge. But I kept my word to protect my family they never had to see him drive down our street or come near our home. He was out of their life and they didn't have to contend with him again. Angel was so glad he was out of our lives and gone for good she did what she called a happy dance of good riddance to bad rubbish.

God's word say's no weapon formed against me shall prosper. I thought what if Konn believed it was his idea to leave but instead it was God picking him up by the neck of his shirt, putting him in his car and driving Konn out of all our life's for the last time. Yet there I was throwing caution to the winds once more time taking things into my own hands before it was over and done with I willfully put myself in Konn's path again.

175

Chapter Fourteen

Divorce & Mania in the Deposition Hearing

There are many emotions abusive men literally take from women while they're trying to destroy their spouse to make themselves look good or macho or whatever they think they are. They really represent an asshole. Sounds unladylike but If fit the description of men making their wives or girl friends responsible for their behavior and shortcomings lacking empathy for their spouse.

I didn't realize how unworthy abusive men made their spouse feel. Sometimes in a way we feel as if we deserve to be treated rotten. I can sympathize sincerely now and know how women felt when cruelty ruled their life. Fear of divorce and being with out my husband was more than the fear of abuse. Fear of trying to survive without finances and insurance was uppermost in my mind. Fear of facing the world alone with no one to support me was not as tolerable as living with an abuser.

Divorce should be spelled P-O-V-E-R-T-Y. Yet all of that is the price tag I put on abuse if I were to continue to take it. It is an important accomplishment for an abused person to overcome obstacles we find ourselves facing through no fault of our own. It's a big deal when your struggling to save yourself and salvage marriage at the same time in whatever way we can while in the midst of aggressive brutality that is forced on your life daily. No one deserves to be treated like they are less than a human being. No one deserves to have someone turn on him or her with rage, wrath and violence. No one should verbally pollute the air condemning their partner for who they are.

I learned some things women must have felt while they're living with a brute in a marriage filled with terror and grief. Why they stayed with the man who put them in an unsafe environment of disturbed, turbulent, tormenting abusive relationships. Almost twenty years ago I asked a friend who was married to an abusive man how she could stand to be with someone that hit her and treated her mean. I told her to tell him to shape up or ship out. In a sad wistful voice, tears in her eyes she said I love him. I want to be with him.

He can't help himself. I'm more afraid of being alone and lonely than to be with my husband. I can't face loneliness.

It's better to have someone than to have no one. I can't live without him. I need him. Even though some of his behavior isn't rationsl all the time sometimes he's nice to me.

I thought he was abused as a child and had a hard life. I believe he was making an effort to change. He accepted Jesus and started to come to church. I loved this couple and wanted to help and encourage him as he tried to overcome what he must have felt inside over all he had been through in his youth. He tried to walk with God in his life. His wife loved God and was such a neat Christian lady. I thought she was a strong woman that had a lot of patience and love she showered on her husband.

I tried to understand what they were going through but I really didn't. I could help them with necessities such as food and clothing but there was no way to know what took place when domestic disturbances occurred. How could I understand or comprehend the manner in which they lived if I didn't live in the same fashion. I had no way of knowing the real hardships people in abusive situations are subjected to in the churning turmoil and explosive atmosphere where anything can be triggered.

Shortly after he was getting his life together he died a tragic death but not before calling out to God. I loved this young man and considered it an honor and a privilege to have been a small part of knowing him.

He's with his Heavenly Father now singing praises before the throne of God and flying with the Angels in Heaven where there is no more abuse, no sadness, and no tears. I thank God for his unconditional love and mercy and for making no distinctions in his forgiveness and grace. I recalled how brave this woman was for standing by her man. I remembered the democratic flippant attitude I had when I asker her why she took being mistreated. I didn't understand why she didn't consider things she went through as being abusive treatment. Rememberance of this sweet lady was like dèjá vu. Because all the things she told me were the same things I repeatedly told people that asked me the same questions in the same manner that I asked her.

It was strange to see myself in the same light I saw my sister in the Lord twenty years ago. It was unusual for me to remember her after all those years I can't recall where I left my glasses and sometimes I forgot the time of my appointments and show up at the wrong time. Something I wrote triggered her back into my remembrance. I'm thankful I thought of her. Seems funny to finally understand where she was coming from in the words she confided concerning abuse she took in her love for her husband and to relate to her words almost twenty years later. At times I thought maybe I didn't love my husband enough to continue the travesty we called marriage. Words were overflowing, spilling and tumbling around in my thoughts as I relived the abuse and heartache with every word I write.

Not everyone can endure and no one should have to tolerate mistreatment in the name of love no matter how much we fear or how much we love or how much we have to give up to come to the conclusion that we are worthy to be treated in a right way and a kind gentle loving manner by the person we entrust with our life too.

The divorce was complicated harsh and unrelenting and intensely affected me. I isolated myself in my home and began to back away from church and things of God knowing full well God was there for me to lean on and was helping me through an impossible situation.

But some times that didn't console me. I was devastated even though I believed God put an end to my being a victim in Satan's lure and I was victorious in Jesus Christ. But I wasn't as tough and brave as I came across and tried to be.

My husband knew how dependant I was on him. How badly I loved him and wanted us to be together. He knew I'd divorce him if he continued to act barbarous and unaffectionate. Feeling as though I was forced to file I still made the final decision to divorce Konn. He wanted to leave and wanted to hold on to me too and he couldn't have it both ways. He knew I wouldn't take much more. After forcing me to file he turned on me with a mighty vengeance and showed who he was all along. The reason he wants to leave surfaced shortly after he left. The pornography and the addiction won out. He has the lustful unclean defiled life style he wanted with someone that has the same morals he has. Having no morals he dove in headfirst.

In reality I didn't want a divorce. My thoughts kept changing. I felt like I just couldn't let him go even though he let me go long before he gave him self the option to hold onto me for life. My heart is breaking yet I can't back down. I thought I was breaking my vows not only to my husband but breaking them to God. I don't take things of God lightly. I took my vow very seriously. I don't just believe in God I believe God. Even after I went to court I still thought of Konn as still being my husband. My definition of marriage was different from the description Konn pulled out of his hat. I believe marriage is more than a commitment to one another. Vows we said before the Lord are much more than words said on our wedding night. It is a contract and a covenant between God and the married couple.

The Bible says you can put your partner away from you for committing the sin of adultery, but God didn't ever condone divorce. I believe the contract between God and a man and wife is binding until death no matter who pursues the divorce. It hurt me more than anything to file and break my contract with God no matter what Konn did in marriage and after marriage. No matter how many times I was told it wasn't my fault. I felt responsible and guilty throughout the divorce and every minute since. I still haven't been able to work through all that happened. In my heart I wanted to protect my children. I was beyond caring about protecting myself. But deep down I still held on to my dreams. Konn and I had a history of going back to one another no matter what the circumstances were one of us always made the effort to call if the other one didn't. Even when we didn't speak or see one another for weeks eventually we communicated.

Even though Konn was making a thrust to come back after all the hullabaloo I had to stand firm in my decision. I wised up to the theory the only way he can be helped is if he recognizes he needs it. I couldn't do it for him. I definitely was not going to allow him to put my family and myself in harms way again. I was through taking mistreatment in any form and I was done protecting his screwy behavior. His actions were his choices not mine. I was no longer going to let him blame me for his behavior.

I honestly thought filing for divorce a second time is going to be a real last ditch wake up call if he is sincere about wanting to come back home with me and on his own cognizance sees a physiatrist. Volunteer to take the chemical imbalance test and follow through working on the staggering problems within his spirit I'd be there for him. I'd have done whatever it took to stand beside him no matter what obstacle got in the way. But first I was adamant in my decision not to let him come back into my life and home or drop the divorce until he followed through. I won't just listen to his words I have to be able to see in his behavior he's going all the way towards recovery.

If he was ever going to commit to recognize he needs to seek help on his own and commit to marriage it would have to be during the six-month reconciliation period the court allows couples to reconsider severing a marriage. Konn knew he could have contacted me through my attorney for he had already done so to retrieve his computer. If he wanted to talk things over it had to be with my attorney present. I'd have consented to meet with

Konn if he were repentant toward recovering from his problems with the help of medical professionals.

No matter how the odds looked the ball was in his court. We had been though the odds many times and managed to get together no matter what they were. He had a choice to reconcile or sever our marriage contract between God and us as a couple even though I was the one to file whether I felt forced to or not. He still had a choice before it was final to recognize his part and do right by both of us.

I couldn't stop thinking in my mind it could still work but knowing in my heart Konn and I together can't and won't every get along together. Light and darkness don't mix. If we turn on a light switch we can see how fast the darkness disappears. We were two individuals living in two entirely different worlds. Our morals and beliefs were completely contradictory. It wasn't until I decided to see the strip club he frequented for myself that I knew for certain just how contradictory they were.

Today I understand by not doing anything about his mannerisms toward me right from the start I was letting him get by with it all.He knew me as clearly as I knew him. He understood what buttons to push to trigger me in all different directions. Although he got by with the whole nine yards and the abusive behavior some of it was not without a struggle. I didn't take kindly to being harmed, abused and treated as if I was brain dead. I took a stand and retaliated. Not being afraid of his eeriness I stood toe to toe with him at times. There were some things I wouldn't back down on.

Sometimes I retaliated in a immature way because it was the only way I knew how to retaliate in the midst of crises. I never handled any crisis very well before I met Konn. No matter what he says in denials my husband was very much aware of the behavior I overlooked to be with him. It bothered me he doesn't concede any recognition toward me for treating him kind hearted and compassionate before, during and after marriage when all odds should have been against my marrying him. When all odds ought to have been against my living with him as long as I did and all odds should have been against my helping him when he asked me to rescue him from going to jail after our divorce.

I didn't think Konn would turn on me exactly the way he did when he reamed me through out the ten months we waited to go to court. After his decision not to follow through with our history of doing whatever it took to contact one another I thought he'd back off and go on his merry bachelor way. His attorney came down on me with the same vehemence Konn did.

She didn't know she was basing her case on her client's lies. Living in a no fault state I thought all we'd talk over was finances. Once more Konn used his mother's mental history when he told her I was mentally ill and took prescription drugs for it every day. He expressed and projected all his twisted behavior as being mine. His attorney kept calling and telling my attorney I was mentally disturbed. While he's trying to make out like I'm a mental case after trying to drive me there I'm having him investigated by a private detective.

The statements he made on the mental condition he tried to force on me along with forcing divorce confirmed the motive to his madness. Without being aware of Konn's behavior and his reasoning his attorney calling mine and telling her stories he told her gave away the truth of why he tried to push me over the edge. All his effort to have me breakdown emotionally was enacted toward me so he could use it against me in a divorce hearing he knew he'd eventually force me to deal with all the time he is manipulating and calculating all his moves.

It really wasn't to bright of Konn and his attorney to push a mental case for it would make him liable to support me for life and he was trying to get out of paying me a dime in alimony.

The virtuous victim never knew he was under surveillance just a few days after I filed. I'm going after the proof and the witness he said I never had. I didn't handle it very well when the mystery women meant for him turned out to be a married stripper. I found out for certain what the rest of his double life incorporated and consisted of while I was visiting my brother in Georgia. I was frantic to hear what detective Heige uncovered in the surveillance so I called him long distance.

He told me my husband was seeing strippers, buying lap dances, sticking money in g-strings and going into a room with them. He blurted out his words so fast it didn't all sink in. As I listened to the news I was shocked to the highest degree and shaking from head to toe. The time was 12:30 am. I needed someone to talk to. I called my friend back home. I was nervous and couldn't think straight. I couldn't believe it was for real. I chose not to believe many things my husband did so I could live with him and myself. It was easier to be in denial than to deal with his problems and perversion. I'd hang up on my friend. Then I'd call the detective back and ask him to tell me what he seen again and what the heck a lap dance was. After he explained I'd call my friend back then I called Heige back then my friend. I was on the phone all night. I offered to pay my brother for the phone calls but he said no he'd pay the phone bill. I walked around in a fog the rest of the time I was there. I tried to hide the way I felt inside as tears poured down my cheeks without warning. I don't know how I'd have made it home if my daughter hadn't been with me. I couldn't concentrate on anything.

First thing I did when we arrived home was to phone detective Heige to fill me in on the details. He said he trailed Konn to the strip club, sat right next to the table Konn and his stripper friend sat. There was another stripper sitting with them for a while. Konn was oblivious to the eyewitness sitting inches from him witnessing the performance he gave in debauchery. Heige said my husband looked real happy grinning from ear to ear. He surmised Konn was interested in a dark haired women sitting next to him and they both acted as if they had known each other quite awhile. After a few minutes the other stripper sitting at the table got up and left Konn and his friend alone.

Konn went outside to the car once and came back in the club with a porno video and gave it to her. They sat talking until it was her turn to take it all off. She got on the stage situated close to the floor in the center of the room and performed a strip dance. When she was through stripping she went directly back over to my husband wearing no top and a g-string she straddled his lap and did a sexual dance short of a sex act. He stuck his head in her naked breasts as she wiggled sexually on top of him. After she worked him into a sexual frenzy he put money in her g-string. They got up from the table, walked up a few stairs near the bar and she took him into a room where the strippers sell sexual favors. They were in the room around 40 minutes. They came down the stairs together and sat at the same table. She stayed by my husband's side until it was time for her to strip again. One of the other strippers came over by Konn and he put money in her g-string too.

What a nice guy giving away money to so many needy people. Detective Heige didn't like the strippers swarming him; he went outside and sat in his truck. He waited three more hours for Konn to come out and leave. Then he followed him back to town to the boarding house where he rents a room. Validating his heart, honor, dignity, self-respect and character is in his pants. Demonstrating and corroborating the outcome pornography and all it advocates had on his life as he pampers the sexual addiction with strippers in a strip club equivalent to a house of ill repute. He actually exists in his fantasies in a den of iniquity with a married stripper. My husband pursued and purchased the bartenders wife every night along with other strippers working in the same club. I couldn't fathom the demoralizing tale I was hearing.

I didn't realize the scene the detective described was moderate in comparison to the scene I witnessed when I decided to see exactly what my husband endorsed and participated in while he betrayed me and everything I valued. I called my attorney to tell her my husband was frequenting a strip club and giving money he wouldn't have to give them if I hadn't helped him attain finances. I had barely $700 a month to live on and needed to meet a $2,500 a month budget plus I still had to pay several thousand dollars in debts belonging to Konn because he couldn't obtain credit and his debts were in my name.

Besides paying his car insurance payments over a year after he left because the insurance company wouldn't let me take him off my policy until we were divorced and he had proof of other insurance or I could be held liable until the divorce is final. My attorney Diane said she would get a hearing for temporary support until we had a court date. In the meantime I wasn't to say a word regarding my husband seeing strippers to anyone especially to Konn. That was a tough request. I had all I could do not to go find him and throw the detectives report at him along with my wedding ring.

During the temporary hearing his attorney Marcy was unwaveringly tearing me apart. The judge was going to award me $1,000 in temporary support until Konn's attorney told the judge I was a greedy money hungry women out to take his money. She said I was living in a nice house on top the hill while poor Konn was living in one room with one stick of furniture. Marcy told my attorney she was going to see to it that Konn doesn't have to give me a dime after I threw him out in the streets to be homeless with out a penny in his pocket.

I didn't have to go to the temporary hearing. It was just his attorney and mine. Diane told me what she said during the hearing. The judge cut the temporary support he was going to give me down to $800 a month. I ended up paying all his bills ten more months while he gave me nothing.

I cried the entire ten months and couldn't control the tears whenever I had a meeting in my attorney's office and she asked me does he know how much he hurt you? I said he doesn't care how much he hurt me.

I had to live with the knowledge of knowing he's giving strippers money that should have been mine after I invested and gave up my income to help him so we could both have finances. I felt it was the same as if he robbed my dead husband using me for finances left through his love to take care of my daughter and me if anything happened to him?

184

By this time I was aggravated with his attorney I wanted to sue her for slander when the divorce was over. However the law doesn't allow anyone to touch an attorney. They can say any liable slander they want to and it's okay with the law if it is untrue and malicious. I was already feeling down and out. It didn't help when I learned his attorney was out to burn me big time. I wasn't sure she was even aware he's manipulating her. I know he was her client but it seemed like she had a personal vendetta toward me and hates me as much as Konn did. At the deposition his attorney looked at me with daggers. My attorney didn't act that way toward Konn she was congenial and very kind to Konn and I was her client so again even my divorce made very little sense by the time it was all said and done.

Konn had Marcy duped. I knew how he used women. She wasn't any different simply because she had a degree in law. She had me put Konn's personal possessions in a cab and sent down to her office and she put his things in her storage locker. I had already given him three carloads of his possessions. His attorney worrying about his personal possessions struck me as being laughable funny. He never took any of his possessions with him when he moved from place to place. When he moved in on me his personal possessions consisted of a can of shave cream, a razor and the clothes on his back. He left with four carloads filled to the brim, a car and $70,000 a year income plus benefits possibly amounting to well over $100,000 with all the insurance benefits. He ended up leaving part of the personal possessions he acquired in our marriage in his attorneys storage locker and the rest he left in his landlords home. Hearing her speak his words through the control he used on her made me cringe. It seemed as if Marcy was calling all the shots along with phone calls she made to my attorney to discuss me. Each time I heard some of the things Marcy said concerning me I decided to use her words to my advantage and I set out to prove her wrong.

I bought a used computer, taught myself to type and proceeded to put facts and figures down for my attorney. Every time his attorney told my attorney anything I set out to prove her wrong. I worked day and night. It was the first time in my life I was totally alone. I always had at least one of the children living with me but my daughter had already moved into her own apartment before Konn's departure. I had no set hours anymore. I stayed up all night most of the time. I didn't have regular meals. All I did was type and worked things out on the computer and wept all the time. My attorney was flabbergasted with all the papers I took to her office. I'd work some thing out dealing with the case and take it to her. Checking further I'd see a mistake or think of something other than what I wrote and redid all the papers again. I took her so many revised copies she had boxes of papers I wrote sitting on the floor in her office for a year. The first time Konn and I saw one another or spoke in five months was at the deposition. At first I wanted to be rotten and ask him if he found his honor and self-respect sticking his head between his stripper prostitutes boobs. I wanted to ask him if he found dignity paying a prostitute to have sex with him in one of the upstairs rooms in the topless strip club while he's still my husband? Maybe ask since he never wanted me to touch him did it turn him on to pay strippers to touch him along with every other man in the place that paid them to do the same thing.

He told me time and again I didn't know when the right time of day was to have sex was and I wanted so badly to blurt out: Konn I didn't know 7 p.m. was the right time to have sex and you didn't bother to tell me it turns you on when naked women sit on your lap. But I never said a snotty word to him.

My attorney told me not to give any information away. We were going to use strip club information as an element of surprise in the court battle I was surely going to have since Konn found an attorney that appeared to have the same bullying personality Konn has. Diane and I based our case on finances and stuck to money issues no matter what Konn and his attorney said. It wasn't easy to look at him knowing what his double life consisted of. Glancing at him during the deposition all I could think of is the mortifying stories Heige told me. I thought; oh my God this was my husband and he stuck his stupid head in the stripper's boobs.

Knowing he wants to be with strippers selling sex really troubled me. It was the ultimate wound. At this point I was still traumatized with shock and terribly brokenhearted, dismayed and unhappy. I was hurting badly when I looked across the table at my husband and all the smart mouth things I wanted to say to him vanished.

I was ambivalent as I could be. I actually looked forward to seeing him at the deposition. I primped for hours wanting to look great. I took him a tape I bought months ago and a pipe I forgot to pack. My attorney put the items in her office. I jumped the gun and asked Marcy if I could give the tape and pipe to Konn. She said I could so I went to get them in the office and gave them to Konn. Diane got upset with me for giving them to him with out asking her permission too. She told me she couldn't get over I came bearing gifts. I told her it is better to treat your enemies with kindness for it catches them off guard and they don't know how to react to mercy and goodness. No one ever understood my feeling for this man but I don't fault anyone. I never fully understood my feelings for him either. I didn't have any idea why I looked forward to seeing him after I heard he wanted us to have a deposition. It hurt to look at him knowing where he had been and whom he had been with. It was mind boggling to deal with the fact the man I slept with deliberately threw me away for a prostitute. He knew exactly where to go to find the kind of women meant for him. I hated that statement as he repeatedly yelled I was not the woman meant for him so many times. Those very words went into the deepest recesses of my heart and soul. My spirit was utterly broken.

No matter how unsure I was feeling I was kind to Konn during the deposition. I was so nervous as I walked in the room. I said hello in a nice voice to his attorney, she glared at me and didn't say anything. I smiled sweetly at him and said hi Konn, how are you? In a sarcastic voice he said hi Rosie how are you right back at me. I never let on that I knew a thing. During one of the breaks I asked Konn if he wanted to step outside and have a cigarette. He said sure and as he started to get up from his chair his attorney growled no, he better stay by her. She didn't let him out of her sight for the six hours we spent at the hearing.

During one of the break times I tried conversing with her. I said she looked familiar. In a harsh voice she said well I don't know why I would be. I think I seen you in my church. She said yes they were at our church a few times and she talked congenially on a subject she could relate to with me. After five minutes she put her guard up and went back to speaking harshly and acting like I'm the wicked witch of the west that abused her client and threw him out in the cold without a penny.

The attorneys chose to question Konn first. My attorney didn't put Konn through any grilling at the deposition. She asked questions on finances and brought out the point I gave him money to live on after he chose to leave, the way I encouraged him and all the possessions I had before marriage I shared with him. He couldn't deny what I did in finances or that I gave him more money after he left than I kept to live on. I had everything down in black and white. He wasn't going to acknowledge anything I did for him or with him. He said I didn't encourage him and he found a job without my help. Konn acted smooth with my attorney trying to win her confidence. I picked up on the way he felt he had her in the palm of his hand. The only question she asked him that wasn't connected to finances was why did you leave home? He got shook and answered a little louder and almost lost it. He said I accused him of cheating and all he was doing the whole time was working on a bible program.

We could have made problems for Konn. He told false stories and perjured himself on the affidavit and in the deposition hearing. After I seen the answers he gave on the affidavit I was confident of the way him and Marcy were going to conduct their defense. She answered a few questions for him using what I'm sure she didn't know were lies he told her. He was playing mind games with the legal system. No one is exempt in the unreal land of Konn. During the deposition our attorneys are not allowed to help their clients or ask questions or interfere in anyway with the opposing clients. We are not allowed to speak except during the questioning. My attorney was in charge of Konn and his attorney was in charge of me.

I was in for it. I wondered if my attorney knew how bad it was going to be. She briefed me on some things and said try to give just yes or no answers. She advised me not to talk about the abuse or the undies and especially not to say what he did with the undies. When I'm asked why did the marriage break up Diane said I was just to say he was cheating. I wonder if she knew what it is like to tell an abused person not to say they were abused. I knew she was trying to avoid having the divorce turn into a mental case. Nothing could have prepared me for the way his attorney conducted her questioning. I saved my copy of the deposition. I didn't think anyone would believe what took place in the confines of the room when it was my turn to be sworn in and questioned. There was a court reporter typing every word said by both parties and the attorneys.

1. The first question was; are you on a mental disability? ....No

I didn't say anything but I thought Konn was brave telling her falsehoods on mental behavior. Playing the role of the pitiful abused husband thrown out of the house without a dime as he walks off with a prostitute stripper. I could have had him committed and buried him in divorce with mental behavior he displayed not only in front of me but in front of my children, friends, neighbors, 911 and my personal councilor documented his behavior and had seen the bruises and all the things I found.

2. Do you take prescription drugs everyday for mental problems?....No

3. Do you believe you know what Konn is thinking?.....................No

I wanted to say who in the world could know what that man thinks he was beamed here from another planet.

4. Did I hear voices talking to me out loud in my head?...................No

5. Did I hear God talk out loud to me?......................................No

God speaks to us through his Holy Spirit.

Konn and Marcy are trying to make me look ridiculous. I wanted to tell her Konn carries on conversations with himself acting like he's talking to an invisible friend both in the house and in the car. He not only talks to himself he answers back in loud voices. I was being a good girl and trying to do as my attorney advised. I don't think Diane knew the questions would be more of Konn's lunacy lies I encountered in the last five years.

I thought questions would deal mostly with finances in a no fault state. I guess they can ask what they want during a deposition. I didn't quite understand for I did know questions and answers we give during the hearing would be used in court and you have to know what you say in the deposition or you're in danger of committing perjury.

I checked with another attorney to get a second opinion. He said the questions were unusual and strange verifying what I already knew for I lived with strange.

6. Did you chase your husband around the house and hit him?.........No

I wanted to say yeah right! Konn did the hitting. As big and as violent as he is I could really get by with hitting him like he'd even give me a chance to hit. I never chased the lunatic anywhere let alone around the house. He'd never have gotten by putting bruises on me if I could have done the things he said of me. She didn't know and maybe she didn't care her client was the mental case projecting what he did in his behavior as being my behavior. I wanted to say he not only hit me but he hit him self all the time, beat his head and eyes in with his fists and attempted suicide twice.

The moment she asked me the question I wished I would have hit him or somebody would hit him. For all the times he hit me and for all the things he said and did in marriage and for what he was doing in divorce. I wanted to slap his face for throwing me away for prostitutes. I wish she would ask me if I want to hit him now I'd say yes now I would like to smack that egotistical mug a good one.

I couldn't stand violence. I detested men hitting women. I didn't even know women hit men. I never even spanked my children. I threw bugs out the door so I wouldn't have to kill them. His attorney is irritating,

7. Did you scream and yell at your husband?.............................No
He did the screaming and yelling.

8. Did you tell your husband after an outing with another couple that you hated him?...Yes but I also told him I didn't hate him I hated the things he did.

9. Did you accuse your husband of seeing other women?..............……Yes

10. Why?………………………………………………………………… I found women's undies. He hid one pair under the mattress of our bed. I came home unexpectedly one day and he had another pair of undies lying on top of our bed as I stood next to him he snatched them up in his hand and shoved them down the front of his pants. His friend kept losing long dirty false fingernails in the car. There are many other things I found relating to women and cheating too numerous to mention.

11. When you found the undies did you ask your husband for an explanation?………………………………………………………………...Yes

Boy that did it. I flipped out at her line of questions. My attorney's advice went by the wayside. I let Marcy have it. I told her Konn is lying to you. My husband is the one that hit me and he ripped all my clothes off outdoors until I stood naked in my front yard because he had a pair of undies in his possession he shouldn't have had to begin with and he wanted them back. I was a new bride and wife that should have meant something to him.

Good grief my husband is the spouse that did the harm. He abused me sexually, physically, mentally, verbally and emotionally. All the things you're asking were all the things he did to me. He used me for his own financial gain.

He is sexually addicted and into pornography; he's not the blameless righteous injured party. You're basing your case on lies and deception. He never ever tells the truth. I related a few gross things he did sexually she didn't ask any more questions dealing with women.

I didn't know Konn would hit me with some of the questions she asked. I knew when she asked why didn't I ask Konn for an explanation about the undies he told her the undies belonged to his ex-wife before they prepared for the hearing. What she didn't know is I had a letter from his ex-wife in my purse denouncing the undies were hers. There was the detective with the lie detector test who knew I wanted to find the truth of who they belonged to and Konn wasn't going to reveal the truth.

I didn't say he told me he masturbated holding the renowned undies on his privates while fantasizing about women while he watches sexually perverted videos. I wanted to blurt that piece of information and the only reason I didn't was my attorney told me it was too disgusting to say in front of the court reporter.

Yes, it was disgusting and sick but it was the reality of what he forced me to exist in. I don't want to hide one thing anymore or protect his guilty butt ever again. I didn't say a word about him playing with strippers and giving them all the money and he wasn't giving me what he was court ordered. His attorney simply sat down and listened as I wept my sad story. She didn't say a word all the time I'm revealing the harmful offensive intolerable behavior he displayed before his new wife. I don't think she could have stopped me if she ran over me with a bulldozer.The next thing she said was if he was so awful why didn't you divorce him sooner? ... ... I did.He talked me into dropping the divorce with more phony promises and dishonesty. I believed he was going to finally do right by me but it was worse after I dropped it.

Who was your attorney? ... ... Diane

She gave Konn a funny look then and went back to asking me a few questions about money. Like why was I in charge of the money, why didn't I tell him what I did with it and with all the money he made how much did I have stashed? He wouldn't listen when I tried to share what I was doing with the finances and he told me not to bother him with anything. I explained he didn't make a sizable income until the last year of our marriage and he took it with him when he left. I supported him a year when he had no income. The second year he made $45,000. His check was not just used for my needs it supported him too. He started to pull away when he began to travel to his job. I was only with him six months during the time of the second job paying the higher wages of $70,000.

The only reason he let me take care of finances is because he owed the IRS and owed State revenue and said he couldn't have bank accounts or the IRS will take his money same as they did before. It was safer for me take care of the finances. I was protecting Konn from losing his finances again. He knows without a doubt I'm honest and above board and I wouldn't ever cheat him or anyone else for he recognized my honesty along with everything else he is denying in this deposition. His attorneys last comments were I better get a job because she was going to see to it he didn't have to give me a dime. She and Konn were trying to break a pre nuptial he had to sign before I'd marry him.

This really sucked. I had money and didn't have to work before I met Konn. They made an issue of my working. I'm sixty years old and disabled. Konn knew I couldn't work. He saw me sleep in a recliner for months at a time. Yet tried to ruin a small disability pension I received amounting to $600 a month. It was all I had to live on after he left and it barely made a house payment. While he's trying to ruin me financially he spent more than $600 on one date with his stripper girlfriend.

I didn't own my home outright yet his attorney made my having a home an issue. She tried to give him credit for the time he lived here and made payments. I had my work cut out for me.

I don't know why but after she got on me I felt bad for her because I knew my husband had duped her into believing his sad story. I knew where Konn was coming from and the exact words he used to deceive her into believing him. I was aware of what he uses to extract sympathy to have people feel sorry for him.

I had to have my defense written in detail ready to show the judge what it would cost Konn to live in my neighborhood in a furnished apartment with cleaning, cooking and maid service I accommodated him with. I wrote papers titled Konn Rodent's financial gain since marriage vs. Rosie Rodent's financial loss since marriage. I ended up using my savings to live on for a year, pay attorney and detective fees. It ate my savings. He deliberately tried to destroy me financially after he had financial gain.

I'm not a martyr but, I gave him money when he had none now he wanted me to have none and he won't give me any. I gave him a home when he was homeless and he wants to see me homeless. It's true he has no heart and no honor. Using the legal system to his advantage. He didn't follow through with anything they ordered him to do. He continued to do things his way and he got by with all of it too.

He didn't have information ready for a July 15 temporary support hearing so it was postponed until July 30th. He got out of another month of paying support. I had to pay my attorney double every time he wasn't prepared for we would have to go over the material we put together all over again or if he didn't provide information for court or if he doesn't show up for court.

I wasn't relying on the legal system. I relied on God's guidance for though I was a broken woman with a downtrodden spirit. God had not forsaken or left me. God never leaves or forsakes those that belong to him and I still belonged to my Savior. I can't do anything without God helping me. Every time I do I mess up big time.

Diane and I had a cigarette together after the deposition. She told me the court reporter was in tears as I spoke. She noticed Konn's mouth was moving ninety miles and hour when I blurted out his abusive behavior and cheating I was glad she noticed him talking to himself or whomever it is he talks to. Due to brainwashing tactics he used to control me I found myself looking for confirmation to all the things I said on Konn's behavior for no one can believe it. My attorney was a Christian and she was great to me.

His attorney subpoenaed my bank records. She thought I was cheating Konn out of money. I proved there wasn't any left. I spent every dime on everyone I knew when it was apparent for months he was getting ready to leave. Being law-abiding and having nothing to hide I gave her my bank records for more years than she asked for.

I asked my attorney to subpoena his bank records directly after his attorney subpoenaed mine. I got more data on Konn's adventures. I had the detective Heige on several more surveillances. We used a women detective one evening. The detectives witnessed him giving the strippers money but they didn't know the amount he was spending. When I got a hold of his bank records the bank debits and cancelled checks told a story only I knew how to tell. The fairytales he told his attorney of his own twisted behavior patterns he projected as mine and the haughtiness of treating me as if I didn't exist was too much.

Treating me like I had never been a part of his life taking care of him and his mother our entire time together was saying the last five years didn't happen. That our marriage didn't exist and the terror he reigned on my life and trauma he put my family through never happened. It was like he had exterminated me. He acted like Mr. perfect but was a far cry from ever being decent. He told my attorney he didn't want to give me a dime after the way I made his life miserable the last four years. As he continued bombarding me with twisted maddening reasoning it became crucially meaningful for me to say the things that welled up inside. For a while I couldn't speak them out. Everything I said came out jumbled and mixed up. I know it was hard to understand what I was trying to relate.

I couldn't concentrate until a twofold message began to manifest in my heart to write the words. To say it did all happen Konn Rodent? I was your wife and you were a part of my life and a part of my history. I was a part of your life and I did exist. I was there and you did everything I saw and everything I heard and every bit of it was despicable.

It was reality and I want reality back in everything I do and say. There is an urgency to tell how pornography does harm innocent people that are exposed to witness sex-addicted perversion. I showed love and kindness toward my husband. In return he showed an evil unfeeling ungrateful attitude along with the desolation and devastation of everything clean and natural. Hearing the same evil hit the air in the deposition hearing was only a sample of life in loony land.

Chapter Fifteen

Accumulating A Harem & Divorce Court

My dreams are like the leaves sailing wildly through the air as the fall wind blows before the winter snows. Leaves blowing here and there cover the ground in a mass of gold and brown until none are left on the trees before the icy freeze.

There are no winners in a divorce. It wasn't a victory when lies unfolded one by one. It didn't make me happy to be right about the addictive lewd fantasies taking over every waking moment of his life. I would rather have been wrong. The saddest downfall was the renegade's absolute betrayal that began the second he begged me to marry him. I thought my dreams came true and assumed it would be wonderful having a husband again to share life with, someone to lean on and gracefully grow old together. The word divorce was ever constant on my mind and continued to affect me in many different ways. Fear of poverty, loneliness, sadness and life without the person I vowed to take for better or worse. The man I loved and wanted as my husband. I'm pathetic he never loved or wanted me. Letting my husband go seemed to be the only alternative I had. Giving him freedom was once more giving him what he wanted. He can have his freedom. As much as I love him I can have my ears stop ringing.

Everything he did in his adventures with strippers in and out of the topless strip club was tearing scars off the wounds of awareness of knowing my marriage was nothing more than a sham. I felt Konn took everything. My wedding, my anniversary, hopes, dreams, plans, my heart, emotions, physical energy, time and money and every piece of me. The grain of hope I held onto was lost in the weeds of waste. No matter what takes place the rest of my life I'll never forget the grueling true tales of my mate in hot pursuit of a specific stripper prostitute. She is a married woman named Toriann. Even though he was hunting and chasing after many other strippers like a hound in heat his interest was in Toriann over the others. I'm familiar with the way he treated someone he wants over other woman he mainly hunts for sport.

My partner spent every day and every dollar escorting Toriann, her family and friends to the same places we went together. It was dreadful acquiring knowledge of my husband wining and dining his new playmate in the same places he knew they might possibly run into me as he sits across the table from her when just a few weeks before he sat across from me. It felt like his taking her to the same places he shared with me was giving her my memories. It struck me as gross when my husband took her to a place that sold strippers clothes and bought her a new strip outfit during the hours he was supposed to be working. The records show he was with Toriann in a matter of ten days after I filed. He said receiving the papers meant he was already divorced. I didn't look at it that way. There's a six-month reconciliation period couples can work things out if they choose too. Our time stretched into ten months as Konn dealt with the legal system by his rules.

No matter how it looked to my husband and I'm sure it looked hopeless. I thought he'd try to win me back. I took tough love steps in filing hoping he'd recognize the wretchedness of his behavior and possibly choose to do whatever it took to help salvage our union. I think I was hopeful because a friend of mine was divorced a year. Her husband didn't run after other women days after his wife left him and filed. He pursued his ex-wife, won her back and they married again and are still together for over 25 years now. Konn liked surprising me and gave me the bombshell of my life when I heard the detectives report and read his bank records. It was a slap in the face or I should say a kick in the head. He knew exactly where to go to be consoled and knew exactly whom to go to.

At the same time he's purchasing what society no longer calls sex with twelve nude dancers he joined a church singles group and dated a Christian lady he met in a Christian setting. In spite of the activities he's engaged in with thirteen women at the same time I looked at the fact he's still married to me. Even though it didn't mean a thing to Konn that he had a wife it meant some thing to me he's still my husband traipsing around with so many women at one time and hadn't been away from home more than a few weeks when he acquired a harem working in a variety of occupations. Occasionally my hubby dated the Christian lady during the day and went to frolic with strippers in the same evening.

"The Great Imposter" led me to believe he's a born again Christian in the same way he led the church singles to believe the same lie. It bothered me to think he was deceiving another Christian woman that has a teen-age daughter. It reminded me of myself when my daughter was fifteen and we started dating. I thought of the way he harmed my daughter's heart with ruthless behavior abusing her mother in front of her putting fear in her heart toward all men. Along with frightening my twelve-year-old granddaughter until she had nightmares of Konn killing all her family.

Seeing 13 different women simultaneously in five months is the number of women I learned of through cancelled checks and a letter Konn wrote to his friend and through Konn's bragging. I'm thankful only God knows how many others there were. This routine is from a man that said everything is my imagination. He doesn't have a problem, he isn't a womanizer and he didn't stare at every woman in his view.

My husband knew going to strippers prostituting sex in private rooms was the one thing I would never get over. It put an end to any hope toward us ever reconciling. He understood it was the ultimate act that would destroy me and us as a couple all the way and it did. After I heard the details from Heige and seen bank records showing the dark foreboding sordid existence Konn whole heartedly chose and threw himself into I withdrew from everything. Everyplace I went reminded me of all we did together.

I'm sure he didn't feel I'd have access to his bank records. It was only the statements for five months time after he left but it was enough to show what he did with finances he didn't give me when court ordered too. There's an ATM machine in the strip club where he debited thousands of dollars from the machine ever hour on the hour. The debits showed places he went, the date, time, city and state and the amount of money spent. Some days he squandered $300 to $600 a day entertaining Toriann, her husband and children. He splurged $200 to $300 a night in the strip club he frequented almost every evening during the five-month period. Several cancelled checks explained a $2.000 computer and equipment he purchased for his stripper gal knowing her for only one and a half months. He also let her use his debit card after seeing her three months. I didn't investigate if she was the one he went with while still living with me but if she was the one then he knew her much longer. I now believe the woman he communicated with behind my back was a stripper too.

I came to the amount of time he spent with Toriann by calculating the time he left home and dates on the cancelled material. The figures described the amount he spent on gas driving one hundred miles almost every day to and from the strip club.

He was taking day's off work and leaving his job early most every day to entertain strippers and him self. Konn didn't care if her husband was just a few feet away tending bar watching my husband stick his head in his wife's boobs. They were one big happy family. I can't comprehend any of it but I can verify it's the unmitigated truth and just the tip of the iceberg of things I saw taking place in the club. The bizarre situation of the all in the family affair was between Konn and his stripper friend, her husband and two sisters working in the same place selling their body too. The last I heard on the love of his life is that Toriann's husband divorced her and Konn is now living in the town she lives and getting ready to reel her in for the kill.

I don't know when he started going to this particular strip club. I didn't have him under surveillance until a few days after he left home. I know he was visiting the club the entire time his attorney and he swooped down on me like vultures trying to make me look mentally ridiculous.

Meanwhile his attorney calls me names, slanders me to the judge, to my attorney, on the affidavit and during the deposition. At the same time he's sweet-talking her to believe the role he's playing as the pitiful, wretched, blameless virtuous victim thrown out of his house with out a dime in his pocket her client is with his harem of prostitute strippers. He was giving the most outstanding performance in his existence I think he missed his calling.

I thought he should have gone to Hollywood with all his talents he might have made millions and possibly won an academy award as he performs him self in all the roles he plays over and over. Creating screenplays he writes with a slight twist in each role to throw you off just a little. At times intentionally leaving clues to make the scripts more sadistic to receive a bigger thrill in the challenge of putting one over on someone. There is no way my husband would have left incriminating evidence of his actions in the house of ill repute if he didn't believe he can do what he wants perjuring and deceiving the legal system.

The control and manipulation doesn't stop with me. He can't survive if he doesn't have complete power over every detail every minute of the day. Everything he does is control, everyone he meets he influences and it's all dominated with deception. I could see the way he manipulated his personal stripper by using money. To delude his attorney he utilized the look at me I was burned in a car accident, my mother passed away and my wife mistreated me.

Being wise to some of his mannerisms and what he uses to dominate situations until it meets his satisfaction I seen the exact way he is trying to call the shots in the divorce not only with his attorney but also with my attorney and the judge. This time I kept one step ahead. It was apparent he was trying to make people think I was absurd so they won't believe the true stories of his behavior. The records show he spent $15,000 in five months on strippers I typed out the bank statements in a budget form listing each canceled check number, savings or check debits. I itemized how much he spent on each individual item including sex he bought and gas for road trips.

Right next to the item I wrote the date, time, place and amount of each purchase and each debit separately and added each column on the bottom of the page for a total of what he spent a day and the number of days he spent it in. For example in five days he spent $1,600. In nine days spent $3,000 etc. I had my attorney give the judge a copy. The first time I filed I recalled his mother asking me if I'd still handle the finances for Konn. She told me he doesn't know how to take care of money. After I seen his expenses in a strip club I know now why she asked me to watch after her son. After I finished working on the finances Konn spent in the strip club on nude dancers selling sexual favors to my husband in a room at the top of the stairs I couldn't put anything into focus. One minute I had a husband and finances. The next I was alone and broke. I missed calling him about little things that happened in my life and in the world news stories as he acts like I have fallen off the planet earth and didn't care if I was dead or alive.

I couldn't deal with Konn taking off into the wild blue yonder acting as if the last five years never happened. He wouldn't speak to me so we could settle the divorce peacefully. After I had a new phone number three months I asked the phone company for my old number back. I thought he might accidentally dial the old number and we could at least talk and try to work things out in harmony.

My attorney finally got a court date December 7,1999. Konn left town the night before and didn't tell his attorney he was leaving. Marcy called my attorney and wanted to know if I knew where he was or a relative she could contact to find him for she was so worried about his welfare he was depressed about his mother dying and the divorce. She just didn't know where he could be or what he might do. He didn't bother to tell his attorney he was taking his stripper friend out of town to a football game spending the time he skipped out on our court day with her. At this time I didn't know exactly where he went but I knew the stripper would be with him. Diane called and said his attorney asked if I knew where Konn was? I told her I wasn't giving Marcy any information. I did know he took off out of town. I had the detective follow him the night before. Heige drove over three hundred miles right behind Konn before I told him to abort the surveillance and go home.

I was glad Konn took off. I was five hours away from going to court and without him there I knew I wouldn't have to go through the crap he and his attorney were going to put me through. I told Diane the events Heige told me about after trailing Konn until three am. I didn't want her to reveal anything to his attorney. I gave Diane his sisters name and said Marcy could tract down a phone number for his sister I wasn't going to volunteer any information to the enemy. Konn had a daughter in town but she had no knowledge of where he would be for he never contacted her.

An hour later my attorney called back and said his attorney was going to call the judge and try to postpone the divorce hearing. At this point I want to get it over with. I had already waited eight months to go to court. I was so unhappy I couldn't stand knowing; while still my husband he was merrily roaming the countryside with strippers. Especially since he desperately wanted me out of the way for so long. In a weak moment two weeks after I filed I called him one time. Not only did I want to see if we could handle the divorce in a friendly manner but my motive was to see where he was at and if he wants to talk things out and I'd consider dropping the divorce after he sought clinical help with truth of his problems.

Konn told his secretary to tell me he wasn't available to speak to me and never returned my call. He told his attorney a cock and bull story and she threatened me with police if I ever call him again. So I didn't.

I begged my attorney to tell the judge we didn't want a postponement we waited eight months already. Tell him Konn and Marcy both knew for two months the hearing was in December. I filed in May. I told Diane you know the opposition is going to ream me it's good he's gone let's get it over with while he isn't around.

I was three hours away from the time I'm supposed to be in court. My attorney called again and said the judge postponed the date until the end of January. I flipped. Diane I want to go to court today I don't care what his attorney thinks about his depression tell her I happen to know he hates his mother, he forced this divorce and he's so depressed he's sticking his head in strippers boobs and buying sex from her because their prostitutes too. Tell her he's a liar and all he told her is a bunch of twisted lies and she acts like his mother not his attorney. I want to go to court when were scheduled to go in three hours this is not fair. Konn is controlling this damn divorce using the legal system to his advantage. We should have thrown him in jail for perjury so he'd have been here today. He pulled the same stunt with his ex wife. The only difference was he didn't have an attorney and didn't bother to show up for court. The judge went ahead and gave her the divorce without his presence there.

This time when he goes to court he has an attorney that intends to stick it to me and he still doesn't show up. I'm glad he took off I don't want him there. When Heige told me Konn took off I was happy he was gone. Diane said Rosie calm down I told the judge you'd be one disappointed little gal. He's giving you a default day January 26, 2000 whether he shows up or not. That's all we can do now. I asked my attorney to do something; anything so we could go to court in three hours it was perfect without him around. She said but if he's not here we won't be able to surprise him with the strip club events.

Man that upset me even more. Diane what difference does that make now he will know by the next court date we have his bank records and he incriminated himself with debits from the ATM machine situated in the strip club.

The element of surprise would have been if we went to court today. We didn't subpoena bank records until two days before our court date so he didn't have time to prepare for the knowledge we acquired with the debits. The only way it would have been a surprise was if all we had was the detectives report as to where he spent our finances. He will know we have his bank statements and waiting another month won't be a surprise.

Okay if we have to wait there's nothing I can do but I want his check garnished today. I want the money he has been court ordered to pay taken out of the next check he receives. He spends over $1,000 a week on hookers and has given me nothing to live on or pay his bills. He has gotten by long enough manipulating the legal system I have a few rights too. If I have to wait another month to go to court that means I have to wait another two months before I have any money. I don't have that much saved anymore.

Diane had his check garnished so when he gets back from roaming the country side he won't have as much money as he thought he would when he returns to town.

I figured Konn left town on purpose and was visiting his sister because there was a home football team playing a game in the town she lived in. I thought maybe he'd be gone a month whether he stayed with her that long or not. He had that much vacation time coming and last year he took the same month off.

I don't know exactly what happened with his attorney two weeks before the default hearing but she dropped him like a hot potato. My attorney thought Marcy could never get a hold of him and he never returned her calls. However by now she seen all the activity on his bank debits when she got her copy of expenditures and that might have been an eye opener. Plus my attorney told Marcy I was being totally honest about all of Konn's behavior.

My attorney called and told me she thought Marcy dropping Konn, as her client was an act of God because she was going to dump on me big time. January 26 we went to court and Konn showed up fifteen minutes before we are scheduled to go into the courtroom. All the talking I did to my attorney about not trusting one word he speaks she asked me if it would be okay to take him down the hall and talk to him to see where he's coming from and maybe shoot him a deal. I said I didn't know what good it would do and I'm not shooting him any deal but she could talk to him if she wanted to. She came back and told me Konn didn't want to give me a dime he was never happy with me and the last three years were the most miserable years in his life it was a living hell. Then he told her another firm bought the company he worked for. They let several people go and he lost his job. She asked me if I wanted to lower the ante. I said absolutely not. I worked ten months on the data I put together. When he gets another job he will continue to earn $65,000 to $100,000 a year.

The only time I talked to Konn was a minute before we went in the courtroom. I told him he betrayed me and asked him if he had a good time taking strippers everywhere he took me and if he enjoyed sex with women he had to pay. He got loud and said I betrayed him. I walked into the courtroom and left him yelling in the hall. Diane heard his loud voice while walking down the hallway. She came in the room, sat by me and asked why did I have to upset him. I told her to let him yell it didn't matter anymore he's not a peaceful person at any given time.

Everything I ever said set him off. He can't handle that I knew the truth about him. I think I'm the only one that knows he's a pervert and what he does when he isn't in church while conning everyone into believing he's a nice guy. We went into the courtroom and Konn acted as his own attorney. He was allowed to question me. A few times he tried to make me look outrageous. I didn't let him get by with anything but I didn't argue or run him down. I simply told the truth. He tried to make me look absurd a few times but the judge stopped him. Again my attorney and I stuck to the finances until the last question. The judge stayed with the no fault laws and didn't allow personal things to interfere with the case. The last question Diane asked Konn was about spending a lot of time and money in the strip club. After he answered the judge stopped this line of questioning from going further and it was over. It didn't matter Konn gave the woe is me I'm out of a job and can't support him self financially the judge awarded me every penny of the $1,500 I asked for a month but he cut the years down to two years. Our marriage was called a short-term marriage in legal terms. It is unheard of to receive alimony in a short-term marriage. I didn't understand the laws reasoning of short term. I believe marriage is marriage whether it is one month or fifty years. Divorce doesn't hurt any less if it is one month or fifty years if one spouse loves the other and the love is not returned. I was sobbing as we walked out of the courtroom and my attorney took me into the rest room but not before I saw the devious smile on my ex husbands face as he walked by us and seen my tears. The tears he put in my heart and eyes were the tears he never once wiped from my eyes. I wept and bawled uncontrollably in the restroom. My attorney knew I loved my husband and my heart was broken from the moment I filed. My attorney was very kind and I felt a kinship with her. She said she didn't have a divorce case quite like ours. Diane stopped me from telling Konn the divorce wasn't final until February 26, 2000. The legal system gives another thirty days to contest or reconcile before it is final.

I felt sad for my husband as I observed him as he questioned me before the judge. I kept thinking of how much I loved him and things I loved doing with him and the bad things didn't seem to matter now that it was over. It took awhile to realize memories I thought about were things he did before marriage before he showed unkind wickedness. We were married three years but we were together five years.

After we went to court it felt like I was going through a type of brainwashing withdrawal much the same as a prisoner of war might have gone through. I had flashbacks and nightmares. I commenced to think every thing was my fault. I probably had it coming. When I wanted to be with him he tried to shake me off and I clung to him. When I tried to shake him off he held onto me. At this point in time I was down on myself I thought about my mistakes and regrets not his.

I thought of the way he cried and asked if he could come home and try to work on our marriage for another year and see what happens. He can act so nice when he wants to come home and the minute he is with me he starts the verbal and emotional abuse all over again.

Nothing made any sense. My heart longed to let him come back but I was too sick and too tired to go through any more deceptive theatrics or have him scare my family again. I just couldn't handle more chaos and confusion or violence.

I can't deal with trying to figure out why he wants to come home each time he chooses to leave, blame me, tell me I had the problem and needed a counselor. Recalling the sick perversion with pornography and verbal emotional abuse he enacted once to often I told him no not this time it's over.

Konn your not coming back because allowing you to come home would mean I'd have to let you bring the woman your cheating and sneaking around with back in with you. I'd have to deal with all the coldhearted cruelty to hide the fact you're a cheating adulterer while your coming down on me merely for breathing.

After I told him no Konn continued to try and get in the house at different hours when he thought I wasn't home. I watched him through the peephole. His face was fierce and scary as he tried to bulldoze his way back in. I kept the door locked at all times and he didn't have a key. He knew if he broke the door down again he'd have to contend with my son in law and possibly go to jail. He left threatening notes in the door and that's when I filed, put a protection order on him and changed the phone number.

Since letting him go was never what I wanted in my heart being with out him was like going through withdrawals just as if I was addicted to wanting and needing his love, desire, devotion and approval more than I needed anything else. I learned an abused person wants the approval of the person that abuses them at any cost. I was determined to protect my family. That meant I couldn't have him coming and going flaunting rampant mistreatment. Even though I told Konn no it's over if it weren't for my family there were times I think I might have weakened and dropped the divorce again. Loving my family helped me to make it to the end.

But I felt it was not only the end of my marriage it was also the end of me. I didn't want to go on without Konn yet I didn't want to go on with Konn after I knew the truth of what he was doing when he left. I was having a bad time. At this time I'm very depressed and unstable. I told complete strangers my husband left to be with strippers. People would be telling me what a nice day it was and I blurted out the things I seen in the strip club. I divulged some of the things Konn did toward me no matter what the conversation was. It seemed harder to deal with divorce than the insanity in marriage. I think one of the many reasons most women feel it's easier to stay in an abusive relationship and be with someone or something familiar than it is to start all over again and fear what the unknown future would hold. Even though all his behavior manifested cruel evil I began to regret letting him go. I felt like I threw him to the wolves. I thought if I hadn't let him go he wouldn't have gone to nude dancers and walked in more darkness now than he did before he left.

I felt as if I failed as a Christian. I was blaming myself much in the same way he blamed me. I began to believe my relationship with Jesus was not what it should have been or he would have seen the light and followed the things of God. It felt like I failed God, my husband, my children, my friends and myself. My failures took in everyone and everything I loved.

I grew weaker in hope and faith and in all the things I held dear. I came to a point in our marriage where I didn't turn to Jesus for guidance and wisdom to know how to handle situations instead I reacted immediately. I'd give anything to undo the part I played in the war of conflicts. I was just fed up with being treated like I didn't have a brain that functioned. I tried telling my husband he had to stop. He wasn't going to get by with treating me corruptly without getting it thrown back in his face in the same way. Then when I'd do something on purpose I knew would disturb him immensely I'd feel sorry and ashamed. It didn't make it right to retaliate by calling him naughty names. All I accomplished by reacting was to keep the fights alive and roaring. I was frustrated with myself whenever I came down on him.

I really was repentant and sorry for some of my behavior, words, thoughts and reactions, times I hurt him, times when he felt I hurt him. I wish I could change some things I did and wish I had not done. Words I said and wish I had not spoken. Most of all I wished I wouldn't have let him get by with the exploiting abuse.

None the less there were times I began to wish I hadn't given up when I did. I kept thinking maybe there was one more thing I could have done to help my husband. My dreams of being with Konn were over. I was alone and lonely again and I wasn't good at either one. Now it's much to late to wish anything more concerning Konn and I. It's all water under the bridge over troubled waters. My wishes are just like the pennies I threw in the river traveling slowly downward in the water till both the wishes and the pennies sunk to the bottom of the river never to be found.

No one understood how the divorce was affecting me. How much I wanted to be with my husband or the great extent I wanted him to do right by him self and by me. I assumed I could be there for him but I wasn't as strong as I thought. I couldn't take any more disturbing mayhem or put my family through any more fear or frustration.

Still it bugged me when people thought it helped me to hear about the things he did. None of it made it any easier and it all had the opposite affect. Their words didn't help. It hurt more to hear people repeat things I already knew. I didn't need to be reminded. They were not I and they were rubbing salt into the already acquired wounds. Although my heart belongs to God first then to me I know better than anyone what my husband did to me and to us. He was still in my heart and my heart is mine alone to decide how I feel and no one else's. I don't deny or condone what he did. I hated what he did. But I loved him. He was still part of my heart much as I wish he wasn't. The whole affair of going through a divorce, knowing about the strip club, strippers, the story the debits told and viewing for myself what takes place inside the club was more than I could muddle through. This was the man I loved and married. I wanted to believe the best about him. Who was he anyway? Why did I have to be so shocked? I was upset with myself since I couldn't discern this was the way it was going to be when I married or when I filed divorce. I thought he didn't know how to get along with out me but he got along very well. I was the one that wasn't getting along well without him.

Being a sentimental romantic fool everything reminded me of Konn. No matter where I was I broke out in tears. I'd think of things I planned for our wedding day and our future and it all came back to haunt me. I bawled nonstop. A familiar song on the radio reminding me of Konn would start a flood of tears. It didn't help when I thought of him having a good time while I was falling apart. If a person loves God they can't help being broken hearted seeing someone they love destroy themselves with addictions they chose that now controls them. It wasn't just the breakup or all the corruption that was getting to me I couldn't stand to see the destruction the addiction unwaveringly was doing to both of us. I wanted to believe he'd accept truth and realize the deception he willfully chose has a hold on him preventing him from living in truth that would set him free. Most of all the addiction thwarts him from seeing the light of God and life everlasting in eternity.

At this time all I can think about is my husband. Nothing else mattered, nothing helped. I didn't care if I talked to anyone or ate or if I ever got up out of bed. I knew when I heard he was with strippers it was really over and there was no going back. I loved Konn and it was too much to handle. I was grief stricken and could not be consoled. My thoughts ran amuck. I was as confused without Konn as I was with him. I didn't want anyone but my husband, I didn't want him to be with anyone other than me and I didn't want anyone else to want him. I threw the mail in the garage and didn't open it. I threw away important letters with out realizing what I was doing. One letter was a tax statement increasing the value of our home and raised our taxes over $140 a month.

We only had thirty day's to protest. Seven months later my daughter told me our payments went up because we didn't protest during the appointed time and it was to late to do anything about the higher taxes. All I could tell her was I don't know what to say I am speechless. I couldn't get the house clean or finish anything. I left the newspaper lay outside for days on end. My children said it was dangerous to leave them laying outside so I tried to remember to pick them up then just threw them away without reading the news. Like the old saying just take it a day at a time sometimes I had to take it an hour at a time. There were too many things happening all at once during the time I learned Konn's preference was a stripper prostitute I was going through grief over a church friend of mine that became very ill. She was a beautiful lady and a wonderful person. I was so wrapped up in what was going on in my life by the time I went to see her in the hospital it was to late she was so sick I couldn't get in to see her. The chemotherapy wasn't working. I didn't know the cancer was as far along as it was and she was dying. Although I knew one thing was certain one thing was for sure she had a destiny with Jesus in Heaven forever. After she heard my husband left me for another woman and I was going through a hard time trying to cope she'd see me in the store and she'd stop and encourage me. She kept telling me what a neat lady I was and it was his loss.

Every Sunday in church she made a point of tapping me on the shoulder and saying hi beautiful lady. When she sat across the isle from me if I caught her eyes they lit up and she always gave me a knowing and encouraging smile.

Here she was riddled with cancer and she cared and was concerned for me. I didn't know as she spoke to me in church one Sunday it would be the last time I'd see her alive. Her kindness and concern really touched me because I knew it was sincere. I wanted her to know the uplifting support I felt from her and she was a blessing. I'll never forget how dear she was to me but I waited to long to tell her. We weren't close friends that hung out all the time. We worked on church projects together and spoke to one another at church and mostly called each other about church business. That's why it was so special when she took time to talk and cheer me up recognizing the pain I was carrying inside as if she could feel the wounds within my heart. I admired her sweet quiet comforting spirit.

During the funeral the pastor shared the last words she spoke before she passed away. Her husband and the pastor stood by her bedside crying and she told them don't be sad. I'm going into the kingdom of God and I will be the angel sitting on your shoulder until you join me in eternity. They were the most beautiful words I ever heard and I shall carry them with me forever. I kept telling myself that was the way our wedding vows were supposed to be and our marriage falling apart tore me up for I wanted to be the angel sitting on my husbands shoulder. I wept over her death for months and still think of her. When I heard how close she was to dying I prayed God take my life she's only 43 please let her live she has two children and a husband that loves her take me instead. I meant every word I prayed with all my heart and soul. I thought my children were older they could get along without me and didn't need me dragging my depression into their lives.

It was as if her death and the loss of my husband in the death of our marriage were all tied together. At that moment I felt like Konn took my life from me. He had a choice and made the decision to put our marriage to death and watched it die along with me. We were married in the same church the funeral was taking place. As the pastor finished speaking I could actually see a vision of us on our wedding day. My eyes shining brightly as I looked into Konn's eyes as we said our wedding vows till death when we part.

I saw myself standing beside my husband, holding my guitar and singing "The Wedding Song" to him. It wrenched me in half. I wanted to be Mrs. Konn Rodent. I was crazy in love with my husband. I thought of my wedding day as one of the most memorable happy events In my life believing with all my heart and soul we'd be by each other's side till one of us departed. I could hardly stand the feelings coursing in my heart knowing without a doubt our vows meant emphatically nothing to Konn. Driving home after the funeral I could hardly see the road as tears blurred my vision. I didn't go back to church for two months.

I came down on myself and kept thinking I should have been stronger and had more patience. I should have done something more to salvage our marriage instead of watching it die too. I didn't know what else to do. I felt responsible for Konn. I don't know if it is in a spiritual way or if it is in a woman's way of still being connected to my husband while he was going on without me. God knows it hurt knowing he was going about his business laughing in the darkness of immorality without one thought of my having been part of his life. Sadness wells up thinking I seen something in him no one else could see. Believing there was something good in him that never emerged and seems buried within. I wasn't able to let go of my husband. Part of me kept thinking of us as still being married and I desired to have that part back knowing I can't have it. It can never be and it never was to begin with except in my dreams. I was as down in the dumps as I could be. No matter what my husband did my heart continued to yearn for my husband to be with me but he no longer wanted any part of me. Even the little part of me Konn held onto for whatever reasons were gone. That was my demise. I wanted to walk in front of a car and end the pain and misery.

Losing his mom a few months before Konn deserted me was a double dose of loss. I was lonesome for both of them. Konn and his mother had been a part of my life the last five years. I missed seeing his mother and I missed going places with her and the phone calls. I felt forlorn and lost without my husband even though I had a family that loved and cared about me a great deal. They didn't understand where I was coming from. They looked at Konn's behavior and couldn't fathom why I felt the way I did about him.

For some reason it was always hard to tell my family my deepest thoughts. I was their mom and I want them to think I was a cool lady too. I acted one way in front of them when I really felt another. They didn't want me to talk about Konn. I couldn't tell them the innermost turmoil I was going through.

Although my personality was always outgoing I became an introvert after the death of my husband five years before I met Konn and went back to being an introvert after the death of our marriage. Actually I didn't wish to share where I was coming from with anyone. I thought what the heck does It matter what I think anyway. I'm nobody why did I think I had to have an opinion about anything. I was down and out and terribly depressed. I have a rough time overcoming the grief of losing someone I love. It isn't easy for me to except their death even though I knew my loved ones accepted Jesus and were saved and they are a part of the Kingdom of God in Heaven. Knowing for certain they're in heaven wasn't enough to console me at the time because I was the one left behind.

It seems like each time someone close to me passes away the feeling of abandonment comes over me. My husband didn't have a choice when he died suddenly yet I felt like he abandoned me. When Konn discarded me in the death of our relationship the same feeling of abandonment hit me in a way I never knew anything would or could. It was more than overwhelming.

209

Being abandoned goes hand in hand with being discarded and rejected and has always been a part of something deep within. I try to keep it in wraps and covered up but it surfaces from time to time. I was never one to want to go back into the past but going back to childhood shed some light on the reason I felt so despondent was due to the fact my parents gave me a form of rejection and abandonment. I lived with a foster family and always felt my parents didn't want me or care about me as a child.

As I grew older I said they came from the old country and didn't know any better and they did the best they could with the circumstances they might have grown up in. My mom was raised in an orphanage and my dad and his brother lived in a poverty stricken country and came to America alone with very little money as teen-age boys. I told my self I understood where they were coming from when they let me live with a foster mom. But now I do wonder if I did comprehend the fullness of the feelings that grew within the small child that felt her parents didn't want to be responsible for her welfare. Or if I consoled myself saying I understand in order to deal with the emotion of abandonment that floods over me when someone leaves me.

I carried the emotional feeling no one truly wanted me until Franklin Latur came into my life. He was the one person aside from my children I felt secure and safe with. Franklin made me feel wanted and accepted just for whom I was not only in words but in his behavior too. Not for what I could do for him but for what I meant to him. My family was happy just to have me near them. My family is my most precious possession and it made me happy to know they liked me near for I liked having them near me too. I experienced what it was to have a healthy loving normal intimate relationship in marriage with my husband Franklin. I knew what it felt like to be desired and the intimacy of looking across a crowded room see Franklin and know exactly what he was saying to me with his eyes He treated me like a queen. Simply a look from him made me feel safe for I could see the love in his soft blue eyes.

I can identify what it is to be a couple wanting to show their love for one another in a healthy sexually intimate togetherness as one. I knew what it was to have soul ties to my partner and to know he had the same soul ties toward me. I was acquainted with what it felt like to have the love I gave him given back to me. I wasn't out there alone. Franklin was devoted and that says it all. He was a true family man that loved his wife and children. He put us first and made us feel we were the most important possession in his life.

I didn't expect my marriage to Konn to be the same as it was with Franklin. There was only one thing I wanted from my husband Konn and that was his devotion to love me back. I loved Konn in a different way than I loved Franklin. I was older and the children were grown up and mostly on their own I was free to do most anything.

After being alone five years and thinking my life was over before I fell in love with Konn the lovechild within was awestruck just to be near him. He became the love of my life. I loved him in a way he will never know or ever appreciate. It was a pure unadulterated child like devoted love that wanted to please him in every way I could. I was thankful to have a second chance with someone I loved and desired believing the feelings were mutual and he felt the same way about me that I felt for him. It isn't easy for me to get to know men. I don't like the dating single scene or getting to know someone's character and habits. I didn't want to be single. I don't want just anyone simply to have someone.

Since Konn left three years ago I haven't seen one person I want to date let alone be with. I still long for Konn but not the way he was. I yearned for Konn the way I dreamed he would be. It's heartrending to say there is not a day goes by I don't think of the way Konn threw me away and the feeling of betraying rejection stays with me and the abused hurt within still wants Konn to accept and desire me. He didn't just throw me away once I ended up putting myself in harms way again after the divorce when I rescued and believed him for a short time once more.

Chapter Sixteen

Describing Scenes I viewed in The Strip Club

The tenacious traumatic betrayal and unfaithfulness was bad enough before I walked in the strip club to witness why my husband cast me aside. But when I walked out of the club I was like a sleep walking zombie and closer to believing I had nothing to live for. I lined up my detective friend Heige to take me to the strip club the day after we went to court January 27, 2000. Heige wouldn't go in. He thought it would be better if he waited outside he didn't like the girls crowding him. I really didn't have any idea what he was talking about when he said the girls swarmed him. I thought they just came around him because he was handsome. I didn't know the strippers propositioned every man that came in the place no matter what they looked like as long as they had money to put in their g-string or go with them into a private room at the top of the stairs. I had never been in a strip club or for that matter any club.

My children would have been appalled if they knew what I was up to. I couldn't believe I'm determined to follow through with the escapade. Aside from wanting to know what his friend looked like I wanted to know what Konn could conceivably spend $15,000 on in five months in a strip club. I carried a picture I had put in a paper sack into the strip club. It was a picture of two bluebirds his mother made and gave us on our wedding night. On the back she inscribed our wedding date, the time and she wrote, " Bluebirds Represent Happiness."

I took the picture with me for the sole intention of giving it to his stripper friend and telling her Konn's mom wanted his wife to have it. Since she was Konn's new wife sexually, financially and in every way they can be as they roam the countryside together, dining out, boating and shopping sprees. Spending every minute of every day together while he's still married to me she should have the picture. She earned it.

I walked in the club by myself I had no idea what I'd encounter. I sat down at a table in the center of the room next to the dance area. A waitress wearing a T-shirt and jeans came over to ask if I wanted anything. I ordered a Coca-Cola. For the first time in my life I viewed demonic activity going on all around me. The stench in the entire place was putrid and the room was unclean. Oddly enough I felt as if I were in a bubble and nothing in the room could penetrate the bubble. There were fifteen to twenty girls working. They all seemed to be wearing five to six inch white high heel shoes. A few strippers had clothes on. Some wore short dresses and several had on long gowns. A few wore sheer robes with very little underneath and quite a few were wearing only a g-string. Which is really nothing more than parading in the nude? The place was known as a topless club.

In the middle of the room was a small dance area just a few inches higher than the floor. One man got up from his seat and walked up to a girl dancing in her g-string and devoured the exposed breast she put in his mouth. With no concern all eyes were on them as he stood there sucking her nipple as saliva ran down his chin and clung to her breast.

Then the dancer lay on the floor held her legs wide apart. First high in the air then spread her legs in the same position on the floor exposing all she owned. Several men went up to the dancer, she allowed them to put their leering faces between her legs and pull her g-string over to the side. While the dancer is taking it all off on stage most of the other strippers are simultaneously dancing next to the males sitting by their tables. Most of the strippers pulled their g string to the side spread their legs and sprawled on men's lap rubbing and straddling them as they performed lewd sex acts on the men's laps. They wiggled back and forth and up and down for lack of a better word right next to the guys family jewels. Some had their breast in the men's mouth as they jiggled on their laps. They were gyrating on gentlemen's laps in every nook and cranny in the place.

A few strippers turned their backs to the men as they dance by the tables and bent over as if to touch their toes putting their behinds as high as they could straight in the air showing and shoving their intimate private parts into transfixed lusting faces of the men inspecting every inch of their body. One stripper with a short dress on was dancing by a table of men showing she wore only a g-string under the dress as she bent over and bared all. Some women walked from table to table talking and allowing the men slipping money in their g strings to touch their bodies.

The guy's eyes looked mesmerized and glazed as they acted worse than animals in a pack. The strippers went from man to man through out the room saliva and other secretions of the men in the place passed from dirty mouth to breast to another dirty mouth. A few men had three different women doing sex acts on his lap individually and then two at a time. One stripper was on her knees by an ugly looking man sitting on the edge of a booth right next to the stripper on bended knees. I don't know what she was doing.

Filth and disease spreading like wild fire as they change partners and wander from man to man. Sexual deviation was taking place through out the room. The women seemed to be catering to whatever the men wanted. Every man is approached the minute he walks in the door and is encouraged to participate in fun and games.

No one seemed to mind I was a stranger in their territory. One of the girls from another state came over to talk with me. She told me most of the girls working in strip clubs don't use their real names and they're from different states. Some stayed several weeks then traveled to other clubs. A few strippers worked in this club a long time and lived in town where the club is located. Most strippers are in their late teens and early twenties. Only a few were in there thirties or forties. Tears were gushing from my eyes. She said I must have loved my husband a great deal to walk in the strip club. Then she went to sit with several men directly across the room from where I was sitting. I was the only woman in the place other than the women that worked there. I'm certain everyone in the place knew I was some ones neglected wife and ignored my presence. They stared at me when I first walked in and as they walked by me and I stared them down.

The filth and stench in the bar was sickening and suffocating. It was hard to breathe. I can best describe all that is taking place as sin, adultery, immorality, fornication, and unrighteous, unclean impurity at the lowest level of degrading ones self. The scenes of perversion can be linked to sexual perversion and pornography-affiliated corruption. How do I describe the agonizing pain welling within as I viewed the basest smut and filth enacted by laughing licentious men grabbing naked strippers selling their nude bodies? Men and strippers on every side of me participating in sex acts on chairs, tables, on the floor, on the stage and in the rooms upstairs. The cliental participated in sexual depravity in front of one another without blinking an eye.

I couldn't stand seeing the reality of knowing my husband participated in the same activity-taking place in the room almost every night for ten months that I can pinpoint for certain. I've no more doubts any more that he took part in the crowded sex orgies for years. It threw me right smack dab into shocking torment. Having sexual encounters with prostitutes and indulging in sex the rest of the perverts in the room were engaging in is the other part of the deceptive secret double life he led and tried so desperately to hide. I became dizzy and felt I was going to faint right then and there. My spirit was completely grieved and wounded.

When I gained my composure I got up from where I was sitting and went up the few steps to the bar. I sat at one of the little tables Konn sat many evenings with the stripper he's infatuated with. There are several stairs in the aisle between the bar and the tables that led to the rooms upstairs where the girls took men and charged $30.00 to finish the frenzied sex job they start downstairs. I did scope out Konn's women as she did a sexual dance on one of the men. Why it's called a lap dance is beyond me. They should call the dance like it is and call it the get turned on dance so the club and the strippers can earn more money.

Konn's girlfriend took one of the men she had been humping in a chair by the hand and walked right past me up the stairs to one of the rooms she took my husband into many evenings. No one selling their body could really know where the other person has been as they passed dirt and germs from the most intimate parts of their bodies from one to the other.

I couldn't get myself to talk to her. I was going to ask the bartender to give the picture to Toriann and tell her it was a wedding gift for Konn's new wife from Konn Rodent's ex wife. I chickened out. I couldn't leave the picture in the filthy squalor of the place or let anyone in there even touch it. As I sat there sick to my stomach knowing Konn made himself at home in the sinful vulgar immorality. I had flashbacks of a few incidents that took place and the undies and other items belonging to Konn's girlfriends. I believe if he knew where to go and who to go to so quickly he must have been spending time in this certain strip club long before me and during our union.

I thought of times he left home four am every morning and times he disappeared for hours on end during the day when he should have been working. I can't deny anything anymore knowing there isn't a shadow of a doubt to hang onto and absolutely nothing he said or did was my imagination. This certain strip club was on the route he drove to and from the state he worked in for a year. I thought of all the hours he must have spent in strip clubs on the many trips he made. I can pinpoint when activity steeped up to force divorce. I wasn't imagining the way his addiction to be with strippers and partake of the sex scene consumed every waking minute until it obsessed his quest to be free of me as quickly as possible. I'll never fully know the reason he made a last ditch effort to come back home after he left. He'd continue to lie and find ways to sneak off to strippers as he persists to harm me.

No wonder he yelled about needing Viagra after joining in all the activity I seen in the room with all the nudies and sex he bought. I under stand now why he came home with far fetched stories of being impotent. What really got to me was the cruelty he displayed throughout and the increased harassment and neglect the last year before leaving. I was mostly upset at myself for taking mistreatment and sexually abusive tormenting words he spoke about not turning him on after seeing what did turn him on along with all the other violating sexual remarks he made.

Every demeaning word he spoke on intimacy and sex haunted me as I sat and viewed what the sex addicted pervert preferred over his wife promising to spend the rest of his life showing how much he loved me. Making an oath that I would be the only woman he will desire sexually and would never look at another women. It was demoralizing to see what his pledges really meant.

One of the filthy slang's he flung at me that stood out the most as I sat in the den of iniquity was when he said I didn't know what passion was and sex was supposed to be between two consenting adults and he never consented to have sex with me, I forced him. I remembered replying marriage is two consenting adults loving one another and consent to have sex is in the act of making love as husband and wife as two intimately become as one. A man and women agree to have sex with one another the moment they say I do take thee as my lawfully wedded wife in the sight of God. Marriage is saying I desire sex with my partner for it goes without saying it is part of the union.

I thought of my husband having the same encounters with the same prostitutes I was observing. It bothered me to think of his reactions toward me if I asked him what his problem was when we went to bed and he acted like he didn't know what it meant to have a sexual encounter with his wife and the way he yelled you're the only whore I have every known you fucking bitch. I was distressed recalling the mean harsh cruel words and ungodly wickedness I had suffered and forgiven trying to hold things together. I was very upset with myself when I thought of all the times he got by with mistreating and manhandling me. It troubled me to no end I was the woman he harmed and used to have money to buy the strippers I was viewing in the sexually degrading acts they were committing with so many different men.

The second I had the flashbacks I was wishing he would walk into the club while I was sitting there so I can throw my engagement and wedding ring in his face.

I got up to leave and was shaking as I made my way to the door. On the way out I noticed the ATM machine by the door where he debited thousands of dollars. I was violently ill and white as a sheet as I stepped out the door into the fresh air. I felt deceived, contaminated, violated and defiled. His behavior toward me was far more than abandonment and betrayal. I finally knew the whole truth and I felt defeated and wiped out. I wasn't merely distraught about my husband. It was the whole scope of the demonic scene I witnessed. The dark deceiving deception of blind lost souls following the blind was as overwhelming and suffocating as the nudity and perversion. My tears have no end.

Heige sat in his truck a few yards away. He was surprised I didn't run right back out the moment I walked in. I told him I was shocked and felt frozen in time. I felt sorry for the women working inside the club degrading and endangering themselves

He said don't feel sorry for the girls working in strip clubs they have no morals. They have the same morals your husband has. That was little consolation to the heart breaking scenes taking place in the satanic den of iniquity. Sometimes it's hard to understand compassion a follower of Jesus has for people they see walking in the same dark fog they once walked in before accepting Jesus as their Savior.

Heige don't you know they're walking in darkness and on the path that leads to destruction. At the risk of sounding like an ignoramus I'm going to say it anyway. Immorality will have no place in the kingdom of God. God is not in the midst of what is taking place inside the confines of the strip club. I believe to walk in darkness is to be out of the presence of God. God can't look upon sin. Why do you think Jesus spoke the words "my God my God why has thou forsaken me?" The Heavenly Father couldn't look upon his own Holy Son Jesus as he hung on a splintered cross-covered with the sins of the whole world with an unconditional love and mercy for all mankind. Imagine being covered with every single human beings sin from the beginning of time to the end of time including ours. He must have felt so alone as he hung there in pain, wood slivers from the cross sticking in his wounds from beatings that left him bleeding and bruised beyond recognition. He was treated like a criminal and he wasn't guilty of anything. Jesus is the only one ever born innocent and without sin.

Imagine loving someone enough to die for them? That's how much God loved us. He gave his only begotten son because he loved us so much he didn't want us to be lost or to walk in darkness. I don't condone the activity taking place in the strip club but an over whelming sadness and compassion came over me for the men and women partaking in the depravity unaware of how lost they are and possibly not caring. Functioning with in the walls of strip clubs is evidently the clue that the people participating in the activity invited the immoral fleshpot of evil into their life through choices they make to live in satanic darkness. It seemed as if demons were jumping from one to other as they are in the act of debauchery with one another.

Konn was a church going person from the time he was a child. He knows what the Bible says and believes in God and Jesus but as a double minded man also feels it's okay to do whatever he wants. Whatever makes him feel good whether it is with sexual depravity or anything else he chooses? He felt it was okay to abuse and cast aside a wife that loved God, her husband and family to chase women he paid for sexual favors. He couldn't behave in the manner he undertook if he believed God and had truly accepted and lived for Jesus. No one can. No matter what his beliefs are I believe although he is not my husband legally he's still my husband till death in Gods eyes and in my eyes.

Being a Christian didn't mean I should let him get by with treating me lousy or like I had no rights as a person to take a stand against deceit and depravity he sanctioned. It wasn't easy living under the gloom of dark with Konn. I didn't just love my husband with the dictionaries description of the word love. I loved him with the love of Jesus within my heart. I tried to show Konn how much I loved him but he felt it was an invitation to stomp me further into the ground, further into the dirt.

I have to look at the fact that Jesus died for my husband and all the people in the strip club too. They are lost by choice but their lost just the same. They are on the path that leads to destruction and eternal damnation and don't believe or maybe they don't understand or even care Satan has a hold on them. I've heard people remark they don't care if they to go to hell to be with their friends believing hell is going to be one big party. Hell isn't going to be one big party. Hell is forever too. It is eternal damnation in never-ending torment. Never to be in God's presence would be hell in itself.

I've heard Konn and other individuals say they don't believe Satan is real. Satan likes that falsehood. If no one believes he is real he already has him or her deaf and blind to the truth, trapped in his cage and pursues people he doesn't yet have a hold on. Tempting them into the same illusory obscurity as those that think Satan is the fictitious little red man with horns and a pitchfork. There's no doubt Satan is real and he is evil and wicked in the exact words Jesus say he is in the bible.

Immorality of the ages is Satan's playground. First the world was destroyed by a flood and then Sodom and Gomorrah was destroyed by fire for the same sins of immorality and depraved sexual perversion that is taking place in society throughout the entire world today.

I Knew Konn well and I'm aware in his reasoning to condone his behavior he felt it was okay to go directly to as many loose women as he wants because I slapped a protection order on him and filed for divorce. He couldn't hold back on plunging into sexual lust that is in his heart for women in the environment he craved during our marriage.

But I wanted to think there had to be something in him that would make him realize he's living like a reprobate wake up and turn from degrading depravity of being with women that sell themselves and recognize a need to turn to God. Instead he dug a deeper hole buying as many strippers as his money could buy.

When someone rejects God and walks in obscurity I don't think I am any better than they are or judge the person but I do judge the act of what is being committed to hurt themselves and hurt others and know it is not the fruit of Gods teachings.

Even though I was never into anything like the scenes I witnessed in the house of ill repute I try to relate myself to the times I walked in darkness thinking what ever I sought to do was okay and whatever anyone else wanted to do was okay. I thought to each his own as long as they left me alone. I was saturated in sin before God rescued me. Since that hour I consider it a gift and a privilege God taught me to have mercy and pray for those who don't know him just as I didn't know for I was not aware until I accepted Jesus that the world's ungodly fun is temporary. I was familiar with what it is like to be a part of the world's fun. At the time it's enjoyable and feels good. I'd go to confession tell the priest my sins and think he had the power to forgive me I'd go right back out and do whatever I want to do all over again. Since that point in time I learned I don't have to go to a priest I can go straight to God for only God could forgive sin.

I can identify with calling myself a Christian and a believer simply because I went to church and believed in God. But I was not a Christian for I didn't strive to follow his teachings. I didn't even know what they were.

I didn't read the bible until I accepted Jesus and was saved by God's merciful grace. Grace his son shed his blood for and paid the price and gave it to all without cost to anyone that reaches out and accepts the free gift of salvation. Many say I believe in God but don't believe what God says but the way he says it is the way it will be no matter how men try to change the meaning. There is only one association and that is God's meaning. When I was first saved I recognized that if I were going to claim that I was a Christian I needed to learn and be taught what I needed to do in order to walk the talk. I still said some of the worlds slang a while. I used to say let's kick ass for Jesus. I'm not discussing a denomination or religion I'm talking about a one on one relationship with the living God and his Holy Son Jesus. Many are in danger of being on the path that leads to ruin because they feel the bible does not apply to them. Konn scoffed at the word saved and born again. But they are the words leading to eternal life. My husband hates me for taking a stand each time he crossed the line to demoralize my life. I wasn't going to give up my beliefs in God and I wasn't giving up on moral principles and values I intend to live by.

No one likes to hear the truth it takes away from what makes us feel good. Who am I to talk of eternal damnation? I'm someone that was on the way to eternal darkness when God rescued me the moment I cried out to him. It takes recognizing we have a need to ask Jesus to put our sins under the blood he shed for everyone and sometimes it takes putting our pride down long enough to identify and acknowledge the need to have Jesus as Savior. Sometimes I think when God looks at us from heaven he sees the people covered with his son's blood and the people who are not covered with the blood. It is so good of God to give everyone the same chance and make no distinctions.

I admit I am weak and wounded in my spirit at this time. But there was a period of time I was strong in my testimony. I've never been weak in loving God and I was not weak in my stand against immorality. I was weak when it came to Konn as he crushed, offended and injured my character.

The amount of dollars spent on pornography shows many people are involved in the depraved perversion pornography promotes through the addiction of worshipping what gives them unnatural pleasure and none of it is part of God's Holy Kingdom. The bible says demons believe in God and tremble they're lost forever with no chance of repenting. We have been given that chance and need to recognize it while we are still alive. Once we stop breathing it is all over there are no more chances or choices to be made and it will be to late to become a child in the Kingdom of God. I have a burden for lost souls for I was lost but now I'm found. It is so important for those who know God to follow his teachings. To tell the unsaved the truth of his saving grace. Sin is sin and one sin is no greater than the other but all sin can be wiped away when we ask Jesus to be number one in our heart and soul and over all we do in this lifetime. For one day in our present lifetime will be our last day.

We have all heard the message of how much God loves us all the same and we don't have to worry a loving God won't let us go to hell for eternity. That's true God loves everyone. I believe there is one thing God requires back if we are willing and that is to love him with the free will he created in us. Love him for who is the "Awesome Holy God" that created us.

If we love God with all our heart, soul and mind we would want to do our best to obey and accept both God and his teachings and strive to live that way. We would just naturally want to please God the same way we want to please our loved ones. We all fall short and mess up at times but we have to continually fight the battle in doing what feels good to us and do what is morally right as we attempt to live for God. That doesn't mean we have to be a stick in the mud or self-righteous. We can have fun and good times it's merely that we seek a different kind of fun than the kind the world sells and advocates and say's were not with it if we don't participate in doing what everyone else considers pleasure and good times.

Christians are not perfect they are only saved. We should never lose sight that the words in the bible are alive and the words are Gods Holy Spirit speaking though Godly men and women that followed God. They were not flawless they stuck their foot in their mouth, made mistakes and some committed adultery. But we fail to recognize the biblical characters repented and didn't continue in their sin. Some of them had a hard row to hoe even after repenting but they kept their eyes of God.

Even though I feel a burden for people walking in darkness and for my husband's choosing the same demonic path it doesn't take away from the way I feel over seeing for myself what my husband was into.

I was so nervous I talked detective Heige's ear off as we drove the fifty-mile trip home. He listened very intently and was very interested. Heige was so nice he knew I didn't have a lot of money so he cut me some slack and let me make payments. He was kind and considerate and became a friend I will cherish. I used his expertise a few more times after we were divorced. I thanked Heige and went in the house and took all my clothes off and took a hot bath. I sent my clothes and coat to the cleaners. The chairs were filthy and gross from the sex acts committed on them. I was afraid of catching a disease just sitting in the smutty dirt and grime in the place. The demonic activity in the strip club was worse than anything I could ever have imagined it would be.

I called crime stoppers and asked why the club I visited was allowed to promote illegal activity? I described a few scenes inside the club and the officer asked if I'd go before the liquor commission? He said they need someone like me to tell what I witnessed. He said they were watching the place. Shortly after I called they sent an undercover agent in the club and he didn't have any success offering strippers big bucks to perform certain sexual acts. To prevent being arrested men don't take their clothes off they ejaculate in their pants while strippers perform sexual favors for money. Sexual touching in the room has the same results as prostitution but it is not called sex. The legal system calls it illegal touching. I thought the officer should have known strippers would be leery of someone offering them $400 to $500 when they only charge $30.00 to relieve sexual frenzy of turning the guys on with naked gyrating they do on their laps whether men take their clothes off or not. The nude dancers would have to know some one as well as they knew my husband to accept the generous offer the undercover agent proposed.

The catch 20 is that it's against a state liquor law to sell liquor and what they call illegal touching at the same time. When I heard the legal systems definition of sex. I wondered if anyone in the legal system knows God created men, women and sex. God being the one to create sex can surely give the best definition of what sex is but even if they don't believe in God as the creator I wonder why they don't believe Webster's dictionaries definition of sex and prostitute and where they find the definitions to words they use to define some of our laws.

Webster's definition of sex....................1) Either of the two major forms that occur in many living things and are designated male or female according to their role in reproduction also the qualities by which these sexes are differentiated and which directly or indirectly function in reproduction involving two persons. 2) Sexual activity or behavior, also sexual intercourse.

Webster's definition of prostitute..............1) to offer indiscriminately for sexual activity especially for money. 2) To devote to corrupt or unworthy purposes.

Immorality isn't prejudice it doesn't care who the people are that it exploits, degrades, and destroys. There are some Christians hooked on pornography too. They have just as hard a time letting go of all it entails in the effect the obsessive sex addiction to pornography has on people that feel it doesn't hurt anything to take a peek. Possibly feeling they can take it or leave it not realizing they may eventually have to over come the bondage it puts them in.

It can happen to those who think it can't happen as long as people continue to feel there is nothing wrong with nudity being displayed everywhere we look and society continues to cop an attitude that says nothing is called sex or adultery.

Everyone seems to have a different definition for the word sex. Today's society uses the definition that suits their need. I didn't think pornography could affect and destroy people that didn't have anything to do with it till it happened to me. It took awhile to figure out when Konn used the word sex it meant whatever he did with women was not cheating or categorized as having sex as long as he didn't do it a certain way or in a certain position. I refused to go before the liquor commission. Officials knew the club had broken the law every night for as long as it's been in business. If I went before the commission the owner would just have to pay a fine and continue to break the law. The officer wrote a letter of reprimand telling the owner to clean up illegal activity he witnessed and sent a letter of violations to the liquor commission. I felt it was a slap on the hand, business continues to flourish. Besides if it had closed someone else would buy the club and the illegal activity would continue.

If I were to do anything about the billion dollar industry pornographers promote in degradation I'd go to the top men running our country now that we don't have the same president in office who didn't know the definition of sex or fidelity in marriage. Some of society accepts the same definition of sex is no longer called sex Konn advocates; sex is no longer called sex unless it is done in a certain way and in a certain position and it is not called sex if your in a private room with a stripper and you keep your pants on while your engaging in what is no longer called sex.

Many are afraid to tell it like it is or everyone will think were a nut. If we call selling sex immoral or call pornography by its given name call it what it really is we would call it sin and destruction of and against your own body and mind. If we say the word sin in connection with anything we'd be ostracized. Call me a nut and ostracize me. I will call indecent, unnatural smut wickedly corrupt distorted filth and all that is connected to it is adultery immoral and sin. I wasn't the one who called it sin and adultery and immoral. I wasn't the one that described sin. Someone else did that 6,000 years ago when men and women and sex were created.

There are people that do not accept God but still have morals and standards and are good family men and women that don't commit adultery or partake of the pornography scene or mistreat their spouse

It's hard to identify with people that choose to damage themselves as they make the decision to put their life in danger for a few fleeting seconds. Taking a chance to catching HIV and every other sexually transmitted disease out there.

Including new diseases being discovered every day linked to having sex where ever and with whomever. The cheating partner takes the disease home and puts their spouse in danger and in harms way. The spouse didn't have any input in the decision made by their promiscuous partner to indulge in buying, selling or having sex outside of marriage. This includes unmarried couples living together too. There should be commitment with people that share their lives and beds with one another. The innocent partner wasn't given the opportunity to decide whether of not they wanted dirt and filth possibly disease the cheating spouse may have caught from someone else's body put inside their body. A partner should have the same right to decide if they want to be clean healthy, disease free and not take a chance to be put in a life or death situation.

If I had the opportunity to talk with people involved in the business of selling the most intimate part of them. I'd ask what does it cost to become a part of the degradation of selling his or her body to anyone that has money? Does it pay what it is worth to take on someone's uncleanness and pass it from body to body? Is it worth the cost of losing their family, possibly their job, their life and their very soul?

How many strippers or prostitutes actually drive a Cadillac or own a condo? I wouldn't be afraid to wager they're far and few between. Can any amount of money take the place of integrity? Someone probably wouldn't give two cents to hear my opinion but I'm giving it anyway. I think a dish washing job can have more self-respect than taking it all off for any Joe Blow. A complete stranger the girls have no idea where their body's been. They just want to use a women's body and don't view who they are as a person. Yes I have had to wash dishes to survive.

Pornography now has freedom to destroy minds as easily as cocaine but you can be arrested and imprisoned if you're caught using drugs. All one has to do to see perversion at it's worst is turn on the Internet and check your email, the debasing advertisements on every kind of perverted sex is at your fingertips. When I learned how to use a computer I couldn't wait to have an e-mail address. The first day I had the e mail address there were advertisements put on my address advocating every kind of sex in the world from incest to bestiality, with any partner and any nationality. It's to overwhelming to list all of the filth that was in my e-mail before I even used it. I didn't know what most of the sexually explicit things they advertised meant or such mortifying sex existed.

Pornography is not viewed as making prisoners of people addicted to it. But they are every bit as much a prisoner as someone needing to shoot their veins with poison.

Just as there are men today that abuse women there are also men that are devoted and treat women and their wife honorably. There are men that wouldn't think of delving into pornography or think of treating a woman abominably and have one woman till death. There are even some animals have only one mate for life and some are cleaner than the men I viewed in the strip club.

After all was said and done shortly after our divorce my husband called and asked for my help. He would not speak to me over a year until he was headed to jail for writing bad checks. I went to his rescue and was thrown into the lion's den yet again. I let myself in for more shocking details and hurt that affected me physically and I have to live with it now for the rest of my life simply for caring about my ex husbands welfare.

Chapter Seventeen

Living in a Car

After viewing the panoramic view of events in the strip club I went into a bottomless depression. It was difficult to have been in his life one minute and thrown away for prostitutes in the next. No one deserves to be treated like an animal that's been dumped on the side of the road. Purely because the owners are tired of their pet and don't want to care for it anymore. The animal stands and looks lovingly forlorn as the owners of his welfare drive away. Knowingly sad, the pet's eyes look trusting as the car drives away and the animal is left to fend for itself in a world it doesn't know. Deep within the animal thought their owner would turn the car around come back and pick them up. Take them to the only home it has known. The animal faithfully sits by the side of the road waiting as the cold night air begins to chill, hunger pains begin to rumble in their stomach and their mouth is dry for a drink of water. The animal instinctively caught on it had been abandoned the moment it was left behind but sat waiting still hoping to see them again. This is how it felt to have someone with you one minute and dump you the next. The pet didn't deserve to be dumped after having been faithful to the owners. They could have taken the animal to a shelter and given the pet a chance to have someone truly love and care for it.

I felt like I was standing in the cold watching my husband laugh and drive away as I shed unending tears asking him not to leave one more time. Thinking how could he keep driving further away not come back immediately comfort me and say he was sorry I can't leave you dear your everything that makes me complete. That was the dreamer in me thinking if he had a shred of love or decency he'd come back. Sometimes I tried to explain things in a similar manner thinking he would say or do something to have peace within him self and with us. He made fun of my words. My councilor kept telling me I wanted to be with the man of my dreams the man I thought he would be.

I can't grasp why Konn was angry and hateful he chose to scurry away. Yet a year after he scampered off and we are divorced I rescued him once again only to see Konn's repugnant hateful mannerisms.

After having no communication for a year I called Konn. His daughter called to ask if I knew how to get a hold of him to tell him his aunt passed away. I jumped at the chance to speak to him so I told her I'd try to contact him. It was over a month after my expedition to the strip club and over a year since we spoke. Even though we hadn't spoken to one another in over a year. Konn still being in my heart meant he was still controlling me to a point. I never got over wanting to know where he was or whom he was with and what he was doing. I found his landlords phone number on the canceled checks. Sounds incredible but after the entire hullabaloo I still want to talk to him. More than anything I want to let him know I was aware of what he is doing since he left home. I thought it was safe to call since he didn't have access to his attorney and the divorce was final.

I was nervous I didn't know what to expect after the harsh treatment he endorsed in divorce. When he heard my voice he was hesitant until I told him I only called to inform him his aunt passed away and where the funeral would be held. He was congenial so I told him about the friend that passed away several months ago because he knew her from church. As we talked he started to brag and rub it in he's seeing a dancer. It took him by surprise when I said I knew whom he was seeing and some of the things he did since he left. You were still my husband what made you think I wouldn't keep track of where you were staying and what you were doing. I knew your address the moment you moved into the rooming house. I was informed of your routine and who your dancer is. I seen her and all that goes on in the house of ill repute you've spent the last year in. He baited me when he said I didn't know what she looks like trying to see if I could identify who she is. I described her but he didn't like my description. I said she was not only a dancer she was a prostitute to every man that goes in the strip club with money to pay her. She doesn't strip her clothes off just for you Konn. Your not the only man to pay to touch your friends intimate parts every man in the place touches your personal dancer.

I described what she looked like along with a few other girls he was attention-grabbing with in the same club. Konn's voice filled with rage. He said I better not touch one hair of her head or he would send a legion of angels after me with him in the lead and he'd slap so many lawsuits on me I won't know what hit me. Absurdly stating I better not hit her the way I chased him around the house and hit and abused him. Turning it on me another time to protect his sex-selling partner, projecting and slanting his behavior. Konn I think one day your going to answer for showing loyalty and devotion to a prostitute while putting your wife in harms way and you were the only partner that did the hitting when you had the opportunity to protect and love your wife. On that note I hung up. I ran to the bathroom and threw up. My bright idea to call only helped me to fall right into vocal insults.

It was obvious he's devoted to the naked dancer as she fulfills his fantasies. At the time I didn't understand why he thought he had to protect his girlfriend from me. The aching words he spoke stung me like a bee sting I am allergic too. It wasn't enough for Konn to know my heart was broken. I found out later he is really protecting himself. He told her I was a threat and would harm her so she would think I'm an uncontrollable nut and I wouldn't have credibility if I decide to inform Toriann about his deeds. The same reason he made a mockery of me to everyone in distorted fabricated tales. He didn't want anyone to hear or believe horror stories I could relate on the ludicrous perversion, mental behavior, suicidal activities and control connected to his tirades.

However being a die hard romantic I thought if only he had said those very words in my defense in our marriage. I'd have stuck to him like glue. They were the very words that would have cemented us so close nothing could pull us apart. I'd have walked on a cloud to the ends of the earth with a smile on my face. The words expressed in his devotion toward her were a definitive insult while I'm in the lowest pit of depression. He was actually proud of his actions.

It's doubtful he'd be in the lead of angels. He'd be more likely to lead a legion of demons not angels. With Konn in the lead no angel would come after me. Angels were all around protecting me from dangers Konn surrounded me with in his quest to consume me. Then in another brief conversation months later he denied saying anything remotely close to what he said. His testimony concerning his friend ended up making me feel more distressed. I knew I shouldn't have called. All I did in my pursuit to let him know I did exist and was aware he went directly to buy indecency was to make his day and allow him to take another piece of me. I felt there was unfinished business between us. There were some things I needed to tell him I never had a chance to say. I want to ask how he could go to the extremes he went to obliterate me with anger and vengefulness. Konn leaving to fraternize with prostitutes was something I couldn't come to terms with.

I want to let him know he continually took all my rights as a human being away. I had the same right to feel hurt as he did, to feel pain and have feelings and the same right to have an opinion and make mistakes just as he did.

I also wanted his input on a few things to see where he was coming from. I want to walk away and not feel guilt and remorse over the things I said. It was essential for me to convey I was sorry for the times I hurt him. I want to repent of my sins and mistakes and follow the sign that says, "What would Jesus do." I was accountable for my words and had a desire to do what I believe is right in the sight of God. It was in my heart to ask his forgiveness no matter what he did. I believe Jesus doesn't want his followers and God's children walked on and abused but there is a way Christians should handle things with out acting like the person that offends us and sometimes I felt I acted like that and I want to lay it all down. I let him know I didn't exonerate any of his behavior I was just taking responsibility for mine.

As it turned out it wasn't the last time we talked or the last hurt I encountered dealing with Konn in the next year. He called the day of the funeral and said if I want to go to the funeral with him he'd pick me up. I told him no I didn't think It's a good idea to come near my home or for me to go anywhere with him. He can offer my condolences. He asked if I want to drive to the funeral and he'd sit with me. I said no it was best if I didn't go. Since he called to ask me to the funeral I called a few days later to ask how the funeral went and how he was holding up. The conversation went back to nude dancers. He went to the police department and signed a complaint saying I harassed him on the phone. The police called and told me if I call him again they will come to my home to arrest me. So I didn't call him. I knew only to well he will do whatever he can to cause problems.

Going to the police because I said something he didn't like was Konn's special brand of revenge. He will never get over being incensed with anger and will never forgive or forget I put a protection order on him so he can't come near my home, my church or where ever I went. Several months later he called and wanted to resolve a 401 K settlement. I wanted to know about the adventures he had without me and I said something that bugged him. He threatened to call the police. Dealing with Konn meant dealing with police too. I hung and left him alone and didn't call back. Shortly afterwards a friend of Konn's came to my home one evening to tell me Konn is going to be arrested for writing a bad $500 check. I told him it wasn't my problem. Konn signed a complaint against me and it was his problem I wasn't speaking to him.

Out of the blue Konn called one evening and said his unemployment ran out, he'd been job hunting and was depressed. He asked me to meet him. I said no and hung up the phone. He called back weeping and cajoling saying he needed my help. I said I don't think it's a good idea for us to see one another. He kept coaxing. Deep down I was curious as to why he called me and against all my better judgment I went to meet him. He proceeded to tell me he put his application in seven different places and he's very discouraged and needs me to build him up and encourage him. Why would you call me? You hate me and signed a complaint against me for saying something you didn't like. How do I know you won't do that again? Will you go to the police department and take my name off their records? He said yes but spaced it off every time I inquired if he reversed the charge.

I knew I didn't have to help him. I shouldn't have helped him but I couldn't help myself. I loved him regardless of who he really is and what he represents. I didn't divorce him in my heart. I never gave up feeling he is still a part of me, still my husband. I felt trapped between the lunacies of falling in the same unreal world Konn resides in and living in the honesty and realism I wanted and tried to reside in.

I knew he was in deep doo doo. Along with the person holding a bum $500 check threatening him with jail he wrote several bad checks to his landlord. Konn's way of confronting his new dilemma is to avoid his landlord and the dude that's ready to throw him in jail. Avoiding his landlord he didn't go in the house until he was sure his landlord was asleep and he got up at the crack of dawn before his landlord was awake and hid in the parks all day long. Occasionally he parked his car a few blocks from where he lives and walked home. Sometimes he slept in his car in front of the landlord's house until his landlord left for work at five am then Konn went inside. The weirdness connected to his predicament is not the fact he's hiding from several people he owes money too. It's the way he deviously persists to act arrogant and superior, nonchalant, laughing and doing things like he doesn't have a care in the world. It doesn't seem to bother him if something is amiss. He always found a way to get around every problem he gave himself and came out smelling like a rose.

Many times he used me to lead his parade. He just gets lost in what ever he's doing and whomever he's doing it with. His life revolves in the same kind of circle of events that could have been avoided to begin with. Konn discerned he could count on me to feel sorry for him and I'd assist him regardless of all he did. He's cognizant of the fact I love him and I'm a

Christian first and foremost and sincere about serving God. He is aware I have a kind heart and a forgiving nature. He knew all the falsehoods he tells denying I helped him otherwise I'd be the last person he would call. He seen me help hungry strangers on the street. My ex husband had no doubt it would melt my heart to know he was hungry and had no money to buy groceries. I put everything aside and once again tolerated Konn exploiting me. I loaned him money to pay the $500 check. I fed him and gave him money for food and miscellaneous things he needed and to buy gas so he can continue to look for a job. He started to call several times through the day and every night he called to say good night. He kept saying he loves me every time he called or seen me. I bought the items he needed to groom properly and look nice to find a job. Sometimes we ate supper together and went to a movie but I was never with him for long periods of time.

I never allowed him to drive down my street. I let him think the protection order was still in effect. I met him away from my home and kept it from my children and friends. I learned not to tell anyone my business for they seemed to think that meant I was involving them and it gave them the right to say or do whatever they wanted to horn in on my decisions. I didn't want anyone's advice or to interfere in anything I did any more whether it was with Konn or whoever. I was sixty years old right or wrong I was going to make up my own mind and mistakes. No one was going to control me another time. I was always so easily swayed.

I knew better than to trust Konn and his reason for calling. He acted thankful for what I was doing to help and as if he truly missed me. I really did miss him and was lonely the entire time we were apart. I began to look forward to his calls and seeing him again. As yet I didn't take down the wall I put up trying to protect myself from further hurt. Never the less In spite of this when he plays the smooth nice guy I start to feel the hold he always had on me tighten. I told him not to even think of touching my hand after all the strippers he touched. He didn't care he was happy to comply.

Here I go again. I encouraged Konn both in words and finances trying to bolster his confidence after not having a job for the last seven months. I told him he'd find a job he is very talented in his area of expertise as a programmer. I convinced him to negotiate a high wage using what he earned on the last job. He wasn't having much success finding a job at first. He had several interviews but they didn't hire him. One interview looked hopeful and I'm sure he'd have taken it for much less money he was so desperate but they didn't hire him. He had a second interview with the same firm which involved having lunch with people he'd be working with to see how they felt toward getting along working with Konn but they voted against hiring him. This was a low blow. He thought having two interviews meant he had the job. He lost his momentum about a month.

I'd been helping him five months when he finally hit pay dirt and landed another high paying job starting at $65,000 a year with a raise every year and better benefits than the last job he had. The minute he got the job I told him okay I was backing off now. He had an income and didn't need me to fill the gap. He asked me not to back off he wanted me in his life again.

He said he is committed to me. If you were not committed in marriage how can you be committed now? He said the famous last words trust me I'm not seeing anyone else you're the only one I want to see. Didn't dawn on me yet going to see him meant I had let the wall down.

When he got the 401 k money refund he paid back the $500 on the check I paid that kept him out of jail. When he got his first paycheck he gave me $300 toward money I spent helping him survive five months. He owed much more than $300. But seemed to be making the effort to pay it back. At first he shared a few things about his new job. He had to put me on his health insurance for six months as part of the divorce settlement. We continued to communicate and see one another. At this time I'm thinking we can at least have peace between us and be friends and friendly toward one another. I didn't buy all he was selling but I gave him the benefit of the doubt and said okay we shall see if you're committed.

One week after he started the job and received his first check he went right back to the strip club and Toriann spending every dime he earned on strippers once more. He didn't have anything to spend on them the seven months he was unemployed and had to make up for lost time. I didn't know at the same time he went back to the club he started dating another stripper. I told him I knew where he went the night he said he had to work late and what I thought of his commitment. Once again the rehabilitated connivers violent temper manifested with out warning and he threatened to call the police if I contact him again. I ignored his threats. He pulled me back into his life and I'll back off when I'm good and ready. I still want to communicate and would like us to have peace and a friendly attitude toward one another since our lives were entwined in some unfinished business. Like paying me back the money I spent helping him survive. We communicated awhile longer and he continued to ask to see me and loan him money every other week.

Eventually I had to back away for good. I wasn't strong enough to with stand Konn's warped sense of values or sadistic cruelty after he landed a job. I couldn't deal with the foul evil mouth and behavior in marriage and his harsh put downs and swearing were worse than before because now he acts exactly like the people he hangs around with in strip joints. Par to course he kept his true self in wraps the five months he needed me to bail him out. That was the part of our relationship that was mystifying. I couldn't grasp anyone being so ungrateful and selfish. I still didn't know how to separate the shock that went with things he can do and say and have no feelings toward his actions. No regrets or regards to the fact I'm a human being that bleeds, hurts, feels and I'm affected by the way I am treated too. During the time he needs my help he remains fairly nice and when he no longer needs anything more his actions are totally opposite. One thing I didn't need to wonder about anymore was how he had the balls to say I didn't do anything to help him, he did it on his own and I was never there for him. That kind of attitude and behavior comes from having no scruples, no conscience, no honor or decency. After our divorce I went to aid him with my eyes wide open. But the fact I'm wise to his behavior made no difference in the shocking out come of all that happened after I rescued him and during the termination to end the circle of abuse once and for all.

Every time I gave Konn assistance to get back on his feet and he no longer needs me he proceeds to eradicate me in the identical uncaring nasty hateful manner. It doesn't matter how much I did to bail him out of his dilemmas and show him I care about his welfare he turns on me. The feedback after bailing him out is once more unbelievable. In spite of everything it's still hard to believe or comprehend he is capable of enacting the same ingratitude. Konn is the first and only person I ever met that is a real genuine selfish ingrate. Being around Konn's mannerisms I feel he appears to have narcissism tendencies both in the way he treated himself and me. Using Webster's new American dictionary the definition of Narcissism… [Beautiful youth of Greek mythology that fell in love with his own image]… 1: undue dwelling on one's own self or attainments 2: love of or sexual desire for one's own body, selfish and self centered.

In addition to the dictionaries definition I'm adding cold hearted, atrocious and merciless.

But in the meantime I ignored what he's up to and just accept having friendly relations. After he secured the job Konn continues to ask me to help him out of several other jams he wove himself into and every other week asks to loan money to make it to the next pay period. I continued to assist him till the villain crossed the line of my tolerance.

I figured calling and asking my help was involving me in his life once more and saying the word commitment up to a certain point gave me the right to know what is occurring in his life while I'm lending a hand. He made his business my business all over again so I decided to find out what is going on with him and us again. I fell in the same trap but the bait was worse than before it stressed me out so bad it triggered diabetes. Sometimes I hit the nail on the head knowing some of his objectives. But shortly after helping him stay out of jail and carry on until he found a job I couldn't comprehend why he chose to live in his car. He earns $5,000 a month and could rent a nice apartment. He had plenty to live on after alimony was deducted directly from his check. Having to pay $1,500 a month in alimony payments didn't leave him with as much to spend on strippers as he spent on them a year ago and probably hurts his impetuous beg spender image. But he still had quite a bit to live on. I made him a budget showed he would have $ 600 a month to blow above his living expenses.

My decision to help Konn wasn't purely because I felt sorry for him it was to help myself too. If he wasn't working I couldn't collect alimony. I wouldn't have much to live on either. Although I'll only receive it a few years I'm the first person to hold him responsible and followed through with collecting. I had no doubt with Konn's experience and my financial assistance and encouragement he'd land a high paying job. Being on friendly terms with Konn gave me access to know where he'd eventually land a job and save me money I'd have to use to hire someone to find where he'd eventually end up working.

I made certain my attorney worded the divorce decree to say if I'm awarded finances they be taken directly out of his paycheck and sent straight to the clerk of the district court when he got a job. Because of the time he purposely didn't seek a job for ten years after his last divorce so he doesn't have to pay his first wife or the IRS. When his first wife divorced him Konn didn't have money to put in g-strings and didn't have a prostitute in the background waiting for him to ditch his wife.

Along with owing his ex-wife, the IRS, the State revenue and three credit card debts the sum total of over $200,000. If he had a job at the time he divorced his first wife he still wouldn't have a dime. That's where I came in after the heat cooled down I became the victim he misused to get his life together and assist him in paying half the debts he owed sixteen years before me. It's still on the court records he owes his wife $40.000. She didn't want to deal with Konn so she let him off the hook and hasn't pursued collecting money he owes her. His mother's last words also impacted my decision to help Konn once more. Her voice was barely a whisper when she asked what is going to become of my Konnie when I'm gone? I said don't worry I'm here I'll take care of him. I felt a twinge of guilt saying I'd be there for him and I wasn't.

I didn't exactly understand why she worried about Konn's well being without her around to keep and eye on him. He was able to make enormous wages giving him more than enough to subsist. I thought of how careful he was about the money he spent when we were together. Like everything in our relationship he taught me what his mother meant by the last words she spoke in my presence before she died. Everything happened so fast after she passed away with Konn becoming incorrigible and uncontrollable I couldn't follow through with words I used to comfort her of watching over and taking care of her son. Of all the stranger than strange behavior he displayed as the curtain fully lifted on another obscurity. It turns out Konn went to the extreme of doing without the barest necessities to survive and lived in his car four months during the winter season simply to have more money to give to women he derives satisfaction from.

I suspected he was up to something inane when I seen his car loaded down with his clothes and computer. It didn't take long to find out why he was carting his possessions around in the back seat of his car. The truth came out when his landlord called and asked if I knew where Konn was. He hadn't seen Konn in weeks and he owed the landlord around $1.000 in back rent payments. He said Konn left most of his things in a mess and he had to clean it up and store his things. He also said he was revolted at the disturbing sex magazines he found cleaning Konn's room and there were nude pictures hanging all over the wall.

Konn didn't care about possessions he left most of the things he acquired and never returned to pick any of them back up. Except one night three weeks after he moved out he went back to pick up his computer without telling his landlord. His landlord called and told me he changed locks after Konn craftily entered his home to get the computer when no one was there.

I finally approached Konn and ask him where he is staying. He said he slept in his car in a parking area by a service station and the parking lot where he's employed. He said he took showers in a truck stop and in the fitness center located in the building he works in. Like most of his behavior it is hard to comprehend living in a car in the dead of winter when he has money to come in from the cold. Living in his car made as much sense as everything else he did in my presence it was like everything connected to his reasoning for doing the things he does and it all makes perfect sense to him.

Every time his behavior seemed like it couldn't become more demented he'd do something to prove me wrong. The manner of his endurance was more than just living like a street person. For reasons known only to Konn he has his rationale on the way he chooses to survive and conduct his behavior. After I knew for certain he gave up a room that cost him only $300 a month is when I came to the conclusion landing another great job and suddenly moving out of his room that is warm in the winter, cool in the summer with access to the entire house and a laundry room could mean only one thing. Moving abruptly had to do with women and sex addiction that controlled all his decisions and the major issue that came between us.

It was nothing new for Konn to live in his car. I remembered when he slept in his car just down the street when we dated. I empathized with him then for he was between a rock and a hard place earning no money and mom changed the locks and he had no place to go.

Living in his car now made no sense what so ever earning $70,000 a year, bonuses and raises. The firm paid health and life insurance, matched dollar amounts in a 401 k savings plan and he resorted to living in his car like a bum. A natural reaction for most people seeing him in the dirty wrinkled clothing he wore and unkempt hair is to feel sorry for him and hand him a buck for a cup of coffee. This bit of madness just to live closer to stripper friends and have more money to spend on them. Moving out of his room to live in his car he doesn't have to pay rent, buys very little clothing or anything else he needs, not paying bills gave him more money to feed his addiction. It seems to be Konn's definition of a normal decent mode of continued existence. It made sense to him within the realm of purpose for living this way.

Besides staying in his car he hung out in the building he is employed. During this time he was still acting halfway nice. He e-mailed me through out the cold winter nights. He said when the cold got to him he just stayed in the building and slept with his head on his desk. Even though we're divorced it hurt me to see Konn on the streets running around in the cold with no coat wearing only a short sleeve T-shirt. I bought him a coat; some warm clothes and gave him blankets. Konn knew me well and utilized his familiarity for all it was worth. He surmised if I knew he lived in his car again it would get to me and it did. I couldn't shake the feeling I was still somehow responsible for him. In the evening when I was warmly tucked in bed I wept at the thought of him sleeping in the cold car and possibly freezing to death. He said he kept warm through the night by running the car heater off and on and lighting candles in a coffee can.

I couldn't imagine what it would be like to sleep in the cold elements of the weather and no place to go except the security of the building he worked in when it was below zero. It was mind boggling to know how he survived. I persisted to ask him to get a room somewhere.

Konn had a knack of having me be the only one who knew things he did and the way he subsists. After a few months of knowing he slept in his car in zero weather I didn't want to be the only one to know he could freeze to death so I told his friend. We were having a harsh unrelenting cold winter. I didn't like feeling responsible for dealing with his inadequacy to survive in a somewhat normal way. It truly bothered me he seemed happy and content with himself and preferred living the way he was over marriage with me. He once told me he was happier living in his car than he was with me. Here I was worried about Konn, acting with my heart instead of my mind.

If I were smart I'd have looked at the fact that he is no dummy in choices he makes. He knows how to get by even when he lives in his car. He resided in his car several other times long before we met. How dumb is it not to pay expenses most everyone has to pay to be comfortable. I am familiar with the way he loves being on the run and driving here and there. He's always been like the roadrunner. We'd drive a hundred miles to have supper. It was nothing for Konn to go a hundred miles every day to see Toriann. He never minded driving 2,000 miles in a day driving back and forth on a job out of town.

He evidently got by with sleeping under a pile of blankets. The weather never seemed to bother Konn either. He took me places in 20 below wind chill. I tagged right along every step of the way freezing my buns off while he had his coat open no gloves or boots. One evening I recalled him taking me to a basketball game when it was 30 below wind chill as we pulled into the parking lot I said Konn it doesn't look like there's a game tonight. He didn't accept the empty parking lot meant there was no game. He took my hand and we walked about a block to the entrance of the auditorium and sure enough the game was cancelled because of the cold. Funny thing is when we dated and were first married up until the time he started screaming in the car at me we did many things together and nothing seemed to matter when I was with Konn. I could walk with him in the cold and it was okay but without him when it's cold out I don't poke my nose outside. There were many things

238

I felt I could do with Konn I don't feel capable of doing alone. I missed that part of Konn.

His motives don't add up to the naked eye but it adds up to him he could make 2+3=4. The way he lives may sound inane to everyone else but it isn't to Konn he invents his ways.

After living in his car four months he rented a motel room around Christmas time. His living conditions can change faster than a speeding bullet and he can exit in any given moment. I also stumbled across the reason he needs to loan money every other week. Along with purchasing strippers, sharing his finances with Toriann he's giving money to another girl friend. According to Konn his new friend ended up conning him out of his whole check one week and he had nothing to live on for two weeks. When that occurred Konn told me he lost his entire check shopping at the mall and didn't know what he was going to do. Several months later I picked up a piece of paper in the car with a note from Janette that said I'll be by early in the morning for $500 I am owed less $350 already paid her. I knew the piece of paper was torn from a tablet in a binder I bought him so she had to be in his room to have access to it. It blew me away to think he borrowed money from me and paid her to sleep with him.

She was a foreign girl so her wording was a little different but there was no mistaking he owed her for something. I asked him who Janette was and what he paid her $500 for? He said Toriann introduced them after he got the job and he didn't owe her she owed him.

Konn told me he slapped a lawsuit on Janette because she borrowed money and wouldn't pay him back. I just assumed she rolled him. He didn't have a checking account any more and after he cashed his paycheck every two weeks he carried $1,200 or more around in cash. I doubt if even Konn would loan her every dime he had and end up with nothing to live on. I filed this bit of loony tunes in the file cabinet as another mystery.

I was the one that lost out. I ended up loaning Konn $350 to survive on in the two weeks he had no money and he paid me back $100. I'm such a dufuss. I'm not patting myself on the back but I was always so kind to Konn. I made lasagna and sweet rolls to take to work when the employees contributed to a potluck lunch. I'd meet him somewhere and take the food to him the night before so he'd have it ready to take to work the next morning.

On his birthday I sent a huge sheet cake and flowers via one of the bigger grocery stores with a florist shop that handled taking both the cake and flowers to the building he worked in so he can share with his co-workers. I was right there Johnny on the spot again. I knew we could never reconcile or ever be romantically involved not because of him but because of me. It bothered me for I was still very much in love with him and in my heart I wanted him to hold me and kiss me. But I knew I'd never let him touch me after all the prostitutes he had his hands on nor would I succumb to his abuse again.

Not being married I could just walk away from him whenever I want and he couldn't do a thing about it and at this point in our new friendship I walked away plenty of times. After a few days we'd start speaking again.

He kept up the facade of leading me to believe he wants to spend time with me. I just want us to be friends so I ignored the deceptions. It was no longer my problem. I had my own ulterior motive for leading him on at times too. Since the dancers don't use their real names I wanted to know the strippers real name he's enthralled with and where she lived and uncover if she is the one he cheated with during our marriage.

It always immensely disturbed him if I found out the truth of his dishonesty. He thought I was a dupe and he's more superior and clever than anyone he encounters. I found out plenty through Konn's carelessness, on the computer and from Toriann's husband. Konn told me he went to the strip bar and the church singles group because he was lonely and needed someone to talk to. I asked how could he have been lonely with the harem he acquired shortly after leaving. He was having more sex in the strip club than Heinz had pickles.

I discovered Toriann's real name on a piece of paper in his car and found her street address and the town she lives in on the computer. One night when Konn asked me to meet him I e mailed back and said here's the name and address of someone you might like to take out instead of me. I knew all along he was seeing her all the time anyway.

It blew his mind I knew her real name. He e mailed back he was going to the town she lives and tell the police I'd harm her and was a threat to her well being. I e mailed him and said go ahead I don't care. I saved your butt from jail and your thanks are threats of jail for me. There is no doubt your aware I'm not a threat to anyone or anything except your deceptions. The only threat you fear is I'll tell her truth to the lies you've told her and the horror dramas you put me in. He was angry I learned her real identity and he didn't contact me for three weeks. He told me he admired his stripper friend because she loved her husband and did anything he wanted her to do just to please him and it is her husband (Lance's) fault she works as a dancer. He makes her strip her clothes off and entice men into a room for money. I learned from Konn that her husband Lance tends bar in the same place his wife prostitutes.

So not only does Toriann have a husband of her own she has my husband too. Konn said he visits their home to see her husband because Lance is his friend too. I think he believes saying she has a husband made everything they did together okay and this is a typical leave it to beaver family.

No matter how you cut it Konn is involved with Lances wife. He wins the entire families confidence first of all pretending to be someone other than the real Konn Rodent, buys the family things and take them places so he can lust after another man's wife behind the guise of Mr. Wonderful. I don't know about these kinds of relationships. All of it sounds pretty bizarre.

The mystery man's ultimate definition of love, marriage, husband, wife, commitment, responsibility, accountability, passion and sex are distorted beyond belief or beyond any planet in the solar systems belief. The word marriage meant nothing in Konn's vocabulary. Why would he care if the woman he wanted was married for goodness sake he didn't care if he was married?

Not only did I put myself in the position to learn much more by communicating with him. I played detective to find out all I could about Konn's rendezvous. I couldn't help myself I had to know. I should get a booby prize or something for seeing him after the divorce let alone rescuing him. I was better off not knowing.

I first contacted Konn to say hey; I'm not dead and buried I'm alive and on the planet earth. There are still some things I felt I needed to get off my chest that he still didn't give me a chance to say. I want to see if I can make heads of tails of what exactly was between us, what his reasoning is for calling me for help and why he bothered to say he's committed again.

I admit after I rescued him I purposely egged him on and messed with him sometimes. Every time I resigned to back off for good I contacted him again. Sometimes weeks went by but eventually I'd e-mail him and we'd be right back to talking and seeing one another. Before he got the job and for a while after wards we talked several times a day and saw one another frequently. As the months rolled by we saw each other less and less. We didn't e-mail or call very often and then we didn't contact one another at all.

I printed some of the e-mail he sent me from the start of our friendship. He used to write several times a day and always said I love you and asked to see me. He even took me to the firm's picnic. He asked me to the Christmas party too. I thought it sounded like fun and I was going to go. I backed out several days before. It bothered me he was starting to depend on me and wants to drive my car. The party was out of town and I was leery of going to far with him. I always made sure I met him in public and stayed close to home. Konn tried to force me to go to the party but it didn't work. He e-mailed I had to go and he'd be waiting for me. He waited an hour and a half in the place we usually met. I never showed up.

In addition I saved a few e-mails he sent during the end of communicating with him. He wanted to push me out of his life in the same manner he used before using gutter language. He said you f---ing bitch, I hate you I really mean it I hate you and his renowned last words burn in hell. The things I want from Konn when I rescued him were totally different from what he wanted. I just want our battles to end on a gracious basis. Instead it went into the war of all our wars and I lost all the battles again. We ended up on a worse note than we ever did.

We didn't necessarily have to see one another or converse all the time just respect where each other was coming from and part in peace. It doesn't matter who was right or wrong anymore. I didn't care if he admitted he is a sex addict and loved porno more than his wife that is between him and God now.

There was one thing I wanted from Konn. It was still significant he accept behavior he was responsible for. He didn't have to apologize. I didn't want him to eat crow. I merely would like him to acknowledge there were things he did that harmed and wounded my heart and spirit. It felt like I couldn't put anything to rest until he sincerely recognized the part he played in all the problems, hurt and pain he indeed inflicted. He left me dangling and I desired to lay things down so I don't have to carry all the pain. Just as he wouldn't give me a chance to have a happy marriage with a husband that should have loved me he will never give me a chance to wipe the slate clean either. I knew I couldn't do a thing about the hurt I felt when he told his friends in the strip club and everyone else including our mutual friends the same embarrassing words he screamed before he left. Like I was the abuser and forced him to have sex when he didn't want to because I didn't know it takes two consenting people to have sex. I was sexually perverted. I didn't want to believe Konn could be that merciless and abominable putting his perversion on me too. In contrast today I believe he is capable of anything and everything.

The words he used to describe my demeanor to everyone were degrading, damaging and reeked of utmost treachery. It was one thing to yell perverse words to me but where he got the mendacity to come up with the grossly malformed, improper and exaggerated stories to condone sexual abuse he displayed is way beyond my perception. In contrast today I don't have to understand the ramblings of a madman.

He made fun and light of every issue and personal habit a married couple can have between them. He took everything from me. I know the tales are twisted mendacity but nonetheless it had an influence on me after all the uncanny mannerisms he displayed he'd go that far to exonerate him self. The wickedly fictitious analogy of me confirmed to me that he has no conscience or remorse. I heard an interesting theory on a Fox news story March 12, 1999 concerning people they say were born with no conscience because it didn't develop in their brain. If someone is born without a conscience they will have no feelings for people they hurt, harm, deceive, and destroy.

They can walk away and go on with their life. They consider themselves blameless as if they never did anything wrong and will constantly accuse others for their conduct. They feel justified in all they do and in things they have done. My theory on the subject is to have no conscience, is to have no heart. I don't think Konn was born with no conscience I feel he became that way with his own self-importance.

The falsehoods he utters demonstrate not one thing about me meant anything to the man that claimed to love me. It blew me away he wouldn't recognize or concede one nice thing toward how good I was to him and his family or confirm the way I rescued his butt so many times. I learned Konn doesn't just hate me it goes way beyond hate. I was about to witness how deep his resentment and detestation of me really is shortly after his girlfriend's husband filed for a divorce. Konn was going to have the woman meant for him no matter what he had to say or do to win Torianns hand. God help the person that gets in his way, which I did.

After rescuing Konn after our divorce I just wanted to crawl in a hole and die. The load I carried in the great weight of loving someone that has that much animosity toward me for endowing him with compassion and financial gain after the malicious divorce was too much to carry around. I was despondent. I didn't watch TV over a year and a half. My friends sent e-mail to keep me up on the news. He couldn't just walk off with strippers he had to continually make me look like a bumble head and the bad guy. I have to believe one day it will catch up to him and he will be caught up in the same position he put me in. By putting everything on me he justified all he did.

Whenever Konn denied ferocious barbaric measures he displayed he was taking away from all he did, from all the heartache I suffered and tears I shed over the lunatic's deeds to hide pornographic sex related incidents he was unquestionably guilty of participating in. He can act like he's innocent as if nothing happened but he can't take away from the fact he isn't innocent and it did happen. He can't deny coming into my home to lie, steal, kill, cheat and destroy me physically, mentally and spiritually in his thrust to advocate destroying what I stood for and who I am. I couldn't help being in emotional turmoil. It was mind boggling he could act like he didn't do a thing to start hostilities between us. He has no idea I have black and white evidence of the embarrassing, shameful, reprehensible existence he imposed on me to exist in. I found a copy of a letter scrunched up in his car whether it was right or wrong I made a copy of it. Since he took the liberty of inviting me back into his life and attempted to undertake the old psyche games I was wise too; I utilized his games to find out all I could about the secrecy of the space invader Konn. I kept the letter and told him that I had it and read it. He didn't seem to care. He acted proud of all his conquests. Finding letters in his car reminded me of the way Konn once made fifty copies or more of a note a waitress wrote him to give to me claiming Konn didn't flirt with her. They were scattered all over the car seats and floorboards. I don't know his reasoning for making so many copies or what goes on in his own little world.

Not only was I weary of the fairytales. I was fed up with him saying I didn't have proof. In the time I was helping him I gathered as much confirmation on his personal sex addiction as I could. One day Konn told me he had to work late and couldn't come to town to make a payment on the money I loaned him. The only time I seen him now was to collect the debt he owes. If he didn't pay me on the day he receives a check he'd space off another two weeks, a month etc. I asked my detective friend Heige if he'd drive me to the town Toriann lived in. I knew he wasn't coming to town to pay me because he is with her.

We spotted him and Toriann by a shopping area. I watched them walk in the store and went over to the sale areas out doors and waited for them to come back out. They didn't see me standing by the sale items and passed right by me on their way back to his car. I said hey Konn and they both stopped. She backed off a little ways like she was afraid of me. I said fancy meeting you here do you have $300 to put on the tab you owe. He was halfway congenial for he can't be snotty and blow his cover in front of Toriann. He dug out his billfold with the wad of bills in plain sight and handed me $300. I said thank you and started to walk away and she walked back over by Konn. I turned around and walked toward them and said aren't you going to introduce me to your friend. He introduced us and I was very sweet. She said so your Konn's ex wife. I said yes I am the wife that loved her husband and he left to be with you. Konn trying not to show anger as he remarked you closed the door on me. I'm not going to argue with you in front of Toriann. I ignored him and talked to her a few more minutes. I asked how she liked riding around in Konn's new car I picked out and loaned him money to pay for it so he'd have transportation to get to work. She said she liked it fine. I told her nice to finally meet you, turned around and walked back by the sale items. As they walked side-by-side to their car she didn't look too happy and his face was beet red he was so livid. Konn opened the door for her, walked over and got in his side and they drove away.

Heige was waiting for me in his van. The van had the kind of windows you can see out but no one can see in. He was parked right next to the spot I stopped Konn and Toriann. When I got in the van Heige said that was the coolest confrontation he ever seen and thought it was a Kodak moment so he videotaped me confronting Konn in front of his girlfriend. We followed them to her trailer house. Konn went inside her home and she sat on her front porch. When he came out he didn't stop to talk to her he got in his car and left. We followed him the fifty miles back to our hometown. He called later in the evening to cuss me out and I merely hung up on him.

Heige asked me why in the heck did I buy him a car? Konn started involving me in his transportation problem. The car I bought him a few years ago had 19, 000 miles and he put 200,000 on it and it broke down. He doesn't maintain his car. He simply drives it until it breaks down. He was riding to work with a friend but every now and then when his friend couldn't drive Konn to work he'd call and ask me if I'd give him a ride. I always said no I'm not driving fifty miles to your job.

One day Konn called and told me his friend was going on vacation for a few days and will I drive him to work at 3 am and hang out in the building until he's off work. I can't drive you or be gone that long my children will worry and I'm not going to lie to them. Konn asked me to call the bus station and inquire the cost and time. I called him back and said it's twelve dollars the bus leaves at midnight. He replied he'd have to take a cab to the building he works at and that's expensive would I take him to work. I said no. He called the next day and said it cost $60.00 to take a bus and a cab will I drive him to work the next morning. I told him no. The next day he called from his job asking if he came to town will I drive him back to work at midnight? He won't accept no and was putting it on me to figure out his life once more by asking me to solve his transportation problem. I told him to go to his relatives in the town he works in and spend those few hours with them. The next day your friend will be back from vacation and you'll be able to ride with him again. After he had a ride to work with his friend again I didn't see him around three months. We weren't really getting along very well.

Then one day he called and said he'd like to have lunch with me and I said okay. He took a bus to a restaurant and I met him there. He said his friend was getting laid off and he needed transportation. He can't get a hold of any money to buy a car and will I use my credit card to rent one for him. Once again making his business my business and once again I'm still trying to figure out his problems for him. I didn't want to be responsible for renting him a car in my name with my credit card. I ended up telling him about a red 88 blazer I seen a couple months ago that my mechanic was trying to sell. It had been well maintained and in excellent shape. I already talked him down to $3,000 the day I looked at it. I asked Konn if I took out a loan to buy the car would he faithfully make payments to me twice a month.

Then I asked if I do this favor will he take care of having the car insured the same day I purchase the vehicle and clear up a driving suspension on his license so he can drive legally? He was shocked I knew about the ticket he received for no proof of car insurance and had been driving over five months on a suspended license. He didn't care if I use my credit card to rent him a car to drive on a suspended license. He will take me down with him every chance he can. That is only one reason I had to check up on him all the time and try to stay one step ahead. Nothing bugged him more than my knowing something he was trying to hide from me. Konn agreed to the terms. The next week I went to the mechanics and bought the car. I had him put the title in just Konn's name and put only my name on the sales receipt so I have proof of purchase in case he tries to get out of paying me.

I took care of everything just like that. Konn had his friend drop him off at the restaurant. I gave him two sets of keys and had him sign a piece of paper I wrote agreeing to the terms to pay the Blazer In full even if it fails mechanically or is wrecked. His friend looked the car all over and said it was a great buy. There was no rust and it looked like new inside and out. It was red with a white design on each side. Konn's friend said he'd have to take me with him if he purchases a car because of the good deal I made. I was always pretty good when it came to wheeling and dealing. I knew it was one reason Konn turned to me about purchasing a car. I could see Konn was impressed with the vehicle. His eyes lit up like a Christmas tree when he seen it but he was acting like acquiring the blazer was no big deal, as if I owed it to him to purchase a car for him.

He didn't say thank you or I appreciate the extra mile you went to find me such a nice car. He didn't say a word. So I asked how do you like the Blazer Konn? He said it was fine and acted like he was in a hurry. Konn I haven't driven it let's see how it drives. He abruptly said why where do you want to go I said nowhere in particular just around a few blocks to see how it feels and maybe stop for a cup of coffee. I want to talk about taking care of the license suspension. I know you haven't done that yet. I loaned him a hundred dollars so he can go to the courthouse in the morning and pay the fine so he can drive legally. He agreed to pay me the money in four days when he received his check along with a car payment.

I wasn't thinking of Konn when I first seen the blazer. I looked at it and inquired because I liked it and thought of purchasing it for myself it had a lot of room in it. I had a small convertible that didn't have much room. I thought for the money it would make a nice car to take on trips. The day I bought the blazer I thought why are you doing this for Konn buy the car and keep it yourself. I thought about him not having transportation to get to work and how much he'd love to have a car with all that room. Crazy as it sounds I didn't realize until I purchased the car I still want his acceptance in something. I want him to see helping him have decent transportation was an act of kindness and maybe he'd accept me just as a kind-hearted person there for him when he needed me or for who I am as a Christian that loved him regardless of his cruelty. I sincerely longed for Konn to see me as the loving person I truly am even though I knew we could never be involved or even remotely close. Accepting him not as my husband but just as a person and just as a friend was a big accomplishment.

I struggled within knowing he's with women other than me as his wife. I didn't have any illusions about Konn using the car simply as transportation to work. I knew he'd take his girlfriends cruising and on dates in it. It was none of my affair anymore. It was only my business when I helped him find a job and he said the word committed. I knew he wasn't but I held him accountable for a couple things a short while. Konn drove off in his new car and that was the end of any bit of civility he might have had in him and the end of our so-called peaceful atmosphere and friendship. I realized being his friend only meant being there when he needs something same as when I was his wife. The payment I collected while he's escorting Toriann is money he owed for the suspended ticket and the first car payment. It ticked me off he tried to space off the first payment. Heige wanted me to yank the car back. I kept a set of keys and he was more than willing to go after it. I told him no it probably has cooties now. Konn can have the car.

I don't want the Blazer after seeing him and her driving around together. He may think he got by with being a smart ass taking me to the cleaners again and that's okay. My reward is not here on earth it is in heaven. When I seen the two of them together I could see Konn's affection toward her. I had a hunch something was going on between them that wasn't happening between them four months before.Konn gave the clue when he stopped contacting me as often and was thankfully ungracious. When I see Konn switching trains in the middle of the track it's a sure sign he's making changes to the program and has something different up his sleeve.

That evening I called Toriann's husband at the strip club. We talked several times before. He was more than willing to tell me a few things. Lance seemed curious about me after Konn made me an odyssey. I asked him what was happening in his life?

He said he filed for a divorce because his wife accused him of cheating all the time. Lance filled me in on several things. I filled him in on a few things. Lance told me his wife wasn't the only woman Konn was with there were seven others he knew of. I said Lance that's old news I already know about ten strippers he went upstairs with. I saw a letter he wrote your wife Toriann explaining why he went to the private room with six other strippersincluding two sisters he mentions as being part of the family. Maybe I have led to much of a sheltered life and things that shock me are not shocking to others but here's the way the letter reads.

Chapter Eighteen

Konn's Parade of Strippers & Prostitutes

I'm undisputedly certain when Konn wrote a letter to Toriann he didn't deduce anyone would have access to the terminology he put on paper.

He began the letter by saying; there's something about me I need to tell you. I have never gone to a prostitute. And I have never had sex with a woman that I didn't think I loved. Since 1975, I have never had sex with a woman I didn't marry. In other words, in the last 25 years I have only had sex with 2 women and married both of them. I think that what Bill and Monica did was sex.

I don't think that what goes on upstairs is sex. But I'm not the kind who wants what goes on upstairs with someone who I don't think is special.

The first day I came in here you and I sat and talked quite a while. If all I saw in you was Toriann we never would have gone upstairs and I never would have seen you again. But I saw through (1) Toriann and I saw that very special person you are inside, and that's why I took you upstairs and that's why I kept coming back.

It's true I've taken others upstairs but it's always been because of you in one way or another.

The first time I met (2) Jolene she was after me to take her upstairs. I kept saying "no" she kept saying it'd be ok with Toriann. I'll ask her to make sure. "One time when I came back from the bathroom. She said, I talked to Toriann and she said it was alright." I didn't want to go up with her. At the time, I thought she was your sister and I didn't want your sister to dislike me, so I did it. That's the only reason.

You forced me into going up with (3) Danielle. The first time I met her, you were after me to take her upstairs. Again I thought she was your sister and I wanted her to like me, so I did.

Neither Jolene nor Danielle is women I would take upstairs on my own.

You asked me to take Lana upstairs too. In fact you ran over to (4) Lana and told her I would take her upstairs after I had told you I didn't want to.

When Lance's mother was in the hospital in South Dakota, I missed you and I came in looking for you a lot. I'd usually just look around, see you weren't here and leave.

(5) Wanda was real nice to me one day. She could see I was feeling kind of "down" and she came up to me and was really nice. She didn't ask for drinks, and wasn't dancing. She just sat and talked and tried to cheer me up.

After about an hour she asked me if I wanted to go upstairs. I figured I owed her that much, so I went up with her.

The other one I took upstairs is the one I feel guilty about. It was a night I had a lot of money in my pocket and I wanted to spend it on you but it seemed like you wanted everybody in the place to spend money on you except me.

You had a drink on my table, but wouldn't drink it. You kept saying, "I'll be right back." Then you'd disappear for an hour and I'd see you at someone else's table. Then you'd come back for a minute and I'd say, "Let's go upstairs" and you'd say as soon as I'm back and then disappear for another hour. And I'd see you at someone else's table again.

One time while you were at someone else's table, I went up to the bar to get a drink. (6) Jody came up behind me and started to rub my neck and back, and asked me to take her upstairs. I was mad at you for refusing to sit with me when I wanted to spend my money on you and I knew you saw Jody rubbing my neck and back.

So I went upstairs with her because I wanted to make you mad.

I'm sorry. I shouldn't have done that. Every night that Jody sees me in there and I'm not with you she tries to get me to take her upstairs again. I've always refused. Please don't ever tell me to go upstairs with someone else. I'd have to like them first before I would ever want to. And there's no one else there I like. Please don't tell me it's wrong for me to take you upstairs because we're friends. To me that's what makes it right.

I took it upon myself to read my husbands lovesick letter but all the same it irked me to be aware at the time my husband wrote the letter to another man's wife and while he's seeing her he's married to me and she's married to the bartender.

I told Konn I read the letter and it didn't seem to bother him. He was proud of his meanderings. He feels the girls want to go to a private room with him because he's irresistible. He said he wrote the letter but he didn't give it to Toriann. That's a toss up.

He didn't care if his words divulge he paid Toriann and five other strippers upstairs as he discloses and acknowledges his addiction to sex with prostitutes and visiting the strip club almost every night whether she is there or not. Although he had no idea anyone else would see the incriminating letter it could be used to blow the whistle on the strippers taking men to private rooms after enticing them with nudity and lap dances. My husband only wrote letters to me when we had discrepancies. I thought maybe they had a little tiff as he pitifully asks Toriann to go to the privileged room to do what they don't call sex. No matter what his definition of sex is, it's called sex no matter what position they're in.

Whenever Konn was seen in the strip club he was always with Toriann. First by detective Heige trailing him to the strip club ten days after we split up. Three months later a woman detective seen him carry a package into the club and give it to Toriann. Ten months later I seen Toriann take one of the men to the private room. A year and a half later, one-week after he started his new job Heige saw Konn with Toriann in the club. There was no mistaking his interest is mainly in Toriann.

A few other strippers I learned of that he took upstairs not mentioned in the letter were (7) Gerri (8) Petula (10) Heather (11) Janette and (12) Pamela. I didn't learn the name of the church lady he met in the Christian singles group he joined so I'll just call her unlucky number (13) from the list I discovered in his little black book of secrets.

Konn is 53 and couldn't handle taking care of one wife yet he's parading as many young naked women into the pleasure seeking room as he can. I think he must have been on Viagra in order to perform every hour on the hour after the famous speeches he made all the time on his inability to perform because he's impotent and needs Viagra. He does a wonderful imitation of a psychotic pathological liar. I don't know how many more nude dancers he actually took upstairs from that certain club. I don't have any inkling of how many more strippers he entertained from other places or if he did. According to cancelled checks he went into another strip club.

The letter was typical Konn reasoning and cop out pleas. Naming six of the strippers he was with while Toriann and he are involved with each other and saying he was with them indirectly because of her. Konn had to be a first-rate nice guy to spread himself and his money to as many of the underprivileged prostitutes as he can. There are usually 20 to 25 girls a night working in this certain club. He had his pick of the litter every few weeks with new strippers coming in and going out of the club all the time. It appears as if Toriann doesn't seem to care if he has a roving eye and body or how many women he's with or how many women she brings to him to engage in his warped addiction as long as he brings home the bacon. In her chosen profession she evidently didn't care how many men she is with either.

I never accepted the lifestyle leading to Konn's love of women that work in the occupation of stripper/prostitute. I'm assuming he's in his glory snagging the kind of woman he desired with the same morals he has. She really is the woman meant for Konn as he so graciously screamed I wasn't. I should congratulate him and send her a thank you card.

The whole extent of the letter was so defeating to the thoughts I entertained during the first few weeks I filed hopeful as a last ditch effort it would be a final wake up call and Konn would do what ever it took to seek help and we'd work things out someway some how.

As Konn's pica dillies unfolded one by one it was difficult to cope with all the emotions that hit me. Surprisingly after I read the words my husband wrote Toriann on how special he thinks she is the feeling that dramatically came over me was the pangs of jealousy.

Feeling resentful I didn't look at the girls working in the club in the realm of what they represent or what they do in their chosen occupation. I looked at the strippers as women he accepted and wanted and it made me jealous because he never accepted or wanted me. I looked at Toriann as competition and all I could think of was he never told me I was special nor did he ever say he was sorry about anything.

It was as if he gave her everything he should have given me. (I was his wife and I should have meant something to him.) The jealously I experienced was in the fact that without blinking an eye he is sexually involved with Toriann and other strippers, yet made a fiasco of our entire marriage and our sex life such as it was.

I felt envious in the hurt I endured when he said I didn't turn him on when he looked at me and yet he's turned on marching girls selling sex into the private room paying them to do God only knows what. I couldn't figure what his reasoning could have been for not showing up on the first court date we had scheduled so he could have been legally free of me much sooner. I don't know how in the world I could have felt covetousness over some thing so disgusting and grossly defective. But I was jealous and it bruised every inch of me. It was the first time I felt insultingly green-eyed of a woman in the flesh and as a whole. As his wife I was resentful of the awareness he lusted other women. I wasn't jealous of the women he fantasized I was upset by the immoral ways he indulged him self in a depraved manner and his mania to keep women's undies in his possession. I never got over the trauma of learning Konn played with female's dirty panties. After the harm he kicked off and instigated with the underwear I reacted in an ornery way. I bought a sexy lacy pair of silk panties and put them in his T-shirt drawer. I reacted and responded to his behavior. I didn't take the initiative to invent the conflicts nor did I start the consistent discrepancies. I basically followed the leader.

I honestly believed if Konn had done nothing to bring about a reaction to the disruptive declaration of disputes I would have had nothing to react or retaliate to or feel the need to show him his behavior was nasty. I left the undies in the drawer to see what he'd do about my declaration of saying; here pervert you want a pair of undies then have a pair of your wife's instead of the filthy panties you hid and only God knows who they belonged to when they end up being a surprise wedding gift for your new bride to find. He knew the message I was sending when I put the lace undies in his drawer. He avoided moving the panties. They stayed untouched in the same spot for months. Then one day he told me he knew why I put them in his drawer and he didn't think it was very nice to keep the undie incident alive. I thought okay let's move on and I removed them. But I never got over the shock and trauma of finding them to begin with.

I was actually envious of his feelings for Toriann because he screamed he didn't want to touch me and could touch her and other strippers and still hunting and chasing Toriann. It was the most horrible of times to recognize how pathetic I was to yearn for my husband and he didn't desire or accept me the entire time we were together. I was jealous he accepted prostitutes and didn't accept his new wife.

I had to leave the computer a while as tears gripped my heart reliving the fullness of all that happened and all the perversion that was more important in the desires my husband favored over me. I prayed for God to help me finish my story and I'm back at it. The expressions he wrote Toriann are mild compared to the last words he spoke to me declaring his undying love for her. The con job he pulled to wheedle a car out of me is the last con game he will ever be permitted to enact with Rosie Rodent. Filing the divorce was a wake up call all right but not for Konn. It was a wake up call to myself. I thought of his activates with prostitutes as an out right act of revenge toward me. After I read the letter definitely not meant for my eyes I remembered my words remaining firm in my loyalty and devotion to be by his side. Telling everyone close to me he's harmless, he doesn't mean anything, he has some good qualities, I love him, he's my husband, I intend to stand by him and make excuses for him all the time.

Chapter Nineteen

Tall Tales & Stress

The story Konn wrote Toriann in relation to marrying the only two women he had sex with represented his first ex wife and me. It was the same speech he gave me. The tale is as fabricated as everything he speaks but I fell for it too. I liked thinking his ex-wife and I was the only two women he had been with sexually in so many years.

At the time I believed him it was before I heard his definition of sex and the rest of his vocabulary and prior to some of the stories he told after we were married. Along with all the other garbage linked to his addictive travesty.

One of the stories he told was on women raping men. Konn said he knows it can happen he was raped. He said his best friends wife came to his apartment when her husband was out of town and raped him. I asked how could she rape him? You were alone when you let her in your apartment knowing her husband was out of town and you had the equipment. He said men can't help it when they are turned on it just happens they have no control over the way the equipment works. I believed him then but after I seen he didn't care if he slept with someone whether married or single I realized it was just one more fabricated tale.

I now believe he was responsible for enticing and seducing his best friends wife sexually. Konn said he felt guilty he had sex with his best friends wife so he told her husband. The couple ended up in divorce court. Seems who ever he's involved with ends up severing their marriage including his own.

Konn related other stories on women he was involved with but the story that stood out above some of the others was the tale he told me and didn't bother to tell his ex wife while they're still married. He said he escorted a woman co-worker to another state. I asked if they stayed in the same hotel and if he accompanied her places and he said yes. He didn't consider not telling his wife he was taking a trip across county with another women was cheating. After he told me the story I kept a closer eye on him.

Once I told him I went in a local clothing store that turned out to be a place that sold strippers clothing and I met and talked to a stripper. He asked me what her name was because he knew a few married women that were strippers and he thought they were nice and only worked as strippers because they could make a lot more money stripping than they could in an office job. I inquired how he came to know them?

Konn said he went with a friend to a local strip club once when he was a bachelor. I thought oh well it was all before me and just a story he shared from his past. It had nothing to do with us. What's important is what he does in our relationship so I didn't put much stock in what he said. After I learned he is a womanizer I didn't ignore any of the tales he told and all his stories troubled me.

I put a lot of emphasis on our hearts for I believe our heart is the most important organ in our body. A heart can be broken and keeps on beating. I'm of the opinion some times we do what's in our heart over what's in our mind. At times we have thoughts in our mind of doing things that are not kosher but don't follow though and actually execute them. They are merely thoughts that flit in and out of our head immediately. I believe the sex addiction was not only in Konn's mind but it was in his heart too and he pursued and sought his heart's desire.

It was at this point I recalled a certain pastor taught me to put things in perspective shortly after I accepted Jesus and started reading and learning the bible. I asked questions on how certain things in the world could happen. He said it was like driving down the street your broke, hungry, don't have a penny in your pocket and you pass by a bank. For just an instant a thought runs through your mind of robbing the bank because it has more money than it needs and you don't have any. But you don't stop to rob the bank you continue to drive by. These are thoughts that should fly right though our mind and shouldn't stop to build a nest in our heads. I felt he gave a good analogy of things we think of to say or do but we don't say them or act on them. The pastor said if everyone acted on every thought they had it could hurt others and themselves. If everyone did whatever feels good and followed through on every thought we have the country would be in anarchy.

How many of us have had bad thoughts maybe even downright evil thoughts even if we don't say anything? When someone is talking superior, nasty, hurting or abusing my thoughts at the time are not very nice. Most of us know we need to keep a check on how we express thoughts and behavior that can harm others. We can't just say or do whatever we want when it comes into our mind without it affecting others. Sometimes saying it like it is may not be the right thing to do. There have been many times I felt guilty about affecting others in things I say and do.

Being together five years and knowing exactly where to go and who to go to Konn wouldn't and couldn't have left his wife and headed straight to the strip joint fifty miles away, spent $15.000 in five months on a strippers if he wasn't led by and carried out what was in his heart as well as his mind.

Even though my husband entertained thoughts and had visions of him self engaging in sex with women exhibiting themselves sexually he could have let them flit through his mind he didn't have to carry the visions out in the flesh.

He didn't have to leave his wife and live out fantasies he dreamed of during our marriage. Thoughts of leaving would have flown through my husbands mind if he were devoted and I had been in his heart as the love of his life and if he thought of me as the only women meant for him when he said I do.

There is no way Konn could act out or entertain thoughts of misusing and mistreating our life together in any way, shape or form if I had been in his heart merely as a woman he respected even if he didn't love me. Thoughts of harming and rejecting me as his wife would have flitted through his head instead of building a nest in his mind. Most importantly even though I wasn't in his heart it didn't give him the right and there was absolutely no reason for subversive, insulting, indignity and shameful, humiliating, harmful damage he executed and demonstrated in reality and acted on the hate in his heart and mind.

The heart is such a beautiful part of us as it holds the many things we love cherish and treasure within our selves. Konn was too blind to see I treasured being his wife and having him by my side because he was in my heart. I was unaware until he illustrated in subversive conduct I wasn't in his heart.

Before I met Konn I was always pretty healthy. I took good care of myself and went in for physicals every year. I had my share of colds and the flu but that was about it. I could function and carry on, work with music, do things with the children and grandchildren without wearing down right away. I went to Israel with a church group.

Konn overlooked the attributes I had before he came into my life. I'm not bragging but I was involved in many things before I met him. I didn't think of myself as the lowly creature he made me feel like when he was through using me for his own egotistic purposes.

Konn is eight years younger than I am. When we met I kept up with him. Sometimes I ran circles around him and I looked younger. I played basketball, went for long walks and did so many things a lot of people my age couldn't do.

I wasn't stressed over every little thing. It took a lot to get to me. I was the person everyone came to for help and solved most any problem anyone confronted me with one way or another. I could throw a meal on the table for 30 people in a moments notice and make it look like fun. I was always active in church functions.

I was a politician and served on the city council and was proficient in achieving different services for the community I lived in which included a new water supply source and a new water plant where my name is engraved on a plaque along with other members serving at the same time. I'm a self-taught artist and educated myself to play piano, guitar and write lyrics and music. I raised four wonderful children whom are all Christians and serve the Lord and would walk through fire for me. I laughed my way through adversities and faced life head on as a realist. I dealt in truth and honesty. I think those qualities attracted Konn and he saw me as someone that took the bull by the horn and accomplished what I set out to do.

I was smart enough to accomplish all Konn targeted me to do for him yet he treated me like I was dim-witted and gave me no credit in all I did for him or with him. I'll be the first one to admit I do stupid things sometimes and I put my foot in my mouth but Konn made a mistake thinking I was stupid and I'd cow tow to all he said till he drove me to the loony bin in exchange for the love I exhibited trying to be a good wife and satisfy him in my actions to give him the best. My counselor said he would never give me credit for anything. She explained that he would have continued to stay with me if I had accepted all his quirks in pornography and all his behavior that went with it. The stress was too much. It not only affected every emotion, it affected me physically.

Looking at the different emotions that affect us and just what stress is. I looked at the facts of my life before I met Konn to get a perception on when and how stress began to affect me. I didn't go through the same kind of stressful anxiety when my husband died. I was grief stricken and heartbroken I was left behind without his gentle spirit ever present beside me. It was heartrending he wouldn't be here to see his daughter graduate, sing at recitals and all the things that went with raising our thirteen-year-old child he left behind. It was sad he wouldn't be around to play with six grandchildren and the grandchild on the way. I grieved because his presence wasn't here for the children to call on, ask his advice and lean on his strong silent gentle Christian spirit but I was not stressed. I was unhappy and mourning he won't be with us to celebrate holidays or dry tears from my eyes, hold me and tell me everything was going to be okay. I wasn't harassed in thoughts I had of my deceased husband. They were loving thoughts of missing him and all he would miss out on with a family that loved him. I was lonely he wasn't by my side. He was my best friend. I missed telling him everything and I longed for the safe secure feeling of catching his eye across a crowded room and seeing the love sparkling in his eyes when he looked my way. I didn't have to worry how I'd make ends meet financially and didn't have to work. I was able to pay the bills once a month, take care of my thirteen year old and send her to a private Christian school. We had all we needed. Not rich just getting by. I was sorrowful seeing my husband one minute and told he was dead in the next. I had a few panic attacks from fear of being without my partner to help me through the storms of life. Throughout the trauma of losing a loved one the emotions I felt overall was sadness and grief they were not stress feelings.

I don't think we can lump everything into one mold. I try to keep the many moods in perspective when feelings of emotion spring up in the different situations I'm faced with at times.

I didn't know what it meant to be really stressed out until I married Konn. The constant tension and nervous duress increased with each passing day. I saw a sign that said "Good Morning Let the Stress begin." That sign seemed to be true to form with the way I felt. Konn called and asked me to help him out of his newest predicament April 2000. I rescued and tried to have a peaceful atmosphere between us until August 2001 before I gave up. All of it took its toll and I'm paying for it today. I'm physically sick most of the time.

I've been clinically diagnosed with type two diabetes. I can get by with pills for now instead of insulin shots. I have to watch everything I eat and do for diabetes has harmful side effects. I believe the diabetes was triggered by stress. I know the approximate time it started according to my physical records and diabetes test I had through the years before, during and after Konn became part of my life.

It worries me to have been afflicted with diabetes I doubt If I can prove it but in my heart I feel diabetes was caused from stress Konn endorsed throughout our relationship with no regard for symptoms I encountered during atrocious behavior consistently displayed. He disregarded all I explained was happening to me physically.

He wouldn't accept his behavior affected his partner and I had feelings and emotions too. His atrocious behavior emphatically cost me not only in finances and emotions it cost me in health too. Statistics are proving stress is the number one cause of death over any other type or cause of death in the United States. When Konn acted up it began to pressure me so bad I'd shake inside from head to toe, my stomach cramped, my heart felt like a vise grip was clamped tight around it and my head hurt. I started to get bad headaches all the time. I became very nervous and my hands shook all the time. My husband had me feeling anxious right from the start. It increased daily with each and every problem he handed me to deal with. Not only did it deeply stress me to discover he masturbated visioning women along with all the other issues connected to his sex addicted habits but with every lie and deception that came to light and every act of mean cruelty. The stress amplified every single time he broke my heart, hurt my feelings, wounded my spirit, rejected, neglected, mocked, scoffed, abused, harmed, hit, ridiculed, twisted and projected his behavior. He caused strain each time he said he hated me and never loved me, abused and downgraded every emotion I had within my heart and personality.

I didn't believe in divorce and I didn't want one but having no alternative after I felt forced to file May 1999 stress increased and the diabetes started to show up as borderline. It stayed at borderline level until Konn came bounding back into my life after we are divorced four months.

My blood sugar level shot up high after I rescued my ex husband and was exposed to the same criteria he sanctions. Now I have to live with diabetes the rest of my life. All I can do is try to control it and pray I don't lose my limbs, or sight, kidneys and my life due to the side effects of the illness. It was my fault and my mistake I put myself in the path of Konn's evil after our divorce. I'm not blaming Konn for going to see him the first time. I should have told him he wasn't my problem any more. I could have stuck to my guns when I told him no it's not a good idea.

During the time I started to help him he stressed me out beyond the gates of no return. I was physically and emotionally on the mend before I assisted him and there I was dealing with the same habits I didn't want to be around to begin with. We did the up and down, round and round ignominy only it was worse because he didn't have any pretence or semblance of decency after practically living in the house of ill repute and he made the people that work in them his family and friends. I had to take classes at the hospital to learn exactly what diabetes was and what I had to do to control my blood sugar level. I didn't know what it really was or how it affects people. The nurse explained diabetes can be hereditary but the genes can lay dormant all your life. But sometimes things happen that can trigger the genes off and puts diabetes in motion. It can be several things but the biggest thing is stress. Stress can cause the blood sugar level to increase to the danger level even in people that don't have the genes. I evidently had the genes because my father was a diabetic that had to take insulin shots. Without the stress the genes could have laid dormant for the rest of my life. My health records confirm the genes were set off during the time I let him back into my life after divorce.

Konn played on the feelings of love in my heart for him along with my Christianity. I thought we could get along after our divorce because I didn't expect anything a wife expects from a husband.

Konn's friendship still included the same attitudes and behavior as when he was my legal husband only worse. He didn't know how to be a friend any more than he knew how to be a husband.

Chapter Twenty

Ending The Nightmare of Abuse

Two weeks after I purchased a car for Konn he calls and screams he hates me and wants me to die. It seems his girl friend wouldn't go out with him one evening because her husband told her Konn hit me and was mean and violent during our marriage.

Konn asked me to call Toriann and tell her he didn't hit me and the stories Lance told her weren't true. I told him no I will never deny the truth to him or her or to anyone else.

My ex husband proceeded to tell me he never lied to Toriann and she is the only woman he ever told the truth to. Konn said he confided things to her he never told anyone else. He went on to say he loves her and now that she's divorced he's planning to ask her to marry him. He blamed me for the disagreement between them and said their tiff should never have happened and things shouldn't have been this way between them. No Konn you're dead wrong about you and Toriann. The prostitute shouldn't have been in your life to begin with. As my husband nothing should have happened between you and your wife and us as a married couple. You begged me to marry your sorry behind and your God vowed wife is the one you should've told the truth to and confided in. The words your speaking are expressions you should've said to your new bride and backed up your words with actions. Your words to her are all the things you should have said to your new bride. You were a married man and your wife is the one that should have meant everything to you the one you should have seen as the woman meant for you and the only woman you should have called special. I was the woman you needed to protect, love and been devoted to. Your bride is the only woman you should've been turned on by and sexually desired when you said I do.

I will never deny anything pertaining to the truth and reality dealing with your shockingly violent monstrous behavior toward me while I was your newly wed bride and wife.

As my husband you did most assuredly ill-treat and hit me. You can interweave and deform the truth by saying I was the one that abused and hit you until pigs fly but it will never change actuality of reality regarding your behavior. All the lies you can muster and speak of me are from the pits of hell. You can't change one thing and neither can I. But I can face the truth and shout from the rooftops Konn Rodent your behavior all transpired in its entirety exactly the way I said it happened. You really are an adulterous scumbag that put me in your proficient reign of terror. You can't control or blackmail me anymore.

I don't know what Toriann's reasoning is for using me for an excuse if the two of you have disagreements or what she told you but I am not getting involved in the games the two of you are playing. I had enough of your sports trivia to last a lifetime. I had as much right to talk to Toriann's husband as you did to pursue his wife while they were married. And the same right to tell him you were violent and mean as you did to run me down to him and all the rest of your friends in the strip club along with the mutual friends we had when we were together.

I never told Konn all the things Lance told me but I let the cat out of the bag when I said Konn go check with the guy down the street that your girl friend is seeing, maybe he can shed some light on the problem you seem to be having with your girlfriend. Although it didn't do one bit of good to say anything because he doesn't pay attention at least I got to tell him what was in my heart. I didn't back down this time and I walked away for good. Konn calling in tears because he had a spat with his girlfriend and asking me to say the behavior he perpetrated never happened was delivering the last blow. It felt as if he were pushing me off a bridge. His last remarks were that I hit him and did things to him too. It was exhausting to try to reason with my ex hubby Nothing ever seemed to click in his head in any semblance of normality in the way things really happened.

I restated correct information to Konn for the last time. I told him all I ever did in the entire time I have known him that I am sorry for and wanted to make amends for was calling him a sob pervert and a few other choice nasty names. Konn; I reacted to some of your sexual travesties in a childish ornery manner. I teased you sometimes and I played a few of your games to uncover the truth. I confronted and held you accountable for your unnatural immoral violent behavior. I was remorseful because I felt it was ungodly to use swear words and nasty names that hurt your feelings. That was all I did and nothing more. I didn't do or say a thing until after I took all your abuse and bull s--t over a year and a half. I was going to demonstrate I had a brain that functioned. I had morals and standards I wanted to live by. That is all I ever did. I told you many times I was sorry I hurt your feelings but I never ever condoned or exonerated anything you did. I was merely taking responsibility for my conduct not yours. You alone are responsible for your behavior.

I let you think whatever you wanted and it gave me leverage to uncover the depraved, demented double life your still leading and wanted me to accept at the same time you tried to make me believe I was hallucinating and imagining it all. Only a loser can do that to another human being.

Along with suicidal attempts and beating yourself in the head every time you didn't want to answer questions you went into the bathroom took your own fist and gave your self a terribly swollen black eye. Saying I did everything you yourself did to your own body or I ran around the house and hit you and gave you black eye's that you gave yourself didn't make it true. I don't have any doubts; Konn Rodent you know what the real truth is no matter how much you try to warp it. You can't ever change the truth. Truth will always prevail over dishonesty and good will prevail over evil. Your aware of all you said and did to make your wife miserable and your hands did hit me on more than one occasion and did tear off my clothes outdoors till I didn't have a stitch of clothes on. I will not deny one thing you did that is actual fact. God will be the judge between thee and me.

The first time you called me a whore I did slap your face and that was the only and the last time I ever touched you in any physical way even though you called me a whore again and again. You got by with calling me filthy names and verbal offenses. You got by with all your bullying behavior because I didn't do anything. I wish now I had done something. You can't erase and take away hurt and pain I felt while I was being mistreated by the hand I thought was going to caress me. You can never acquit and validate your inane selfishness simply by saying you never did anything and that is the end of it as far as your concerned but it is not now nor was there ever an end to any of the terrible ordeals you enacted toward me. The triumphing truth that you will never be able to change is the truth that I emphatically did suffer by your cruel hands.

Yet you have the audacity to ask me to lie for you or do anything to help you in your quest to marry or live with the stripper prostitute you've been involved with from day one because your corrupt deception has no boundaries.

I'm telling you for the last time Konn, if you had done nothing and had not abused and mistreated me to begin with I wouldn't be able to say that you did. The same goes for the fact that if you had done nothing we wouldn't be going through a divorce and we'd still be married. The truth and reality is undeniable and it's not up for grabs, it's no longer in your hands to dissect. If you had done nothing I would have no reason to say Konn Rodent is without a trace of doubt the most extremely unkind, callous, uncaring, evil unspeakable, deceivingly dishonest, manipulating, nasty, malicious person I had the misforutne to meet. All that is merely one drop of water in the bucket of dung you consistently rubbed my face in with everything you exhibited in our marriage. I won't hide anything you did under a rock anymore. I definitely will not now nor will I ever tell Toriann or anyone else anything but the truth.

I believe you're a predator. I will never tell Toriann what you're asking me to say to clear the way for you. I will not protect you or do anything to accommodate your love life with the prostitute you desired our entire marriage. Harming and hurting and saying you never loved me and didn't want me for a wife. Why the heck you went through the motions to marry me, begging me to be your wife using God, as your witness will always be a mystery and beyond comprehension.

This is the end of our conversation and the end of trying to have a friendly atmosphere between us. I came to your rescue because I wanted peace between us. You never gave in to giving me anything I needed from you so I give up. Don't call or contact me anymore. We have nothing more to say to one another. All I can ever do for you is continue to pray you will see the light of God and face the truth about your self before it is to late. I am physically ill and I don't have time to be involved in anything linked to you.

I didn't tell him Lance said he thought Konn could possibly have a violent temper and that's when I told Lance yes he does have a violent streak he hit me and was cruel our entire marriage. I don't know what he told his wife or what she confronted Konn with. My daughter asked me if Konn hit me and I told her no he wouldn't ever hit me. I will never deny my husband relentlessly, without ceasing, abused me physically, emotionally, metally, sexually and verbally. He never stopped battering me verbally, mentally, sexually and emotionally. All the abuse was continual and on going.He shoved me around so many times and held me captive preventing me from leaving the house when he was violent. I learned all of it is the same as physically hitting. He put bruises on me every time he grabbed me and held me captive. Konn only got by with hitting me brutally hard around seven times but hitting me one time was one time too many along with trying to shove me out of a speeding car. I'd say all that is cause to divulge I was the partner that was physically abused. It upset me that he had the audacity to tell everyone including his delusional self that I chased him around the house and hit him. Each time he said he did nothing, he took away all he did toward me and took away the truth of abuse as he wreaked havoc on my life. I was going to follow through with having him arrested if he touched me physically one more time and I was going to tell my sons. He knew by this time that I'd follow through to expose him. I'd show bruises to everyone he worked with too and he wouldn't be able to keep his secrets hidden.

Konn had an image to uphold in front of everyone that doesn't know the real Konn that I knew. I couldn't stand one more moment around the person that set out to destroy me misleading and misinforming every one to believe he is the pillar of the community, Mr. Wonderful, Mr. Good Guy and Mr. Innocent all rolled in one. My daughter caught my husband grabbing me outside one day as I was trying to open the car door. She told Konn I'm keeping my eye on you so get your hands off my mom and don't ever touch her again, he let loose real quick. He tried to jostle and shove me around in many manhandling ways like when he wouldn't let me out of the house or grabbing my arms while he screamed in my face but he didn't get by with battering me physically after I let him know how I was going to retaliate.

My son Paul took boxing lessons and fought some matches I was afraid he'd get in trouble if he hit Konn. My sons would never permit Konn to touch me if they had known. For some reason he was afraid of my family. So after a fashion he watched the physical realm of abuse. But began to accuse me of hitting him to cover up his activity toward hitting me if I decided to tell on him. But Konn steadily kept up and increased battering me in every other humanly possible way already out there in the world and all the new ways he invented that wasn't out there.

After harassing me about transportation he started to call and threaten me one week after I found and bought a car for him. He said I didn't have the right to warn Toriann about him. What I did to him was just like what the terrorists did to the twin towers in New York. He said so many hateful ungrateful things it did get to me. I was more stressed than ever and that's when my blood sugar went from borderline and shot up to type two. Feeling I went above and beyond the call of duty as a Christian, his wife, as his ex-wife and just as a decent person to make amends and have peace with my ex husband I couldn't tolerate the death wishes he made toward me.

I decided to tell Lance the truth about my husband hitting and his violence because I was aware Konn was going to do all in his power to be around her and eventually either marry or live with Toriann and she has a thirteen-year-old child. Whether it was any of my business or not every time I hear he's going be around another child I can't help but think of the way he behaved in front of my teen and twelve year old grandchild with no regard that they were children influenced by grown up behavior. I felt like I want to protect other children from his mania when I hear they will be subjected to existing in his presence.

I cringed when the 53-year-old Mr. Konn told me he befriended and was helping one of his stripper's 14-year-old baby sitters that was on drugs and he was seeing a nineteen or twenty year-old stripper that had a small child. He told meToriann introduced to him. Shortly after romping around with the thirty-five years younger stripper Konn said she owed him money and kept his computer and he took her to court and procured a policeman to go to her apartment and help him retrieve his computer out of her apartment after they had a falling out. I was hip to the fact that Konn's reasoning for asking me to deny the truth of his violent behavior to his girlfriend was so he can continue in dishonesty with Toriann. She doesn't deserve to be under his dilemmas any more than I did no matter what her occupation is. However she still continues to see him. After being privy to learn more of his bizarre situations concerning his character in the double life he is leading there's one thing I absolutely know for certain there's no way I'll ever feel sorry or pity for him in this lifetime.

He was more than vehemently hateful as he persisted to call a while longer. If I seen it was him calling on caller ID I wouldn't answer the phone. He called every day for weeks and left hate messages. He left twenty hate and threatening messages one day when I was out of town. He sent hate e-mail letters along with phone threats.

He knew I was diagnosed with diabetes and threatened to take me off the health insurance policy I was still on at the firm he works for if I didn't call Toriann. He continued to call and leave messages numerous times saying how glad he is I was sick, hoped I died and he really hated me. On one message Konn said Jesus hates you Rosie and so do I, I really hate you.

One time he called and said everything can be wonderful between us if I call Toriann and tell her he was very good to me in our marriage and he never abused me. If I don't call her he will hate me. Konn harped about the money he was court ordered to pay and called it blood money. He kept this up over a month until I e mailed him I was going to send his boss a copy of hateful swearing he e-mailed me on the firm's computer on company time and a copy of a tape I made of his death threats. I was going to give a copy to the police if he didn't stop contacting me.

He didn't appreciate one thing I did to help him during the fifteen months after we are divorced to keep him out of jail, assist his survival, care about his welfare, escort him places, and went in hock to purchase the vehicle he's driving. It was time to stop rescuing his behind and back off forever. Subsequent to all that was said and done I realize I can still be stunned at the attitude the ungrateful degenerate cops when I won't do what he asks. I become perplexed he could have done all he did once more during the time he called and asked me to rescue him because once again I couldn't conceive anyone behaving so deviously corrupt.

The thing is now were not speaking I'm not collecting any of the payments toward the car. Toward the end of trying to be on a peaceful basis I would meet him every two weeks just long enough to collect the payment. One day several weeks before Christmas I met him to pick up a payment at a well lit busy restaurant. I thought I'd take him a Christmas gift when I went to pick up the money, no big deal it was my way of saying you can hate me and send me death wishes but I am a Christian and I'm not going to hate instead I will give a gift in love because I am not Konn I'm Rosie. His thoughts are not my thoughts. His heart is not my heart. I got in his car to collect the payment because the restaurant was packed and there were cars coming and going. I noticed he put a sign on the dash of the passenger side that said Goddess and told me it symbolizes how he feels toward Toriann and how much he loves her. I thought he is sicker than I gave him credit for.

I collected the payment and asked for more than he handed me. He still owed money I loaned during the weeks he ran out of cash that is above the car payment.

He gave me $25,00 over the payment. I got out of the car and went home sicker than I was before I picked up the money. He called an hour later and said you can have the gifts back I hate you. I told him I bought the gifts in love if he doesn't want them he can throw them away or give them to someone. I didn't want them back and I don't care what he does with them. On Christmas day he called and left a nice message saying thank you for the gifts. Several days later Konn called and left a message he's in town and can I meet him he has a payment for me. I ignored the message to collect the payment. I had enough of the ambivalent atmosphere. One time he's okay one time he's not okay, heck with him. I don't want to hear one more word about how much he loves a prostitute or anything else he has to say. I don't want to look into his wicked malicious face ever again.

After he left the hate messages on my machine I screened all my calls. When he is angry I know it's his calls without checking caller Id for he calls every five minutes all hours of the night and early morning.

I wasn't about to put myself in the line of fire again. I called his work number when I knew he wouldn't be there and left a message. I told him I don't care to see you any more than he cared to see me, send the payments in the mail. It was the last time he'd hear my voice again. It's been months since I left the message and he never sent me a dime and I know he has no intention of sending what he owes.

I haven't done anything as yet but I intend to have an attorney slap a lawsuit on my ex husband to collect the money he owes on the car and money I loaned him to survive in the last year and I'll include the pain and suffering I endured hearing the threats and death wishes. He's still responsible for the reprehensible conduct to deliver hate and death wishes. No one has the right to do whatever he or she wants to harm and hurt another human being. I taped most of the calls and I intend to hand a copy of the tape to an attorney as evidence to the fact Konn felt he had the right to threaten me on my answering machine in my home evidently feeling he doesn't have to pay the consequences. The threats were directed toward damaging me even more during the same time I was going through emotional trauma learning I contacted diabetes I will have to live with for the rest of my life. One of my friends told me why bother trying to collect anything from him it won't do any good to take him to court people get by with the kind of things I went through all the time. Win, lose or draw I think abused people need to take a stand to let perpetrators know they can't get by with treating another person inhumanly.

I went above and beyond the call of duty and the call of Christian to help my husband both during and after marriage as he continued to believe he could do what ever he wants toward my life. I want to make a statement to Konn and possibly others that got by with treating their partner despicable as the spouse tries to simply please them.

The only advice I can give to anyone in an abusive relationship is to seek guidance right from the start. The first time someone strikes out whether it is physically, verbally or emotionally. God gave us the medical profession to heal, console, guide and teach us with wisdom what we need to know to cope with issues we don't know how to deal with. Don't be ashamed of what your going through look at what the situation really is. Don't hide behind a smile and denial the way I did. No matter what the spouse says no matter how sorry they sound. It doesn't get any better, it gets worse. Each time we forgive an abusive spouse it allows them to continue and abuse increases. I know the same fear of losing finances and what facing loneliness is like. I came to the conclusion stayingwith a mean bullying abusive louse because we fear losing finances is the price tag we put on the cost of abuse. It's the price we paid for staying in a toxic relationship and no amount of money is worth the cost the abused spouse pays.

Loneliness is easier to cope with than a loud screaming voice breaking an eardrum with insults. We can wait a lifetime and that same voice that puts us down will never speak a kind loving word no matter how long we stay with them. No matter how much abuse we take before taking a stand and making a mark toward equality that includes not having to take being mistreated from a threatening bully.

All Along I wanted to do nothing more than show kindness to Konn as another human being. That didn't give him the right to treat me cruelly. I refuse to maintain a victim's attitude. I have so much to say and so little time to say it in. With God's help I am victorious. I feel I am living proof there is victory in Jesus. For without God I know I would not still be here. I thank God for watching over me. I thank my children and friends for being there. The question most people ask is how can I say God was there for me when I was going through adversity? Why didn't God let me know I was marrying a man that didn't love me? It was not God's fault I chose to marry Konn. I made the decision with my own free will. God didn't intend for me to have the loveless marriage I encountered. It was my husband's decision to destroy and make our marriage and my life miserable. It was never God's intention or will for my life.

I paid dearly and the cost was big time, not just in dollars but in emotional anguish and grief, bruises, tears, shattered dreams, marriage and divorce and the hurt and scars my family endured too. I regretted I was responsible my daughter was subjected to live in the midst of a maniac's terrible actions. He didn't care she was a child and had been through the death of her beloved dad. I didn't realize what it was doing to her as I protected and rationalized his behavior that exhibits no regrets or respect for anyone but him self.

Reliving some of the memories as I wrote I looked at my mistakes and heartache over the love and fairness of the attitude I had that Konn is my husband I have to stand by him in the tug of war to keep peace between the family and my partner. All I tried to accomplish was in vain to a man that has no heart or conscience. The divorce was equally hard on my family. When the divorce was over I felt like what kind of mother was I to bring this monster into my daughters innocent life when I was the only parent she had. Even though I never dreamed he'd act barbarously in front of her and my entire family.

I'm sorry for not seeing the whole picture of how badly Konn's behavior was affecting my youngest child and she will probably remember the things she heard and witnessed the rest of her life, along with my daughter and granddaughter enduring the sight of violent gestures Konn acted out in their sight. I can't forget my grand daughter growing up next door to her grand mother that loved her and wanted her to have normalcy and happiness and three of her young years were marred with screaming night mares of Konn hurting or killing her grandmother. As I wrote I thought of my family when Konn asked me to deny the mendacious behavior he committed to his personal prostitute. I thought of the way I protected him and denied his actions as it continually increased. There is no way I will ever deny any of his conduct to anyone ever again. I pray I can forgive myself for allowing his behavior to affect everyone that's dear to me and for letting it go on as long as it did before taking a final stand.

A valuable lesson I learned is that we should know who we are, know what we stand for and never allow anyone to take it from us. I wanted to stand for God, honor and morals and all that is good and decent, clean and beautiful. I realized to late I allowed my husband to take away my dignity, all I stood for and believed in. I can no longer be what everyone wants me to be anymore and feel as though I failed everyone close to me and myself. Who I was got lost in the process of wanting to please my husband, those I loved and just about everyone I was in contact with. I can't live in anything that deals with unreality anymore or allow anyone to control and manipulate me.

I'm partially at fault for allowing my world to shatter no matter how unknowingly naive or how trustingly innocent I was I should have walked away when deception first reared its ugly head before our marriage. If not then I should have made a move to end it when perversion and cruelty followed close behind on our honeymoon. I'm at fault for letting my husband get by with abusively mistreating me as a person for so long and calling it love.

Never the less even though I consider myself to be a realist and a hopeless romantic and dreamer when my dream shattered the whole adventure was like walking through a fog. There was no light to show where your going and you have to push yourself to keep walking until your completely through it, until your totally outside of the fog standing in the light where I am standing once more and it feels great.

I will not allow myself to be the heart of a victim Konn Rodent or anyone else can put in harm's way ever again, so help me God.

Printed in the United States
703900003B